Sm'algyax

A Reference Dictionary and Grammar
for the Coast Tsimshian Language

Sm'algyax

A Reference Dictionary and Grammar for the Coast Tsimshian Language

Compiled and edited by
John Asher Dunn

University of Washington Press
Seattle and London

Sealaska Heritage Foundation
Juneau

Originally published in two volumes by the National Museums of Canada, Ottawa, as (1) *A Practical Dictionary of the Coast Tsimshian Language*, Canadian Ethnology Service Paper No. 42, 1978; and (2) *A Reference Grammar for the Coast Tsimshian Language*, Canadian Ethnology Service Paper No. 55, 1979. The pagination of the original publications has been retained for the main texts of this one-volume edition.

Reprinted by permission of the Canadian Museum of Civilization

Library of Congress Cataloging-in-Publication Data
Sm'algyax : a reference dictionary and grammar for the Coast Tsimshian language / compiled and edited by John Asher Dunn.
p. cm.
Rev. ed. of: A practical dictionary of the Coast Tsimshian language. 1978; and A reference grammar for the Coast Tsimshian language. 1979.
Includes bibliographical references and index.
ISBN 0-295-97419-2 (alk. paper)
1. Tsimshian language—Dictionaries—English. 2. English language—Dictionary—Tsimshian. 3. Tsimshian language—Grammar—Dictionaries.
I. Dunn, John Asher. Practical dictionary of the Coast Tsimshian language.
II. Dunn, John Asher. Reference grammar for the Coast Tsimshian language.
III. Title.
PM2494.Z5D86 1995 94-31488
497'.4—dc20 CIP

The paper used in this publication meets the minimum requirements of American National Standard for Information Sciences—Permanence of Paper for Printed Library Materials, ANSI Z39.48-1984. ∞

CONTENTS

Sealaska Heritage Foundation

One Sealaska Plaza, Suite 201 • Juneau, Alaska 99801-1249 • (907) 463-4844
Fax (907) 586-1807

The Sealaska Heritage Foundation is pleased to sponsor the reprinting of this new, combined edition of John Dunn's classic *Dictionary and Grammar for the Coast Tsimshian Language.* These two works were originally published as separate books in 1978 and 1979 by the Canadian Museum of Civilization, but they have been out of print for some time, although the demand for them has continued.

In Alaska and British Columbia, there is renewed interest in the Tsimshian language. As noted in the preface, in the early 1990s, Tsimshian language teachers in British Columbia adopted the spelling system used in this book. Thus, it has helped to establish a standard writing system for Tsimshian. We believe this combined reprint will be used by teachers, students, and the Tsimshian community in general for many years.

We thank John Dunn for his encouragement and cooperation in the project. We thank the Canadian Museum of Civilization for granting permission to do this facsimile reprint, and we thank the University of Washington Press for its support of the publication and distribution of this edition.

The Sealaska Heritage Foundation is happy to help make these important works once more available.

Dennis Demmert
Executive Director
January 1995

PREFACE TO THE 1995 EDITION

In 1990 the Bilingual Programme in Prince Rupert School District 52, under the supervision of its First Nations Advisory Council, adopted the orthography and spellings in the *Practical Dictionary of the Coast Tsimshian Language* (with the revisions listed below, page xi) as the standard for instructional materials. The Bilingual Programme was directed by Vonnie Hutchingson, with the very able assistance of Susan Marsden. The First Nations Advisory Council included representatives from all of the coastal British Columbian Tsimshian villages and from all of their Band Councils.

This spelling standard has been observed in the publication of the bilingual series Suwilaay'msga Na G̲a'niiiyatgm (Teachings of our Grandfathers), which was organized and prepared by Vonnie Hutchingson and Susan Marsden. The series—consisting of seven volumes as of January 1994—was edited by Pauline Dudoward, John Dunn, Verna Helin, Ernie Hill, Jr., Vonnie Hutchingson, Susan Marsden, Beatrice Robinson, Marie-Lucie Tarpent, and Mildred Wilson. It was approved by the Tsimshian chiefs and elders, and published by the Ministry of Higher Education for the Province of British Columbia.

The Tsimshian chiefs hold the copyright to the series in trust "for Tsimshian Children Present and Future." When the first seven volumes arrived from Vancouver, the printing was blessed by the four ranking Tsimshian chiefs. These volumes have become a model for the development of instructional First Nations language materials throughout the Province. They effectively establish the original edition (1978) of the accompanying dictionary as the spelling authority for Sm'algyax.

This spelling standard is also currently applied in the classroom by the four School District 52 teachers of Sm'algyax: Pauline Dudoward and Verna Helin, both from Port Simpson; Beatrice Robinson from Kitkatla; and Mildred Wilson from Hartley Bay. For each of these excellent teachers, Sm'algyax is the home (first) language.

John Dunn
Norman, Oklahoma

LANGUAGE CONSULTANTS AND CONTRIBUTORS

Alfred Anderson, Clarence Anderson, Daphne Anderson, Louisa Anderson, Johnnie Clifton, Josiah Dundas, Elizabeth Dundas, Ernie Hill, Jr., Ambrose Robinson, Arthur Robinson, Cora Robinson, Violet Robinson, Dick Wilson, and Mildred Wilson, all of Hartley Bay, British Columbia

Dorothy Brown, Josephine Brown, Frank Ryan, Maude Tolmie, Kathleen Vickers, all of Kitkatla, British Columbia

Arnold Booth, Alfred Eaton, Martha Eaton, Mary Guthrie, Harold Hudson, all of Metlakatla, Alaska

Paul Starr of Kitselas, Kitkatla, and Prince Rupert, British Columbia

REVISIONS TO THE 1978 DICTIONARY

A Tsimshian language committee, consisting of Pauline Dudoward, Verna Helin, Beatrice Robinson, and Mildred Wilson, as well as John Dunn, Ernie Hill, Jr., Vonnie Hutchingson, Susan Marsden, and linguist Marie-Lucie Tarpent have made the following revisions to the 1978 edition of the dictionary.

1. Throughout, gyiV, kyiV, and k'yiV have been replaced by giV, kiV, and k'iV.

2. Revisions in the following list often move from a spelling with more phonetic detail to one that is more phonemic, i.e., closer to lexical representation.

Original Spelling	Revised Spelling	Gloss
aa'pax	a'ap'ax	remember
badzi	badza	lift
g̱alts'aap	g̱alts'ap	village
g̱anyeetk	g̱aniiyatsgm	grandfathers, ancestors
k'ooli	gooli	scalp
k'yi'nam, k'yi'lam	gi'nam, k'i'lam	give
gwanüks	gwenks	spring of water
xaldawxk	haldaaks	medicine
hiduu	hidu	fame
hoygyax	hogyax	correct
łiłuungit	łałuungit	slave
łgwüslis	łgusliis	nephew
kb'i'nsxn	kbiitsxn	ten
k'wili	k'wilii	three (round and abstract
'naaxł	'neexł	killer whale
'nłoomsk	nłoomsk	respect
płaksk	płaksk	exhausted
sg̱anakt	sg̱a'nak	length, length of time
snyeekw	snyaakw	hold
t'u'utsk	t'uu'tsk	black, iron, knife
waa	'waa	find
weel	waal	do
wüliil	wiliil	rub
woo	'woo	invite

ABSTRACTS FOR THE DICTIONARY AND GRAMMAR

PART I

A Practical Dictionary of the Coast Tsimshian Language represents a contemporary complement to the work of Franz Boas (1912) and Amelia Susman (1940) since it was compiled in the time period from 1968 to 1977. Likewise, it represents a geographic complement to the Tsimshian materials because it contains data from Kitkatla and Hartley Bay. The earlier research had been conducted in Metlakatla and Port Simpson. Each lexical entry includes (1) a practical transcription, (2) morphological information, (3) English glosses, and (4) phonetic transcriptions showing the local variants. In addition, there is a description of the practical writing system and an English index.

PART II

A Reference Grammar for the Coast Tsimshian Language is a nontechnical introduction to the phonology, morphology, and syntax of Coast Tsimshian as it is currently spoken in Metlakatla, Alaska, and Port Simpson, Kitkatla, Hartley Bay, and Prince Rupert, British Columbia. The grammar contains sections dealing with pronunciation and sound changes, word formation (morphology), and syntax. At the end of the grammar there are summaries showing the basic sentence types and their grammatical relationships.

PART I

A Practical Dictionary of the Coast Tsimshian Language

PREFACE TO THE 1978 EDITION

The compilation of this dictionary began in the summer of 1968, when my wife Luceen and I moved to Kitkatla, British Columbia, to study the Coast Tsimshian language. Our field research was supported by the National Museum of Man and the American Philosophical Society and was supervised by Professors Bruce Rigsby and Stanley Newman.

We worked in Kitkatla from July through September, then moved to Prince Rupert, British Columbia, where we continued our research through November. We returned to Prince Rupert for further field study in August and September of 1971, this time supported by the National Endowment for the Humanities. In 1972, I began working as a linguistic consultant for the Alaska State Operated Schools and then for the Annette Island (Metlakatla, Alaska) School District after the state-operated system was dismantled. This professional contact has given me many opportunities for collecting additional data. Arnold Booth, the director of the Metlakatla Bilingual-Bicultural Program, and his assistant, Mary Guthrie, who are both native speakers and accomplished linguists, have been most enthusiastic about my research and have spared no effort to help me.

In the summer of 1974, the people of Hartley Bay, British Columbia, invited me and the Tsimshian-speaking people from all the coast villages to come to Hartley Bay for the purpose of developing a practical writing system. Arnold Booth, Mary Guthrie, and I accepted the invitation. With the help of Daphne Anderson and Elizabeth Dundas, both of Hartley Bay, we undertook an intensive study of phonetics and the general principles of transcription, then adapted the Hindle/Rigsby orthography of *A Short Practical Dictionary of the Gitksan Language* (1973) to the Coast Tsimshian language. This is the orthography used and described in the present dictionary. Our work has been enthusiastically supported by Johnnie Clifton and his wife Helen and by Mr. and Mrs. Ernie Hill, Jr.

During the summer of 1974 and the autumns of the following two years, I was able to continue the collection of language materials in Hartley Bay. I received support from the Provincial Museum of British Columbia in 1975 and 1976 for this research. In 1975, I was commissioned by the Urgent Ethnology Programme of the Canadian Ethnology Service to prepare a dictionary of the Coast Tsimshian language.

I want to thank Jeff Leer for his helpful comments and suggestions concerning certain orthographic problems. The orthography is a matter of controversy among Tsimshian people, but it was designed to be as close to the Gitksan orthography as possible. Both the Tsimshian and the Gitksan orthographies have been designed in accordance with those practices that are currently most generally accepted for practical writing systems. While I wish to acknowledge my great debt to the people mentioned in this preface and in the list of contributors, I alone am responsible for any shortcomings in the dictionary and orthography.

John Dunn
Norman, Oklahoma
1977

TABLE OF CONTENTS

KEY TO TSIMSHIAN PRONUNCIATIONS

VOWELS

Tsimshian spelling	*Phonetic Symbol*	*Nearest English Equivalent*
a	[a]	a as in hat
a̲	[ɑ]	a as in father
a̲	[ʌ]	a as in about

Note: the underlining diacritic for the vowel a̲ is an optional diacritic. A competent speaker of Tsimshian should find it unnecessary.

e	[e]	e as in grey
e	[ɛ]	e as in net
i	[i]	i as in machine
i	[ɩ]	i as in hit
o	[o]	o as in hope
o	[ɔ]	o as in fought
u	[u]	u as in rule
ü	[ï]	u as in rule, but with the lips unrounded
ü	[ɨ]	u as in just, when it is an unstressed adverb.
aa	[a·]	a as in hat, but prononunced with greater length.
áa	[a·ʌ]	a as in hat, but with greater length and with an a̲-like diphthong similar to that found in some dialects of the Southeastern United States.

Note: a dipthong diacritic marks an optional pronunciation feature and can generally be omitted according to the preference of the writer.

a̲a̲	[ɑ·], [ʌ·]
á̲a̲	[ɑ·ʌ], [ʌ·ʌ]
ee	[e·], [ɛ·]
ée	[e·ʌ], [ɛ·ʌ]
ii	[i·], [ɩ·]
íi	[i·ʌ], [ɩ·ʌ]
oo	[o·], [ɔ·]
óo	[o·ʌ], [ɔ·ʌ]
uu	[u·]
úu	[u·ʌ]
üü	[ï·]

CONSONANTS

b, d, g, h, k, l, m, n, p, t, w, and y are pronounced as in English.

dz	[ʒ]	dz as in adze
k'	[k?]	k pronounced with a

		simultaneous closure of the vocal cords. This closure is released as the k is pronounced.
'k	[ʔk˺]	k pronounced with a simultaneous closure of the vocal cords. This closure is unreleased during the pronunciation of the k.
k̲	[q]	k pronounced with the tongue pulled back against the soft palate.
k̲'	[qʔ]	
'k̲	[ʔq˺]	
'l	[ʔl]	
ł	[ł]	an s-like sound produced with the tongue in position to pronounce an l.
'm	[ʔm]	
'n	[ʔn]	
p'	[pʔ]	
'p	[ʔp˺]	
s	[s], [š]	s as in sand; sh as in shape.

Note: s can be pronounced in either of the two ways described according to the preference of the speaker.

t'	[tʔ]	
't	[ʔt˺]	
ts	[c]	ts as in hats

Note: ts is never pronounced as ch in church.

ts'	[cʔ]	
'ts	[ʔc˺]	
'w	[ʔw]	
ẅ	[ÿ]	w pronounced with the lips unrounded.
'ẅ	[ʔÿ]	
x	[x̣]	an h-like sound produced with the tongue in position to pronounce a k̲
'y	[ʔy]	
k'y	[kʸʔ]	the k and y are pronounced simultaneously
k'w	[kʷʔ]	the k and w are pronounced simultaneously
'	[ʔ]	a glottal stop
l̲	[ḷ]	l as in careful
'l̲	[ʔḷ]	
m̲	[ṃ]	the second m in medium
'm̲	[ʔṃ]	
n̲	[ṇ]	n as in medicine
'n̲	[ʔṇ]	

Note: a competent speaker of Tsimshian can distinguish the syllabic consonants, l̲, m̲, n̲, from their non-syllabic counterparts, l, m, n, by their characteristic position within the word. Because of this fact the underlining diacritic is optional for these letters.

THE ENTRY

Each entry is numbered. Variants of the same entry carry the same whole number, but with different decimal numbers, e.g.,

> 195. DASX *squirrel* (from Metlakatla)
>   195.1 desx *squirrel* (from Hartley Bay).

Entries with the same lexical root or stem which vary only in terms of grammatical (not lexical) affixes are also given different decimal numbers of the same whole number, e.g.,

> 806. HOOKS *come*
>   806.1 hooksk *be with*
>   806.2 hooksn *be put with*.

Because of this numbering system, the entries are not in absolute, but only approximate, alphabetical order. The primary function of the numbering system is to facilitate the English index.

Immediately following the number for each entry is one or more words in capital letters. If the first of these words is followed by a hyphen, it is a proclitic rather than an independent word. If the first word in upper case letters is followed by a comma, it is an independent lexical item as it will stand in a sentence without a syllabic-initial suffix. If the second word in upper case letters is followed by a hyphen, it represents the spelling of entry when it has a syllabic-initial suffix. Any word in upper case letters which follows the first word and which is not followed by a hyphen represents a plural form of the word.

Following the capitalized portion of the entry, i.e., the Tsimshian lexical item, is a notional part-of-speech characterization, e.g., *n.*(noun), *v.t.*(transitive verb), and English glosses with occasional ethnographic elaboration. Finally the entry indicates the pronunciation, in phonetic notation, of the singular and plural forms. Each pronunciation description is tagged to indicate the local source, e.g., hb (Hartley Bay).

ABBREVIATIONS AND SYMBOLS

adv. adverb

anat. anatomical term pertaining to the human body

B brother('s)

Ch child('s)

D daughter('s)

excl. exclamation

F father('s)

H husband('s)

hb. Hartley Bay

hum. human

ichth. pertaining to fish (ichthology)

i.e., that is

interj. interjection

interr. interrogative

k. Kitkatla

lit. literally

M mother('s)

m. Metlakatla (Alaska)

n. noun

naut. nautical term pertaining to boats

num. numeral

orn. pertaining to birds (ornithology)

physiol. physiology

plur. plural

pr. Prince Rupert

pron. pronoun

S son('s)

spec. specifically

v.i. intransitive verb

v.t. transitive verb

W wife('s)

Z sister('s)

♀ female speaking

♂ male speaking

TSIMSHIAN-ENGLISH DICTIONARY

1. A- at; from; on; to, toward. [ʔa] hb,k.

2. A- easily. [ʔa] m.

3. AA. *n.* an edible root; a root medicine (antidote for food poisoning). [ʔa·] hb.

4. AADIT, AADID-, AK'AADIT. *n.* fisherman. [ʔá·dɩtʰ] hb,m. [ʔɑkʔá·dɩtʰ] hb.

5. AADMHON. *v.i.* catch fish with a net; fish with a net; net fish. [ʔà·dm̥hɔ́n] hb.
   5.1 aadmhoon, ga'aadmhoon. [ʔà·dm̥hɔ́·n] pr. [gɑ'à·dm̥hɔ́·n] pr.
   5.2 admhon. [ʔàdm̥hon] hb,k,m.

6. AADMMÜSOO. *n.* net for catching sockeye salmon. [ʔà·dm̥ɨsó·] hb.

7. AADMÜÜX. *n.* net for catching coho salmon. [ʔà·dm̥ɨ́·x̣] hb.

8. AADZAK, AADZAG-, AX'AADZAK. *v.i.* long enough; reach across. [ʔá·ʒʌqʰ] pr. [ʔʌx̣ʔá·ʒʌqʰ] hb.
   8.1 aadzax. [ʔá·ʒʌx̣] k,m.

9. AADZAKS. *v.i.* arrogant; haughty; proud; snobbish. [ʔá·ʒʌks] k,m.
   9.1 adziks, adz'adziks, ak'adziks. [ʔáʒɩks] k,m,hb. [ʔaʒʔáʒɩks] hb. [ʔakʔáʒɩks] hb.

10. A'ADZIK, A'DZIG-. *v.i.* straight. [ʔaʔáʒɩkʰ] m,pr.
   10.1 a'dzik. [ʔaʔʒɩ́kʰ] hb.
   10.2 a'tsik, ak'a'tsik. [ʔáʔcʼɩkʰ] hb. [ʔakʔáʔcʼɩkʰ] hb.

11. AAK, AAG-, GA'AAK. *n.* edge; mask; mouth; rim. [ʔa·qʰ] pr. [gɑʔá·qʰ] pr.
   11.1 aax, aag-. [ʔa·x̣] k,m.

12. AALIKS. *n.* servant. [ʔá·lɩks] k,m.
   12.1 áalks, áalks. [ʔaʌlks] hb,k,m. [ʔaʌlks] hb.

13. AALX, AL'AALX. *v.i.* bold; brave; courageous. [ʔa·lx̣] k,m. [ʔalʔá·lx̣] k.
   13.1 alax. *v.i.* angry; brave. [ʔálɑx̣] hb.
   13.2 alx, ak'alx, al'alx, ga'alx. *v.i.* angry; brave. [ʔalx̣] hb. [ʔakʔálx̣] hb. [ʔalʔálx̣] hb,k. [gɑʔálx̣] hb.

14. AAM, AM'AAM. *v.i.* good; well. [ʔa·m] hb,k,m,pr. [ʔʌmʔá·m] hb,k.
   14.1 aam-, am- good; goodly; well. [ʔa·m] pr. [ʔam] m.

15. AAMADZAP, AAMADZAB-. *v.t.* complete; fix. *v.i.* completed; fixed; fixed well; good-looking; handsome; intact; pretty. [ʔà·maʒʌ́pʰ] hb,k,m.
   15.1 aamdzap, aamdzab-. [ʔa·mʒʌ́pʰ] pr.
   15.2 aamadzadzap, aamadzapdzab-. *v.i.* faultless, perfect.

[ʔà·maʒʌpʒʌ́pʰ] hb,m.

16. AAMGASGAAWT, AAMGASGAAWD-. *v.i.* medium sized; of a good size. [ʔà·mgạsgá·wtʰ] pr.

17. AAMNDEP, AAMNDEB-, AAMNGADEP. *n.* an accurate/good assessment, estimate, evaluation, measure, measurement, reckoning; a goodly amount, quantity, size. [ʔà·mn̩dɛ́pʰ] m,pr. [ʔà·mn̩gạdɛ́pʰ] m,pr.
17.1 amindep, amindeb-, amingadep. [ʔàmɩn̆dɛ́pʰ] m,pr. [ʔàmɩngạdɛ́pʰ] m,pr.

18. AAMSGADAPDUUT, AAMSGADAPDUUD-. *v.i.* of a small size. [ʔà·msgạdʌpdú·tʰ] pr.

19. AAMSGANAK, AAMSGANAG-. *v.i.* just far enough; just long enough (of space or time). [ʔà·msganákʰ] m,pr.
19.1 amsganak, amsganag-, amsgaganak. [ʔàmsgạnákʰ] m,pr. [ʔàmsgạgạnákʰ] m,pr.
19.2 ˈaámsgaˈnak. *adv.* after a while. [ʔà·msgạʔnákʰ] hb.

20. AAP, AAB-. *n.* father (address; woman speaking; F) [ʔa·pʰ] hb,m.
20.1 ap, ab-. *n.* father (address; archaic). [ʔapʰ] k.

21. AA'PAX. *v.t.* remember. [ʔá·ʔpˀạx̣] k,m.
21.1 a'pax, ap'a'pax. [ʔáʔpˀạx̣] hb,k,m. [ʔʌpʔáʔpˀạx̣] hb.

22. AAT, AAD-, GA'AAT. *v.t. & n.* net; seine. [ʔa·tʰ] hb,k,m. [gạʔá·tʰ] hb.

23. ÁATK, ÁATG-, ÁATK. *n.* night. [ʔa·ʌtʰkʰ] k,m. [ʔa·ʌtʰkʰ] k.

24. A'AYAAẄK, A'AYAAẄG-. *n.* aurora borealis; northern lights. [ʔàʔạyá·ẅqʰ] pr.

25. AAYUWAN. *v.i.* stay away for a long time. [ʔá·yuwan] k,m.

26. ABUU. *v.i. & n.* a few; some; several. [ʔabú·] hb,k,m.

27. ADAAHN. *n.* phosphorescent algae. [ʔadá·ɬn̩] hb.

28. ADABIIS. *v.i.* beautiful (non-human subject) [ʔàdabí·s] hb.
28.1 adabiis. *n.* butterfly. [ʔàdabí·s] m.

29. ADAGAN. *n.* ghost bread (sulphur polyporus, red polypore, fir polypore, multizoned polystictus, artist's fungus, oyster pleurotus, sapid pleurotus, lenzites. [ʔàdagạ́n] hb.

30. ADAWX, ADAWG-, ADAWX. *n.* folktale; legend; title; story. [ʔadáwx̣] hb,k,m.

31. ADIGULTÁA, ADIGULWAN. *v.i.* continue; endure; last, remain. [ʔàdigultʔá·ʌ] hb,k. [ʔàdigulwán] k.

32. ADIGWIL- continuing. [ʔadigʷɩl] hb.

33. AGWI-, AGWII- distant. [ʔagʷi] k,m. [ʔagʷii] hb.

34. AGWIBIIP, AGWIBIIB-. *n.* great uncle (address; FMB, MMB).
[ʔàgwibí·pʰ] k.

35. AGWIDZI'IS. *n.* great aunt (address; FFZ, FMZ, MFZ, MMZ).
[ʔàgʷiʒíʔis] k.

36. AGWIIŁEMS, AGWIIŁMŁEMS. *n.* granddaughter's husband; grandson's wife (address and reference; DDH, DSW, SDH, SSW). [ʔàgʷi·ɬɛ́ms] hb.
[ʔàgʷi·ɬm̩ɬɛ́ms] hb.
36.1 agwiłems. [ʔàgʷiɬɛ́ms] k,m.

37. AGWIINÜBIP, AGWIINÜBIB-, AGWIIGANÜBIP. *n.* great uncle (reference; FMB, MMB). [ʔàgʷi·nəbípʰ] hb. [ʔàgʷi·gɑnəbípʰ] hb.
37.1 agwinübíip, agwinübíib-. [ʔàgʷɩnɨbíʌpʰ] k,m.

38. AGWIINÜGWAT, AGWIINÜGWAD-, AGWIIGANÜGWAT. *n.* uncle; uncle-in-law (address and reference; FB, MZH). [ʔàgʷi·nəgʷátʰ] hb.
[ʔàgʷi·gɑnəgʷátʰ] hb.
38.1 agwinügwat, agwinügwad-. [ʔàgʷɩnɨgʷátʰ] k,m.

39. AGWII'NTS'II'TS, AGWIIGA'NTS'II'TS. *n.* great aunt (reference; FFZ, FMZ, MFZ, MMZ). [ʔàgʷi·ʔn̩cʔí·ʔc˃] hb. [ʔàgʷi·gɑʔn̩cʔí·ʔc˃] hb.
39.1 agwints'i'i'ts. [ʔàgʷɩncʔíʔiʔc˃] k.
39.2 agwints'i'i'ts. [ʔàgʷɩn̩cʔíʔiʔc˃] k,m.

40. AGWII'O'OS, AGWIITXAL'O'OS. *n.* second cousin (address and reference; FZDD, FZDS, FZSD, FZSS, MBDD, MBDS, MBSD, MBSS). [ʔàgʷi·ʔɔ́ʔɔs] hb. [ʔàgʷi·tx̣alʔɔ́ʔɔs] hb.
40.1 agwi'o'os. [ʔàgʷiʔɔ́ʔɔs] k,m.

41. AGWIL- aside. [ʔagʷɩl] hb.

42. AGWILWAN. *v.t.* set aside (plural object). [ʔagʷɩlwán] hb.

43. AHOO. *n.* common scoter. [ʔahó·] hb.

44. AK'OM. *n.* (the place) behind one, to one's back. [ʔakʔɔ́m] m.

45. AK'OO. *n.* back (anat). [ʔakʔɔ́·] m.

46. AKS, AK'AKS, AKS. *v.t.* & *v.i.* drink. *v.i.* be wet. *n.* water.
[ʔaks] hb,k,m,pr. [ʔakʔáks] k,hb. [ʔaks] k.

47. AKS- opening up. [ʔaks] hb,k,m.

48. AKSLSGMMAADM. *n.* sleet. [ʔàksl̩sgm̩má·dm̩] m.

49. AKSYAA, AKSWAALXS. *v.i.* accumulate, increase (of fungus or trash); brighten (of the sun or fire); get fat (of humans); spread across (of the wind). [ʔaksyá·] hb,m,k. [ʔakswá·lx̣s] hb,m,k.

50. AKSYAADZIWS. *v.i.* dawn. [ʔaksyà·ʒíws] hb.

50.1 aksyaagwadziiws. *n.* dawn; daybreak. [ʔaksyà·gʷaʒí·ws] m.
50.2 aksyaakwdziws. *n.* dawn; daybreak. [ʔaksyà·kʷʰʒíws] hb.

51. ALAAYS, AK'ALAAYS, AK'ALEEYS, HUK'ALAAYS. *v.i.* lazy. [ʔalá·ys] hb,k,m.
51.1 ak'alaays, ak'aleeys. *plur.* (several are) lazy. [ʔàkʔalá·ys] hb. [ʔàkʔalɛ́·ys] hb.
51.2 huk'alaays. *plur.* (always) lazy. [hukʔalá·ys] hb.

52. ALAH, GA'ALAH. *n.* chimney, smoke hole, vent; the boards used to shelter and cover the smoke hole of a house. [ʔaláh] hb,k,m. [gàʔaláh] hb.

53. ALASKW, ALASGW-, AK'ALASKW, HUK'ALASKW. *v.i.* weak. [ʔaláskʷʰ] k,m.
53.1 ak'alaskw. *plur.* (several are) weak. [ʔàkʔaláskʷʰ] hb.
53.2 huk'alaskw. *plur.* (always) weak. [hùkʔaláskʷʰ] hb.

54. ALDAH. *n.* fir. [ʔaldáh] hb.

55. ALGYAGASK, ALGYAGASG-. *n.* big man; chief; noble. [ʔálgʸʌgàskʰ] k,m.

56. ALGYAX, ALGYAG-, AL'ALGYAX. *v.t. & v.i.* speak, talk. [ʔálgʸʌx̣] k,m. [ʔalʔálgʸʌx̣] hb,k.

57. ALO-, ALU- conspicuously; openly; plainly; standing out. [ʔalo] k,m. [ʔalu] hb.

58. ALOBAA, ALOK'OOɫ. *v.i.* run quickly. [ʔàlobá·] k,m. [ʔàloqʔó·ɫ] k,m.
58.1 alubaa, aluk'aɫ, huk'alubaa. [ʔàlubá·] hb. [ʔàluqʔáɫ] hb.
58.2 huk'alubaa. *plur.* *n.* a fast runner. [hùkʔalubá·] hb.

59. ALUGYIGYAT, ALUGYIGYAD-. *n.* talking chief; spokesman. [ʔàlugʸigʸátʰ] hb.
59.1 alugyigyet, alugyigyed-. *n.* people who live in the open, i.e., not in fortifications, i.e., people who are not fearful of raids. [ʔàlugʸigʸɛ́tʰ] hb.
59.2 alugyigyet, alugyigyed-. *n.* coastal Tsimshian peoples (as opposed to the Skeena River Tsimshian). [ʔàlugʸigʸɛ́tʰ] k.

60. Aɫ-, AɫGA-, AɫGADI- not. [ʔaɫ], [ʔaɫgʌ], [ʔaɫgʌdi] hb,k,m,pr.
60.1 akadi- [ʔákʌdi] hb,k,m,pr.

61. AɫDIGAWS, AɫDIGAWS. *n.* hummingbird. [ʔàɫdigáws] hb,k,m.
61.1 aɫdigaws. *n.* woodpecker. [ʔàɫdigáws] hb.

62. AɫGADIGOO. *n.* nothing. [ʔàɫgʌdigó·] k,m.

63. AɫOO. *v.t.* praise. [ʔaɫɔ́·] m.

64. AɫOOM, HAK'AɫOOM. *n.* sail. [ʔaɫɔ́·m] hb,k,m. [hàkʔaɫɔ́·m]
64.1 aɫo, hak'aɫo. [ʔaɫɔ́] hb. [hàkʔaɫɔ́] hb.
64.2 haɫo, hakhaɫo. [haɫɔ́] hb. [hakhaɫɔ́] hb.

65. AŁOOMBÓOT, AŁOOMBÓOD-. *n.* sailboat. [ʔaɨɔ̀·mbɔ́ʌtʰ] hb.
65.1 hałoombóot, hałoombóod-. [haɨɔ̀·mbɔ́ʌtʰ] m.

66. AŁOOMGYEMK, AŁOOMGYMEG-, HAK'AŁOOMGYEMK, HAK'AŁOMGYEMK. *n.* flag. [ʔaɨɔ̀·mgʸɛ́mkʰ] hb,k,m. [hakʔaɨɔ̀·mgʸɛ́mkʰ] k,m. [hakʔaɨɔ̀mgʸɛ́mkʰ] hb.

67. AŁOOMXSO, HAK'AŁOOMXSO, HAK'AŁOMXSO. *n.* sailboat. [ʔaɨɔ̀·mx̣só] hb,k,m. [hakʔaɨɔ̀·mx̣só] k,m. [hakʔaɨɔ̀mx̣só] hb.

68. AM- serving for. [ʔam] m.

69. AM- useless; without purpose. [ʔam] m.

70. AMAALK, AMALG-. *n.* crust; scab. [ʔamá·lkʰ] k,m.
70.1 amalk, amalg-, ak'amalk. [ʔamálkʰ] hb. [ʔàkʔamálkʰ] hb.
70.2 amelk, amelg-, amelik. [ʔɑmɛ́lkʰ] k. [ʔamɛ́lɩkʰ] k.

71. AMADAALK, AMADAALG-. *v.t. & v.i.* praise; speak well of; worship. [ʔàmʌda·lqʰ] hb,k,m,pr.
71.1 amadaalx, amadaalg-, ga'amadaalx. [ʔàmʌdá·lx̣] hb. [gɑʔàmʌdá·lx̣] hb.
71.2 amadaal'kask, amadaal'kasg-, ga'amadaal'kask. [ʔàmʌdá·lʔqˀɑskʰ] hb. [gɑʔàmʌdá·lʔqˀɑskʰ] hb.

72. AMANÍITS, AMANÍIDZ-. *v.i.* careful; cautious; watchful. [ʔàmanɩ́ʌcʰ] k,m.

73. AMAP'AAS. *v.i.* attractive; beautiful; handsome; pretty (human subject). [ʔàmʌpʔá·s] hb.
73.1 amap'as, amamaxs. [ʔàmapʔás] hb,k,m. [ʔàmamɑ́x̣s] hb,k,m.

74. AMAWAAL, AMAGAWAALT. *v.i.* rich; wealthy. [ʔàmawá·l] hb,k,m. [ʔàmagɑwá·ltʰ] k.
74.1 amagaweelt, amagaweeld-. *plur.* [ʔàmagɑwɛ́·ltʰ] k.

75. AMGAN. *n.* red cedar. [ʔamgɑ̣́n] hb.

76. AMGO'INSK, AMGO'INSG-. *n.* anything enjoyable, e.g., a flower garden; entertainment, e.g., a dance. [ʔamgɔ̣́ʔɩnskʰ] pr.

77. AMGOL. *v.i.* only (human subject). [ʔamgɔ̣́l] k,m.

78. AMGYEEK, AMGYEEK-. *n.* shore animals and plants; seashore life. [ʔamgʸé·kʰ] hb.
78.1 amgyeeka. [ʔamgʸé·kʰɑ] hb.

79. AMGYÍIK, AMGYÍIG-. *n.* black duck; surf scoter; white-winged scoter (*Melanitta deglandi, M. perspicillata*, but not *Anas rubripes*). [ʔamgʸɩ́ʌkʰ] hb,k,m.

80. AMHALAAYT, AMHALAAYD-. *n.* shaman; mask and headdress of a shaman. [ʔàmhalá·ytʰ] hb.
80.1 amhaleyt, amhaleyd-, amhakhaleyt. [ʔàmhaléytʰ] hb,k,m. [ʔamhàkhaléytʰ] hb,k,m.

81. AMHAW. *n.* voice. [ʔamháw] k,m.

82. AMÍILK, AMÍILG-. *n.* disguise; effigy; mask. [ʔamí·ʌlkʰ] k,m,pr.
82.1 axmíilk, axmíilg-. [ʔax̣mí·ʌlkʰ] k,m.

83. AMKSIWAH. *n.* driftwood; European. [ʔʌ̀mksɩwɑ́h] pr.

84. AMP'AAL. *n.* cottonwood. [ʔʌmpʔá·l] hb,pr.

85. AMSAHÓON. *n.* fish trap; weir trap. [ʔʌ̀msɑhɔ́ʌn] hb.

86. AMSGABUU. *v.i.* abundant; adequate; ample; enough; plentiful. *n.* a batch; enough; a lot; plenty; a sum. [ʔàmsgɑbú·] k,m,pr.
86.1 amsxabuu. [ʔàmsx̣ɑbú·] k,m,pr.

87. AMUKS. *v.t. & v.i.* listen; obey. [ʔamúks] k,m.

88. AMUUS. *n.* corner of a house (inside). [ʔamú·s] hb.

89. AMYAAT, AMYAAD-. *plural of* wáatk.

90. ANAAS, AK'ANAAS. *n.* hide; pelt; skin. [ʔʌná·s] hb,k,pr. [ʔàkʔʌná·s] hb.

91. ANAAY. *n.* biscuit; bread. [ʔʌná·y] k.
91.1 aney. [ʔanɛ́y] k.

92. ANN'ANEEX. *n.* duck. [ʔànʔané·x̣] k,m.

93. ANHAAT, ANHAAD-. *n.* side (anat). [ʔanhá·tʰ] k.

94. AN'ON, GA'AN'ON. *n.* hand. [ʔanʔɔ́n] k,pr. [g̣àʔanʔɔ́n] k.

95. ANOOL, AK'ANOOL. *v.t.* allow; give permission. [ʔanɔ́·l] k,m. [ʔàkʔanɔ́·l] k.

96. ANOX. *v.t. & v.i.* agree. [ʔanɔ́x̣] k,m.

97. AP, AB-, HAKHAPS. *n.* bee, bumblebee, wasp. [ʔapʰ] k,m. [hakháps] k.

98. AP- pertaining to one's being, essence, nature. [ʔʌpʰ] hb.

99. AP'ADZIKSMGYET, AP'ADZIKSMGYED-, AP'AK'ADZIKSMGIGET. *n.* snob. [ʔʌpʔàʒɩksm̥gʸɛ́tʰ] hb. [ʔʌpʔakʔàʒɩksm̥gigɛ́tʰ] hb.

100. APLOGAWDI. v.t. empty, make empty. [ʔaplog̣áwdi] k,m.

101. APSXAWGAN, HAKHAPSXAWGANGAN. *n.* wooden spoon. [ʔapsx̣áwgɑn] k,m. [hakhapsx̣àwg̣ɑng̣ɑ́n] k.

102. AS. *n.* soapberries. [ʔas] k,m,pr.

103. ASDI- from the front to the middle of the house; to make a mistake.

[ʔásdi] m.

104. ASDIWAAL. *v.i.* to have an accident; to make a mistake. [ʔàsdiwá·l] hb.

105. ASGAABAX. *n.* chatterbox. [ʔasgá·bʌx̣] hb.

106. ASII, GASASI, GASISII. *n.* foot, leg (anat). [ʔasí·] hb,pr. [g̣àsasí] m. [g̣àsɩsí·] hb.

107. ASOOT' ASOOD-. *n.* sea egg. [ʔasó·t^h] k,m.
107.1 asuun. *n.* sand dollar; sea urchin (spec. *Strongylocentrotus droebachiensis*). [ʔasú·n] m.
107.2 asuut, asuud-. [ʔasú·t^h] hb.

108. AW'AAWS. *n.* curly hair. [ʔawʔá·ws] hb.
108.1 aw'aawsk, aw'aawsg-. [ʔawʔá·wsk^h] m.

109. AWS, AWS. *n.* sand. [ʔaws] k,m,pr. [ʔaws] k.

110. AWT, AWT-. *n.* porcupine. [ʔawt^h] hb,k,m,pr.
110.1 awta. [ʔáwt^{h}a] hb,k,m,pr.

111. AWÜL- aside; away. [ʔáwɨl] m.

112. AWÜL'MAG, AWÜL'MAG-, AWÜLT'AŁ. *v.t.* put aside; put away; sidetrack. [ʔàwɨlʔmág̣] k,m. [ʔàwɨltʔáɬ] k,m.

113. AXBESX, HAKHAXBESX. *v.t.* saw. [ʔax̣bɛ́sx̣] k. [hàkhax̣bɛ́sx̣] k.

114. AXŁK, AXŁG-, AX'AŁK. *v.t.* & *v.i.* achieve; accomplish; arrive; reach. [ʔax̣ɬk^h] k,m. [ʔax̣ʔáɬk^h] m.

115. AYAALTK, AYAALTG-. *v.i.* fortunate; lucky. [ʔayá·lt^{h}k^h] hb,k,m.

116. AYA'AGAS. *n.* a good hunter. [ʔayáʔʌg̣ʌs] k.

117. AYAAWÜX, AYAAWÜG-. *n.* custom; law; precedent; precept. [ʔayá·wɨx̣] m.
117.1 ayaawx, ayaawg-. [ʔayá·wx̣] k.

118. AYAM. *v.t.* throw. [ʔayám] k.

119. AYAWA, AYALUWA. *v.t.* & *v.i.* shout; yell. [ʔàyawá] k,m. [ʔàyaluwá] m.

120. AYAWÜL. *v.i.* adequate; competent; proficient; skilled; successful; talented. *n.* adequacy; competence; proficiency; skill; success; talent. [ʔayáwɨl] k,m.

121. AYIN- no. [ʔáyɩn] k.
121.1 ayn- [ʔayn] k.
121.2 aynɬ- isn't it? [ʔaynɬ] k.

122. AYTK, AYTG-, AK'AYTK. *v.t.* call by name. [ʔayt^{h}k^h] hb,k,m.

[ʔakʔáyt^{h}k^{h}] hb.

B

123. BÁA, K'OL. *v.i.* run. [ba·ʌ] hb,k,m,pr. [qʔol] hb,k,m,pr.
123.1 baah, gol. [ba·h] k. [g̣ol] k.

124. BAAL, BALBAAL' BÜBAAL. *v.t.* feel; guard; handle; keep; touch (agent subject, i.e., to feel or touch something for the purpose of seeing if it's still there, still safe). [ba·l] hb,k,m,pr. [balbá·l] hb. [bɨlbá·l] pr.

125. BÁAL. *v.t. & v.i.* try. [ba·ʌl] k,m,pr.

126. BAA'LX, BELBAA'LX, BÜBAA'LX. *n.* corpse, ghost. [bá·ʔḷx̣] hb,k,m,pr. [bɛlbá·ʔḷx̣] k. [bɨlbá·ʔḷx̣] m.
126.1 ba'lx. [báʔḷx̣] pr.

127. BAAŁ, BIŁBAAŁ. *v.t.* burst; butcher; cut open; spread; stretch. [ba·ł] k,m,pr. [bɩłbá·ł] m.
127.1 beł, bibeł. [bɛł] k. [bibɛł] k.
127.2 baałk, baałg-, labaalxk. *n.* abdominal surgery. [ba·łk^{h}] k,m,pr. [lʌbá·lx̣k^{h}] k.

128. BAAS, LÜBAAS. *v.i.* afraid. [ba·s] hb,k,m,pr. [lɨbá·s] hb.

129. BÁASK, BÁASG-. *v.i.* blow (of the wind). *n.* wind. [ba·ʌsk^{h}] hb,k,m,pr.

130. BABÁA. *v.i.* tremble; quiver (of the chin). [bʌbá·ʌ] m.

131. BADZI. *v.t.* lift. [báʒi] hb.

132. BADZIT'ÓOL. *n.* elephant seal; hooded seal; sea elephant. [baʒitʔó·ʌl] hb.

133. BAK, BAG-. *v.t.* taste. [bɑq^{h}] k,m,pr.
133.1 bax. [bɑx̣] k,m,pr.

134. BALAAS. *n.* haddles; hakes; bastard halibut. [balá·s] hb.

135. BAN. *n.* abdomen; belly. [ban] k,m.
135.1 ben, gaben. [bɛn] hb,k. [g̣abɛ́n] hb.
135.2 bin. [bɩn] hb,pr.
135.3 binbentk, binbentg-. *v.i.* swim with a backstroke, i.e., belly up. [bɩnbɛ́nt^{h}k^{h}] pr.

136. BANA. *n.* bag-net, scoop net (for olachen). [bána] k,pr.
136.1 bena. [bɛna] k,pr.

137. BA'NBA'N. *v.i.* break bread. [bʌʔnbáʔn] k,pr.

138. BAPŁÓON. *plural of* płóon.

139. BASAGN, BÜSBASAGN. *v.t.* divide. [básagn̩] k,m,pr. [bɨsbásʌgn̩] pr.
139.1 basaxk, basaxg-, büsbasaxk. *v.t.* separate; split. [básʌx̣kʰ] k,m,pr. [bɨsbásʌx̣kʰ] pr.

140. BATSK, BATSG-, ŁAMAXSGAT. *v.i.* arrive. [bacʰkʰ] hb. [ɬamáx̣sgʌtʰ] hb.
140.1 betsk, betsg-, maxsk. *v.i.* arrive; come in; stand (up). [bɛcʰkʰ] k,m,pr. [max̣skʰ] k,m,pr.
140.2 betsgn, maxsn. *v.t.* place upright; plant; stand (up). [bɛ́cʰgn̩] pr. [max̣sn̩] pr.
140.3 be'tsn. *v.t.* place upright. [bɛ́ʔcˀn̩] k,m,pr.
140.4 batsgn. *v.i.* arrive in a boat. [bácʰgn̩] hb.

141. BA'WIS. *n.* monkey; bigfoot. [báʔwɩs] hb.
141.1 ba'wüs. [báʔwɨs] hb.
141.2 BA'OS. *n.* monkey; any animal that can imitate human behaviour with great alacrity and deftness. [báʔos] k,m,pr.

142. BAX- up. [bax̣] hb,k,m,pr.

143. BAXBÉEGA'AKS. *n.* gale; waterspout. [bax̣bɛ̀·ʌɣaʔáks] k,m,pr.

144. BAXBOGMGYEMK, BAXBOGMGYEMG-. *n.* butterfly. [bax̣bɔ̀gm̩gʸɛ́mkʰ] hb.

145. BAXGAKSÜÜLGYIMXS. *n.* half-tide (coming in). [bàx̣gaksɨ̂·lgʸɩmx̣s] m.
145.1 baxgaksüülmxs. [bàx̣gaksɨ̂·lm̩x̣s] hb.

146. BAXSE'IK, BAXSE'IG-. *v.t.* pull up along the ground; stretch up along the ground. [bax̣sɛ́ʔɩkʰ] k,m,pr.
146.1 baxse'ky, baxse'gy-. [bax̣séʔkʸˀ] k,m,pr.
146.2 baxse'y'k, baxse'y'g-. [bax̣séʔyʔkˀ] k,m,pr.

147. BAXYAA, BAXWAALXS. *v.i.* go, move, walk up along the ground. [bax̣yá·] k,m,pr. [bax̣wá·lx̣s] k,m,pr.

148. BEE. *n.* lungs. [be·] hb,k,m,pr.
148.1 beeh. [be·h] hb.

149. BEED, BÜKBEED. *n.* bed. [bɛ·d] hb. [bɨkbɛ́·d] hb.

150. BÉEGA'AKS. *n.* storm (at sea; on the water). [bɛ̀·ʌɣaʔáks] k,pr.

151. BEEX, BEEG-. *v.t.* tear; tear up. [bɛ·x̣] hb.
151.1 béex, béeg-. [bɛ·ʌx̣] k,m,pr.
151.2 be'ax, be'ag-, baxbe'ax. [bɛ́ʔʌx̣] k,m,pr. [bax̣bɛ́ʔʌx̣] pr.
151.2 béexk, béexg-. *v.i.* tear bark from a cedar tree. [bɛ́·ʌx̣kʰ] k,m,pr.

152. BIAAXŁ. *n.* cliff. [bia·x̣ɬ] pr.
152.1 biyaaxł. [biya·x̣ɬ] k,m.

153. BI'AGN, BIBI'AGN. *v.t.* deny; tease. [bíʔʌgn̩] hb,k,m,pr. [bɩbíʔʌgn̩] hb.

154. BIIŁTSÜK, BIIŁTSÜG-. *n.* red sunset. [bí·łcʰɨkʰ] k,m,pr.
154.1 *n.* red sunrise (omen of weather change). m.

155. BII'K, BII'G-. *v.i.* lie; tell a lie. *n.* a lie. [bi·ʔk˃] hb.
155.1 bi'ik, bi'ig-. [bíʔɩkʰ] k,m,pr.

156. BIIN. *n.* thrush (orn). [bi·n] hb.

157. BILAAN. *v.i.* put on a belt. *n.* belt. [bilá·n] k,m,pr.

158. BILAX, BILAG-. *n.* moss. [bɩláx̣] hb,k,m,pr.
158.1 blax, blag-. [bl̥áx̣] hb.
158.2 büīlax, büīlag-. [bɨláx̣] hb,k,m,pr.

159. BILHAA. *n.* abalone. [bɩlhá·] hb,k,m,pr.
159.1 blhaa. [bl̥há·] hb.
159.2 büīlhaa. [bɨlhá·] hb,k,m,pr.

160. BIP, BIB-. *n.* uncle-in-law (address; FZH). [bipʰ] k.

161. BIẄAATK, BIẄAATG-, BIẄAATK. *n.* phosphorescent algae. [biÿá·tʰkʰ] hb,k,pr. [biÿá·tʰkʰ] k.

162. BIYAALS. *n.* star. [biyá·ls] hb,k,m,pr.
162.1 biyeels. [biyɛ́·ls] hb,k,m,pr.

163. BIYAALSM'ÁATK, BIYAALSM'ÁATG-. *n.* evening star. [biyà·lsm̥ʔá·ʌtʰkʰ] hb.

164. BIYAALSMGANŁAAK, BIYAALSMGANŁAAG-. *n.* morning star. [bīyà·lsm̥ganłá·kʰ] hb.

165. BLAGMLÓOP, BLAGMLÓOB-. *v.i.* & *n.* mossy-green (colour).

166. BNIM-, BNM-, BÜNIM- pretending to. [bn̥ɩm], [bn̥m̥], [bɨnɩm] hb,m.

167. BÓOT, BÓOD-. *n.* boat. [bɔ·ʌtʰ] hb.

168. BU- plural. [bu] hb,k,m,pr.
168.1 ba- [bʌ] k.

169. BUHBUU'AKS. *v.t.* & *v.i.* splash. [buhbù·ʔáks] hb.

170. BU'NSK' BU'NSG-. *v.t.* & *v.i.* splash. [búʔn̥skʰ] hb.

171. BUPTAL. *plural of* ptal.

172. BUPTEELTK, BUPTEELTG-. *plural of* pteeltk.

173. BUPTS'AAN. *plural of* pts'aan.

174. BUPTS'IH. *plural of* pts'ih.

175. BÚU, BEBÚU. *v.t.* & *v.i.* await; wait. [bu·ʌ] k,m,pr. [bɛbú·ʌ] m,pr.

176. BÚU, GABÚU. *v.t. & v.i.* blow (animate agent). *v.i.* have an orgasm; sound (e.g., of a whale). *n.* orgasm. [bu·ʌ] k,m,pr. [gabú·ʌ] m.
176.1 buu. *n* noise. [bu·] k,m,pr.

177. BU'IL. *v.t.* warn. [bú?ɩl] k,m,pr.
177.1 bu'ɨ. [bu?ɨ] hb.
177.2 búul. [bu·ʌl] k,m,pr.
177.3 buultk, buultg-. [bu·ltʰkʰ] hb.

178. BUUS. *v.i.* split. [bu·s] k,m,pr.

179. BU'Y. *v.t. & v.i.* get out of the way (of). [bu?y] k,m,pr.

D

180. DAALG, DAALG-, DÜDAALG. *v.t.* rebuke, scold, talk to in a mean manner, upbraid (m). *v.i.* talk (pr). [da·lg̣] m,pr. [dɨda·lg̣] m,pr.

181. DÁAŁ. *n.* madam, miss, my dear (polite address to a woman of any rank). [da·ɨ] pr.

182. DAAMSAX, DMDAAMSAX. *v.i.* faint; pass out. [dá·msʌx̣] m,pr. [dm̥dá·msʌx̣] pr.

183. DA'AS. *n.* aunt (address; FZ). [dá?as] k.

184. DAAW, DUDAAW, DÜDAAW. *v.i.* frozen. *n.* ice. [da·w] k,pr. [dudá·w] pr. [dɨdá·w] pr.
184.1 daw, dudaw. [daw] k,pr. [dudáw] pr.

185. DA'AXK, DA'AXG-. *v.i.* able (with verb complement). [da?áx̣kʰ] pr.
185.1 da'axɨk, da'axɨg-, daxda'axɨk. *v.i.* able (with verb complement); succeed. [da?áx̣ɨkʰ] hb,k. [dàx̣da?áx̣ɨkʰ] hb.

186. DAGA'AW. *n.* sea anemone. [dag̣a?áw] hb.

187. DAKŁ. *v.t.* tie around. *v.i.* around (encircling). [dʌkɨ] m,pr.

188. DAL, DILDAL. *v.t., v.i. & n.* fight. [dal] k. [dɩldál] k.
188.1 dal. [dʌl] k.
188.2 del. [dɛl] pr.

189. DALBAKSK, DALBAKSG-. *v.t.* shorten. *v.i.* shrink. [dálbʌkskʰ] pr.
189.1 delbaksk, delbaksg-. [dɛ́lbʌkskʰ] pr.

190. DALPK, DALPG-, DILDALPK. *v.i.* short. [dalpkʰ] k,pr.
190.1 delpk, delpg-. [dɛlpkʰ] k,pr.

191. DAP, DAB-, DAP. *v.t.* count; measure; try (give judgement). *n.* liver; trial. [dapʰ] k,m. [dapʰ] k.
191.1 dap, dab-. [dʌpʰ] k,pr.
191.2 dep, deb-. [dɛpʰ] pr.

192. DAM. *v.t.* hold; keep. [dʌm] pr.
  192.1 damks. *v.t.* squeeze. [dɑmks], [dʌm̥ks] pr.
  192.2 dmwaaks. *v.t.* squeeze. [dm̥wa·ks] pr.

193. DAMXƚ. *n.* friend. [dɑmx̣ɨ] m,pr.

194. DA'ÓOX. *n.* cheek (anat). [dɑʔɔ́·ʌx̣] m.
  194.1 see t'oox.

195. DASX, DIKDASX. *n.* chickaree; chipmunk; squirrel. [dasx̣] k,m,pr. [dɩkdásx̣] k.
  195.1 desx. [dɛsx̣] hb,k,pr.

196. DAWE. *n.* billy goat; domestic goat. [dɑwɛ́] hb.
  196.1 dawee. [dawɛ́·] hb,m,pr.

197. DAWƚ. *v.i.* depart; go away; leave. [dawɨ] pr.

198. DAX- firmly. [dɑx̣] m,pr.

199. DAXDAM, DAXDMDAM. *v.t.* hold fast; hold tight; restrain. [dʌx̣dʌ́m] pr. [dɑ̀x̣dm̥dɑ́m] pr.

200. DAXLAMOL. *n.* Oregon junco (orn). [dɑ̀x̣lɑmɔ́l] hb,

201. DAXƚ, DAKDAXƚ. *n.* hammer. [dɑx̣ɨ] k. [dʌkdɑ́x̣ɨ] k.

202. DAXƚMLÚUT, DAXƚMLÚUD-. *n.* sledge hammer and wedge. [dɑ̀x̣ɨm̥lú·ʌtʰ] hb.

203. DAXS, DAXS. *n.* flounder. [dɑx̣s] hb,k. [dɑx̣s] k.
  203.1 daxsn. *v.t.* throw flat on the water; make skip along the surface of the water. [dɑ́x̣sn̥] k,pr.

204. DAXSMT'ÁA, DAXSMWAN, DAXSMWEN. *v.t.* & *v.i.* mind; obey. *v.i.* sit still. [dɑ̀x̣sm̥tʔá·ʌ] k,m. [dɑ̀x̣sm̥wán] k,m. [dɑ̀x̣sm̥wɛ́n] k,m.

205. DAXWANS. *n.* adze; Indian hammer. [dɑx̣wʌ́ns] hb,k.

206. DAXYÁAGWA. *v.t.* hold fast; hold tight. [dɑx̣ʌyá·ʌgʷɑ] pr.
  206.1 daxyaakw, daxyaagw-. *v.t.* hold in one's hand; keep in one's hand. [dɑx̣yá·kʷʰ] m,pr.

207. DAYTS. *n.* alaria algae. [daycʰ] hb.

208. DEENTK, DEENTG-. *v.t.* lead by the hand, [dɛ·ntʰkʰ] m,pr.

209. DEESGYEN. *n.* whetstone. [dɛ·sgʸɛ́n] m,pr.
  209.1 deesgyin. [dɛ·sgʸɩ́n] m,pr.

210. DEEWL. *n.* burial payment. [dé·wl̥] hb,pr.

211. DEEXƚGAGYEMK, DEEXƚGAGYEMG-. *n.* halo around the moon. [dɛ̀·x̣ɨgɑgʸɛ́mkʰ] hb.
  211.1 dexɨgagyemk. [dɛ̀x̣ɨgɑgʸɛ́mkʰ] m.

212. DIBÁA. *v.t.* attempt. *v.i.* struggle; try. [dibá·ʌ] k,m.

213. DIBOOYGIT, DIBOOYGID-. *n.* shrew (zool); masked shrew; pigmy shrew. [dɩbó·ygɩt^{h}] hb.

214. DIDIT'IIL. *v.i.* go quickly. [diditʔí·l] hb.

215. DIDII. *plural of* la̱xdii.

216. DIDUULS, DILDUULS. *v.i.* alive. [didú·ls] hb. [dildú·ls] hb.
216.1 didúuls. [didú·ʌls] m,pr.

217. DII, DIDIIYA. *n.* hill; mons; mons veneris. [di·] hb,m. [didí·ya] m.
217.1 díi. [di·] hb,k,m.

218. DIILM̱X, DAXDIILM̱X. *v.t.* & *v.i.* answer. *v.i.* reply; respond. [dí·lm̩x̣] hb. [dax̣dí·lm̩x̣] hb.
218.1 díilm̱xk, diilm̱xg-. [dí·ʌlm̩x̣k^{h}] k,m,pr.

219. DÍILTK, DÍILTG-. *v.t.* & *v.i.* take revenge (on). [di·ʌlt^{h}k^{h}] k,m.

220. DITXAKS. *n.* high tide. [dɩtx̣áks] k.
220.1 ditxa̱ks. [dɩtxʌ́ks] hb,m.

221. DM̱- non-past. [dm̩] hb,k,m,pr.

222. DOO. *plural of* sgüü.

223. DOOŁ. *n.* tripe. [do·ɬ] m,pr.

224. DÓOS. *n.* the opposite side; the other side. [dɔ́·ʌs] pr.

225. DOOYA̱XS. *v.i.* strong. [dɔ́·yʌx̣s] m,pr.

226. DOX. *plural of* gáa; gyaa.

227. DUKWŁG̱N. *v.i.* drown. [dukʷʰɬgn̩] m,pr.

228. DÚUBASG̱A'NIS. *n.* base of a mountain; foot of a mountain. [dú·ʌbasg̣aʔnís] pr.

229. DUULA̱. *n.* tongue (anat); lumber; shiplap. [dú·la] k,m,pr.

230. DÚULALEK, DÚULALEG-. *n.* flame. [dù·ʌlalɛ́k^{h}] k.

231. DUUŁK, DUUŁG-, DIKDUUŁK. *n.* basket (large, cedar). [du·ɬk^{h}] hb. [dɩkdú·ɬk^{h}] hb.
231.1 dúułk, duułg-, dikdułk. *n.* basket (made of cedar bark; used for collecting seaweed; has a strap for over the shoulder and a cloth top closed with a drawstring). [du·ʌɬk^{h}] k, pr. [dɩkdúɬk^{h}] k.

232. DUUP, DUUB-, DÜPDÚUP. *n.* base of a mountain; foot of a mountain.

[du·pʰ] pr. [dɨpdú·ʌpʰ] pr.
232.1 dúup, dúub-. [du·ʌpʰ] pr.
232.2 duupxs. *n.* heel (anat). [du·px̣s] hb,k.

233. DUUS, DIKDÚUS. *n.* cat. [du·s] hb,k,m,pr. [dɩkdúʌs] k.

234. DUUSMGYILHAWLI. *n.* bobcat: cougar; lynx; mountain lion. [dù·sm̩gʸɩlháwli] hb,m,pr.

235. DUWAY, LUWAY. *v.t.* & *v.i.* paddle (e.g. a canoe).

236. DÜÜ. *plural of* dzak.

DZ

237. DZABÁA, DZAK'OL. *v.i.* lame; run a short distance. [ʒʌbá·ʌ] m,pr. [ʒʌq?ǒl] m,pr.
237.1 see ts'übaa.

238. DZABUUKSK, DZABUUKSG-. *n.* spitoon. [ʒʌbú·kskʰ] m,pr.
238.1 dzapuuksk, dzapuuksg-. [ʒʌpʰú·kskʰ] m,pr.

239. DZAGA- around (encircling). [ʒʌɣ̣ʌ] hb,k,m,pr.

240. DZAGAGANAAXS. *n.* bridge. [ʒʌ̀ɣ̣ʌg̣aná·x̣s] pr.

241. DZAGATGUBAA. *v.i.* run around in circles. [ʒʌ̀ɣ̣ʌtʰgubá·] hb.

242. DZAGAYÁA, DZAGAWAALXS. *v.i.* & *v.i.* go across; move across; walk across. [ʒʌ̀ɣ̣ʌyá·ʌ] k. [ʒʌ̀ɣ̣ʌwá·lx̣s] k.

243. DZAGMDAAWŁ. *v.i.* go ashore. [ʒʌ̀ɣ̣m̩dá·wɬ] pr.

244. DZAK, DZAG-, DÜÜ. *v.t.* kill. *v.i.* dead; die. [ʒakʰ] k,m. [dï·] hb,k,m,pr.
244.1 dzak, dzag-. [ʒʌkʰ] pr.
244.2 dzek, dzeg-. [ʒɛkʰ] hb.

245. DZAK'WÜSK, DZAK'WÜSG-. *n.* animal (i.e., land animal; does not include flying animals nor water animals). [ʒákʷ?ɨskʰ] hb,pr.

246. DZALEE. *n.* an old fish. [ʒʌlɛ́·] k,m.

247. DZAŁ, DZÜDZAŁ. *v.t.* consume; eat up; lose. [ʒaɬ] hb. [ʒɨʒál] hb.
247.1 dzeł. *v.t.* eat up. *v.i.* lose. [ʒɛɬ] pr.

248. DZAP, DZAB-. *v.t.* build; construct; make. [ʒapʰ] hb,k,pr.
248.1 dzep, dzeb-, dzapdzep. [ʒɛpʰ] hb,k,pr. [ʒʌpdzɛ́pʰ] pr.
248.2 dzapk, dzapg-. *n.* crest (family insignia). [ʒapʰkʰ] k.
248.3 dzapol. *v.t.* build; make. [ʒápʰol] k.
248.4 dzepk, dzepg-. *n.* crest (family insignia). [ʒɛpʰkʰ] k.

249. DZA'WEST, DZA'WESD-. *n.* laughing berries; salal (*Gautheria shallon*); smiling berries. [ʒa?wɛ́stʰ] k,m.

250. DZAXAGAYT, DZAXAGAYD-. *n.* flying squirrel. [ʒàx̣agáytʰ] k.

251. DZAX'OOTK, DZAX'OOTG-. *v.i.* naked; nude. [ʒʌx̣ʔɔ́·tʰkʰ] hb,m,pr.

252. DZEEX. *v.t.* give (i.e., freely, not expecting a return). [ʒe·x̣] hb.
 252.1 dzéext, dzéexd-. [ʒe·ʌx̣tʰ] pr.
 252.2 ndzuh. "Give it to me." [n̩ʒúh] hb.

253. DZEEYEƚ. *n.* fish trap; fish weir. [ʒe·yɛ́ɫ] m,pr.

254. DZEM. *v.t.* & *v.i.* boil. [ʒɛm] k,m,pr.
 254.1 dzim. [ʒɩm] pr.

255. DZE'PL. *v.t.* play with compulsively; handle compulsively. [ʒɛ́ʔp̓l̩] pr.

256. DZEYEET, DZEYEED-. *v.t.* trap. *v.i.* go trapping. [ʒɛyé·tʰ] pr.

257. DZIGAWS. *n.* salmon, split open and dried. [ʒɩg̣áws] m,pr.

258. DZIGYIDZÍIP, DZIBYIDZÍIB-. *n.* & *adv.* tomorrow. [ʒɩgʸɩʒí·ʌpʰ] pr.
 258.1 dzügyidziwp, dzügyidziwb-. [ʒɨgʸɩʒíwpʰ] pr.

259. DZÍIBLK, DZÍIBLG-. *v.i.* all burned up. [ʒíʌbl̩kʰ] pr.

260. DZÍILK, DZÍILG-. *v.i.* melt. [ʒi·ʌlkʰ] pr.

261. DZIIS, DZIKDZIIS. *n.* salmon trap; fish weir; a wickerwork weir for catching seals or salmon in the falling tide. [ʒi·s] k. [ʒɩkʒí·s] k.
 261.1 dzíis. [ʒi·ʌs] k.

262. DZI'IS. *n.* grandmother (address; FM, MM). [ʒíʔis] pr.

263. DZIIẄ, DZIKDZIIẄ. *n.* dolphin; porpoise. [ʒi·ÿ] hb,k,m,pr. [ʒɩkʒí·ÿ] k.
 263.1 dziẅ. [ʒiÿ] hb.

264. DZIIWKWSA. *v.i.* bail water out of a canoe or boat. [ʒí·wkʷʰsa] m,pr.
 264.1 see ts'iiwkwsa.

265. DZIIWS. *n.* daylight; daytime. [ʒi·ws] pr.
 265.1 dzidziws. "It is still daylight." [ʒiʒíws] hb.
 265.2 dziws. *n.* daylight; daytime. [ʒiws] hb.

266. DZINDEH. *adv.* when. [ʒɩndɛ́h] pr.

267. DZOGA- across. [ʒɔ́g̣a] hb.

268. DZOGM- ashore; in (to land from the water). [ʒɔ́g̣m̩] hb.

269. DZOGMBAASK, DZOGMBAASG-. *n.* onshore wind. [ʒɔ̀g̣m̩bá·skʰ] hb.

270. DZOGMHAWAAS. *n.* south wind. [ʒɔ̀g̣m̩hawá·s] hb.

271. DZÓOK, DZÓOG, GADZOOK. *v.i.* ashamed. [ʒoʌqʰ] k,pr. [gaʒó·qʰ] k.
 271.1 dzóox, dzóog- lidzóox. [ʒoʌx̣] k,pr. [liʒoʌ́x̣] k.
 271.2 dzox, dzog-. [ʒox̣] hb.

272. DZOOKS. *v.t.* drain the water off of; dry. [ʒo·ks] m,pr.
 272.1 *see* ts'ooks.

273. DZOOɬ. *v.i.* slide down. [ʒɔ·ɬ] hb.
 273.1 dzóoɬ. [ʒɔʌɬ] pr.

274. DZÜGWIITS, DZÜGWIIDZ-. *n.* large sea urchin (spec. *Arbacia punctulata, Strongylocentrotus franciscanus, Echinometra lucunter*). [ʒɨgʷí·cʰ] hb.

E

275. ÉEPN. *v.i.* light (of weight). [ʔé·ʌpʰṇ] k,m,pr.

276. ÉESK, ÉESG-. *v.i.* promise. [ʔe·ʌskʰ] k.
 276.1 esk, esg-. [ʔeskʰ] hb.

G

277. GÁA. *v.i.* come. [g̣a] k.
 277.1 gah. [g̣ah] k.

278. GA'AADMHOON. *plural of* aadmhoon.

279. GA'AAK, GA'AAG-. *plural of* aak; aax.

280. GA'AAT, GA'AAD-. *plural of* aat.

281. GAAGɬIK, GAAGɬIG-. *n.* house mouse; rat. [gá·gɬɩkʰ] pr.
 281.1 gaakɬik, gaakɬig-. [g̣á·kɬɩkʰ] m,pr.
 281.2 gagɬik, gagɬig-. [g̣ág̣ɬɩkʰ] pr.
 281.3 gakliik, gakliig-. [g̣ákli·kʰ] hb.

282. GAAK, GAAG-. *n.* swan. [g̣a·kʰ] k.

283. GA'ALAH. *plural of* alah.

284. GAALMX. *n.* Nass-Gitksan language. [g̣a·lṃx̣] hb.
 284.1 geelmx. [g̣e·lṃx̣] hb.

285. GA'ALX. *plural of* alax; alx.

286. GA'AMADAALX. *plural of* amadaalx.

287. GAAMGANTS, GAAMGANDZ-. *n.* oars. [g̣á·mgʌncʰ] hb,m.
 287.1 gaamgn. *v.t.* pry. [g̣á·mgṇ] pr.

288. GAAN. *n.* skunk. [g̣a·n] hb.
 288.1 geen. [g̣e·n] hb.
 288.2 geyn. [g̣ɛyn] k.

289. GA'AN'ON. *plural of* an'on.

290. GA'APAYTK, GA'APAYTG-. *v.i.* fall down (patient subject). [ga?apʰáytʰkʰ] m.
290.1 *see* k'a'apaytk.

291. GAAPK, GAAPG-, GAXGAAPK. *v.t.* rake; scratch. [ga·pʰkʰ] k,pr. [gaxgá·pʰkʰ] k.
291.1 gaa'pn. *v.i.* be scraped. [gá·?p'n̩] m.
291.2 gaapxan. *v.t.* paw; rake; scratch. [gá·pxʌn] pr.
291.3 gaapxs. *n.* border; sill (i.e., of a window or door). [ga·pxs] pr.

292. GA'AWIS. *n.* new-born baby girl. [gá?awɩs] pr.

293. GAAX, GAAG-, GAAX. *v.i.* & *n.* black; raven. [ga·x] k,pr. [gax] k.
293.1 gaax, gaag-, gakgak. *n.* black bass; Pacific sea bass. [ga·x] hb,k. [gakgáqʰ] k.
293.2 gáax, gáag-. *n.* black bass. [gaʌx] k.

294. GA'AY. *n.* wing (anat). [ga?áy] pr.
294.1 gak'ay. [gaq?áy] pr.

295. GAAYDI BAA'LX. *n.* mushroom. [gà·ydɩbá·?lx] hb.

296. GAAYDI TS'U'U'TS. *n.* glans (penis); mushroom. [gà·ydic?ú?u?c'] m.

297. GAAYDMBOOSN. *n.* rimmed hat (from "boss's hat (hb) or Boston hat (m)). [gà·ydm̩bɔ́·sn̩] hb,m.

298. GAAYDMTS'AALXS. *n.* hooded coat. [gà·ydm̩c?á·lxs] hb.

299. GAAYɫK, GAAYɫT-. *n.* a large dish (made of a single piece of hemlock bark). [ga·yɨkʰ] pr.
299.1 gayɨ, gagayɨ. *n.* dish; plate. [gayɨ] k,pr. [gagáyɨ] k.

300. GAAYT, GAAYD-. *n.* billed hat. [ga·ytʰ] hb.
300.1 gayt, gayd-, gagayt. *n.* hat. [gaytʰ] k,pr. [gagáytʰ] k.

301. GAB, GAB-. *v.t.* & *v.i.* eat. [gʌb] pr.
301.1 ga'psk, ga'psq-. *v.i.* eat berries off the tree. [gʌ?p'skʰ] pr.

302. GABALAAS. *n.* bat; mosquito larvae. [gabalá·s] k.
302.1 ga'pilaas. *n.* mosquito larvae and pupae. [gʌ?p'ɩlá·h] hb.

303. GABAXSK, GABAXSG-. *v.i.* jump in fright. [gabáxskʰ] pr.
303.1 galiibaaxskh, galiibaaxsg-. *plural of* goos.
303.2 galiibaxsk, galiibaxsg-. *plural of* goos.

304. GABEN. *plural of* ben.

305. GABILAH. *n.* gun. [gʌbɩláh] hb.
305.1 ga'pilah. [gʌʔpʾɩláh] m.

306. GABOGMP'AXS. *n.* corduroy pants. [gabògm̥pʔáx̣s] hb.

307. GABOOK, GABOOG-. *n.* cockles. [gabɔ́·qʰ] m.
307.1 gaboox, gaboog-. [gabɔ́·x̣] hb.

308. GABÚU. *plural of* búu.

309. GADEELPK, GADEELPG-. *n.* anchor. [gadɛ́·lpʰkʰ] hb,m,pr.

310. GADÍIŁGMWAS. *n.* fringed blanket. [gadìʌɬgm̥wás] hb.

311. GADIISK, GADIISG-. *v.i.* braid one's hair into one braid on the side of the head. [gadí·skʰ] pr.
311.1 *see* k'adiisk.

312. GADNAADA. *interr. pron.* who? [gadná·dʌ] pr.

313. GADOOLT' GADOOLD-. *n.* male humpback salmon. [gadɔ́·ltʰ] hb.

314. GADZAA. *n.* cross; an "X". [gaʒá·] m.

315. GADZAK, GADZAG-. *plural of* ts'ak.

316. GADZAKEEẄ. *n.* gigartina algae. [gaʒakʰé·ẅ] hb.

317. GADZIKS. *v.i.* declare bankruptcy; sell out (*lit.* throw water on everything). [gáʒɩks] pr.

318. GADZOOK, GADZOOG-. *plural of* dzoox.

319. GAGAATS, GAGAADZ-. *n.* dogfish. [gagá·cʰ] k.

320. GAGAAWS. *n.* horn (of any animal). [gagá·ws] pr.
320.1 gagaws. *n.* antlers (hb,m); buck (with horns) hb. [gagáws] hb,m.

321. GAGAWN. *plural of* k'awn.

322. GAGAYKT, GAGAYKD-. *plural of* gayk.

323. GAGAYŁ. *plural of* gayɬ.

324. GAGAYT, GAGAYD-. *plural of* gayt.

325. GAGOK, GAGOG-. *n.* dried fish nose. [gagóqʰ] m.
325.1 gagox, gagog-. [gagóx̣] m.
325.2 gagox. *n.* fish brains; forehead (*hum. anat*). [gagóx̣] pr.

326. GAGOOM, GAGOOM. *n.* sea gull. [gagó·m] k. [gagó·m] k.
326.1 gaguum. [gagú·m] k,pr.

327. GAGIGYET, GAGIGYED-. *n.* common people. [gàgɩgʸɛ́tʰ] hb.

328. GAGTS'II. *plural of* xts'ii.

329. GAGWÜNUU. *plural of* gwünuu.

330. GAHAYDMX. *plural of* haydmx.

331. GAHÚUD, GAHÚUD-. *n.* beads on a string; necklace. [gahú·ʌd] m,pr.
331.1 gahuut, gahuud-. *n.* beads. [gahú·tʰ] hb.

332. GAHUUST, GAHUUSD-. *plural of* huust.

333. GAK'AA'LK, GAK'AA'LG-. *plural of* k'aa'lk.

334. GAKGOM. *plural of* goom; goom.

335. GAKK'ATSIWELT' GAKK'ATSIWELD-. *plural of* k'atsiwéelt.

336. GAKŁKUM'YEE. *plural of* łkum'yee.

337. GAKŁÜÜLSK, GAKŁÜÜLSG-. *plural of* łüülsk.

338. GAK'OOŁ. *v.i.* shiver. [gak?ɔ́·ɬ] m.

339. GAKPAL. *plural of* kpal.

340. GAKSAA. *plural of* ksaa.

341. GAKSÍILT, GAKSÍILD-. *plural of* ksil.

342. GAKSK, GAKSG-, LIWDSK. *v.i.* wake up. [gakskʰ] k. [liwdskʰ] k.
342.1 gyaksk, gyaksg-. [gʸakskʰ] k.
342.2 gakst, gaksd-. *n.* rattle. [gakstʰ] k,m.

343. GALAAK, GALAAG-. *v.i.* cracked. [galá·kʰ] hb.
343.1 galaakt, galaakd-. [galá·kʰtʰ] pr.

344. GALAALTK, GALAALTG-. *plural of* láaltk.

345. GALAAẄ. *n.* cedar. [galá·ÿ] pr.

346. GALAPLIIB, GALAPLIIB-. *n.* thunder. [gàlʌplí·b] pr.
346.1 galaplíip, galaplíib-. [gàlʌplíʌpʰ] pr.
346.2 galiliip, galiliib-. [gàlɩlí·pʰ] hb.
346.3 galiplip, galiplib-. [gàlɩplípʰ] k.

347. GALAXUN. *n.* fence. [galáx̣un] k,m.

348. GALBEELTK, GALBEELTG-. *num.* two (of canoes). [galbé·ltʰkʰ] pr.

349. GALDM'AKS. *n.* bucket; pail [gàldm̩?áks] k,pr.

350. GALDMALGYAX, GALDMALGYAG-. *n.* talking chief; chief's assistant.

[gàldmálgʸax̣] hb.

351. GALDOO. *n.* camp. [galdó·] k,m.
351.1 galdzox. [galʒóx̣] k,m.

352. GALDZAP, GALDZAB-, GALDZAPDZAP. *n.* town; village. [galʒápʰ] k. [gàlʒʌpʒápʰ] k.
352.1 galts'aap, galts'aab-. [galtsá·pʰ] k.

353. GALGA'AAYSUU. *n.* knee. [gàlga?á·su·] pr.

354. GALGAL'ÜÜNG. GALGAL'ÜÜNG-. *n.* an empty box. [gàlgal?ɨ́·ng] pr.
354.1 gal'üüng. *n.* coffin. [gal?ɨ́ng] pr.

355. GALGOLIK, GALGOLIG-. *plural of* k'oolx; k'oylk.
355.1 galgolx. *plural of* k'oolax.

356. GALIIMSK, GALIIMSG-. *v.t. & v.i.* spend lavishly; throw away. [galí·mskʰ] pr.

357. GALIILP, GALILLB-. *n.* hip (of roof); house beam. [galí·lpʰ] hb.

358. GALK, GALG-. *n.* creeping raspberry (*Rubus pedatus*).

359. GALKSIŁÓOSK, GALKSIŁÓOSG-. *n.* nose ring (*note*: worn only by the nobility). [gàlksiɬó·ʌskʰ] pr.

360. GALKSIYAAN. *v.t.* go through (e.g. the door). [gàlksɩyá·n] hb.

361. GALMOOS. *n.* crab. [galmó·s] k.
361.1 *see* k'almoos.

362. GAL'OD, GAL'OD-. *v.t.* let go (of). [gal?ɔ́d] pr.

363. GAL'OOS. *n.* stomach. [gal?ó·s] k.
363.1 gal'os. [gal?ɔ́s] hb.
363.2 gal'o'os. [gal?ɔ́?ɔs] m,pr.
363.3 *see* o'os.

364. GALSGANTK, GALSGANTG-. *num.* three (of canoes). [galsgántʰkʰ] pr.
364.1 galtsgan. *num.* three (of long objects). [galcʰgán] hb,pr.

365. GAŁDIK. *v.i.* be to one side. [gáɬdɩkʰ] pr.
365.1 gaɬdik- to one side. [gaɬdɩk] pr.

366. GAŁDIKSGÜÜ. *v.i.* lie at the side. [gaɬdɩksgɨ́·] m,pr.

367. GAŁDIKYAA. *v.i.* go aside; go into the woods; walk to one side. [gaɬdɩkyá·] m,pr.

368. GAŁIK, GAŁIG-. *plural of* ɬik.

369. GAŁINGIITX. *plural of* ɬingiitx.

370. GAMAATS, GAMAADZ. *n.* starfish. [g̣amá·cʰ] hb,k.

371. GAMGAANTK, GAMGAANTG-, GAGAMGAANTK. *n.* door. [gamgá·ntʰkʰ] hb. [g̣àgʌmgá·ntʰkʰ] hb.
371.1 gamgantk, gamgantg-. *n.* door (*note*: archaic). [g̣amg̣ántʰkʰ] pr.

372. GAMGOOD, GAMGOOD-. *v.t.* pity. [g̣amg̣ó·d] pr.

373. GAMIILG, GAMIILG-. *v.i.* play. [g̣amí·lg] pr.
373.1 gamiilg, gamiilg-. [g̣amí·lg̣] m,pr.

374. GAMŁABIISK, GAMŁABIISG-. *n.* shavings. [g̣ʌmɨʌbí·skʰ] pr.

375. GAMT'U'TSK, GAMT'U'TSG-. *n.* charcoal, coal, lava (i.e., volcanic rock; note: used as a cooking stone). [g̣amtʔúʔcʰkʰ] hb.
375.1 gamt'úu'ts. [g̣amtʔúʌʔcʾ] k.

376. GAMO. *plural of* mmo.

377. GAMO'MG, GAMO'MG-. *plural of* mo'mx.

378. GAMÚUKT, GAMÚUKD-. *plural of* muk.

379. GAN, GANGAN. *n.* stick; tree. [g̣an] k,pr. [g̣angán] k.
379.1 gan- long; wooden. [g̣an] hb,k,m,pr.
379.2 -gan, -gn, -xn long; wooden. [g̣an], [g̣ʌn] hb,k,m,pr. [g̣n] hb,k,m,pr. [x̣n] hb,k,m,pr.
379.3 gantk, gantg-. *v.i.* have an erection (*physiol*); erect (*physiol*); stiff. *n.* erection (*physiol*). [g̣antʰkʰ] m,pr.

380. GANA- to keep doing something; continuing to. [g̣ana] pr.
380.1 gani- [g̣ani] hb.

381. GANAAG, GANAAG-. *n.* foot or leg of a deer; deer tracks. [g̣aná·g̣] m,pr.
381.1 ganaak, ganaag-. [g̣aná·qʰ] m,pr.
381.2 ganaax, ganaag-. [g̣aná·x̣] m,pr.
381.3 ganaaẅ. *n.* drying rack. [g̣aná·ÿ] pr.
381.4 ganaaxs. *n.* ladder; steps. [g̣aná·x̣s] pr.
381.5 ganéexs. [g̣ané·ʌx̣s] pr.

382. GA'NAH. *n.* mast (*naut*). [g̣áʔnah] hb.
382.1 ganałóo. [g̣àna ɨóʌ] hb.
382.2 *see* sganhałóo.

383. GANAHAAYTK, GANAHAAYTG-. *v.t.* lean against, stand against. [g̣anahá·ytʰkʰ] pr.

384. GANAŁ. *plural of* naał.

385. GANAW. *n.* frog; toad. [g̣anáw] hb.
385.1 ganaw. [g̣anáw] k,pr.

386. GANAWELII. *n.* carrying strap (note: a long strap, 1½" x 6', used for carrying things by tying them to the head). [g̣anawɛ́li·] pr.
386.1 ganiwaal. *v.i.* continue; keep doing (something). [g̣aniwá·l] hb.
386.2 ganiwilaweel. *v.i.* continuously do (something); always be doing (something). [g̣àniwɩlawɛ́·l] hb.

387. GANDAAWŁMGOOT, GANDAAWŁMGOOD-. *v.i.* shift position; take a rest. [g̣andà·wɬm̥gó·tʰ] pr.

388. GANDAH. *n.* skate (*ichth*). [g̣andáh] k.
388.1 gandeh. [g̣andɛ́h] hb.

389. GANDZÓOŁ. *n.* foreskin; prepuce. [g̣anʒó·ʌɬ] m.

390. GANHAAYK, GANHAAYG-. *n.* sparks.

391. GANHADA. *n.* Raven Clan; Raven Phratry; Raven Tribe. [g̣anháda] k.

392. GANHADAAY. *n.* wheel (*naut*). [g̣ànhadá·y] hb.
392.1 ganhadeey. [g̣ànhadɛ̌·y] hb.

393. GANILÍIMI. *v.t. & v.i.* keep singing. [g̣ànilíʌmi] hb.

394. GANIWNAKS. *plural of* 'naks.
394.1 ganiwnskt, ganiwnskd-.

395. GANLUTGUBAA. *n.* block (*naut*); double block (*naut*). [g̣anlùtʰgubá·] hb.

396. GANŁÁAK, GANŁÁAG-. *n.* morning. [g̣anɬáʌkʰ] k.

397. GANŁAAN. *n.* armour. [g̣anɬá·n] pr.

398. GANŁABIISK, GANŁABIISG-. *n.* drawknife; drawshave; spokeshave. [g̣ànɬʌbí·skʰ] pr.

399. GANOODZIT, GANOODZID-. *plural of* noots.

400. GANOOKSINSK, GANOOKSINSG-. *n.* gunnel (*naut*). [g̣anó·ksɩnskʰ] hb.
400.1 ganooksnsk, ganooksnsg-. [g̣anó·ksn̩skʰ] hb.
400.2 gan'ooksnsk, gan'ooksnsg-. [g̣anʔó·ksn̩skʰ] m.

401. GANP'IYAAN. *n.* chimney; stove pipe. [g̣ànpʔiyá·n] hb.

402. GANSALGOS. *n.* swing (recreation apparatus). [g̣ànsalgós] k.

403. GANSIGÍIDASK, GANSIGÍIDASG-. *n.* yeast. [g̣ànsɩgí·ʌdʌskʰ] pr.

404. GANTS'AA'TS, GANTS'AA'DZ. *n.* sticks used to spread out a skin for drying. [g̣ancʔá·ʔcʼ] pr.

405. GANTS'IIT, GANTS'IID-. *n.* clam siphon. [g̣ancʔí·tʰ] hb.

406. GAN'UKSGIŁÉE. *n.* boom (*naut*). [gan?ùksgiɨéʌ] hb.

407. GANUUT, GANUUD-. *n.* week. [ganú·tʰ] hb.
407.1 ganuutk, ganuutg-. *n.* Sunday. [ganú·tʰkʰ] m.

408. GANYEETK, GANYEETG-. *n.* forefathers; grandfathers (*plural of* niiya). [ganyɛ́·tʰkʰ] k,m.

409. GANYÜSYETSA. *n.* suspenders. [ganyɨsyɛ́cʰa] hb.

410. GAP'AXS. *plural of* p'axs.

411. GAP'EELTK, GAP'EELTG-. *v.t. & v.i.* wink. [gap?ɛ́·ltʰkʰ] pr.
411.1 gapsl. [gápsl] m.
411.2 *see* k'asíipsl.

412. GASASI. *n.* legs; sun rays (*plural of* asii). [gàsasí] m.
412.1 gasasii. [gàsʌsí·] pr.
412.2 gasüsíi. *plural of* sii; síi.

413. GASGAATSK, GASGAATSG-. *v.i.* rough. [gʌsgá·cʰkʰ] m,pr.
413.1 gatsgaats, gatsgaadz. *n.* dogfish shark. [gacʰgá·cʰ] hb.

414. GASGAAWT, GASGAAWD-. *v.i.* be of a certain size (Note: *used with* aam- *and* 'wiileeksm, *but not* ɨgu-).
414.1 *see* aamgasgaawt.
414.2 *see* 'wiileeksmgasgaawt.

415. GASGADZAX. *n.* ants. [gasgáʒʌx] hb.
415.1 *see* k'ask'adzn.

416. GASGOOS. *n.* stork. [gasgó·s] k.
416.1 gasgos. *plural of* k'os.

417. GASIHON. *plural of* sihóon.

418. GASK'U'UNSK, GASK'U'UNSG-. *plural of* sk'úunsk.

419. GASSTUNŁ. *plural of* stúunɨ.

420. GASUUNS. *plural of* suuns.
420.1 gasúuns. *plural of* súuns.

421. GATGYET, GATGYED-, GATLEET. *v.i.* strong. [gatgʸɛ́tʰ] k,pr. [gatlɛ́·tʰ] k.
421.1 gatgyetk, gatgyetg-. *v.t.* jerk; push; throw down. [gatgʸɛ́tʰkʰ] pr.

422. GATGYETGABAASK, GATGYETGABAASG-. *n.* gale; strong wind. [gatgʸɛ̀tgabá·skʰ] pr.
422.1 gatgyetgmbaask. gatgyetgmbaasg-. *n.* gale; squall. [gatgʸɛ̀tgmbá·skʰ] m,pr.

423. GATLEET, GATLEED-. *plural of* gatgyet.

424. GATS, GADZ-. *v.t.* pour; spill. [gacʰ] pr.

425. GATS'AA'TSAX, GATS'AA'TSAG-. *plural of* ts'ak; ts'ax.

426. GATS'ALTS'AL. *plural of* ts'al; ts'a'l; ts'e'l.

427. GATS'AŁ. *v.t. & v.i.* swallow. [gacʔáɬ] k.
427.1 *see* k'adzał.

428. GATS'AWGYIT, GATS'AWGYID-. *plural of* ts'awx.

429. GATS'ÓOXS. *plural of* ts'óoxs.

430. GAWAGANI. *n.* the act of making peace. [gawagáni] m.

431. GAWDI. *v.i.* all. [gáwdi] pr.

432. GAWIŁEE. *n.* blood veins. [gawiɬé·] pr.

433. GAWLG, GAWLG-, GALGAWLG. *v.t.* wind around (as a string). [gawlg] pr. [galgáwlg] pr.

434. GAWN, GANGAWN. *v.t.* chew. [gawn] pr. [gangáwn] pr.

435. GAWS, NAK'AWST. *n.* hair. [gaws] k,m,pr. [naqʔáwstʰ] k,
435.1 gawsk, gawsg-, gàsgawsk. *v.i.* narrow; thin. [gawskʰ] k,pr. [gasgáwskʰ] k.

436. GAWSGMGAN. *n.* pole. [gàwsgmgán] m,pr.

437. GAX. *n.* ground hog; woodchuck. [gax] pr.

438. GAXAAX. *n.* berries in bloom (i.e., the white flowers); foam. [gaxá·x] pr.

439. GAXBA-, GAXPA- sometimes. [gáxba], [gáxpʰa] pr.

440. GAXBA'ALASKW, GAXBA'ALASGW-, GAXBA'AK'ALASKW. *v.i.* sometimes weak. [gàxbaʔaláskʷʰ] hb. [gàxbaʔàkʔaláskʷʰ] hb.

441. GAXŁIIẄ. *plural of* xɬiiẅ.

442. GAXPAWEEL. *v.i.* do (something) sometimes. [gàxpʰawɛ́·l] pr.

443. GAXGOOMTK, GAXGOOMTG-. *plural of* k'oomtk.

444. GAXGÜÜS. *plural of* xgüüs.

445. GAXGYET, GAXGYED-. *plural of* xgyet.

446. GAXHAY. *plural of* xa; xay.

447. GAXSAN. *plural of* xsan.

448. GAXSGYEN. *plural of* sgyen.

449. GAXSO. *plural of* xso.

450. GAXTS'II. *plural of* xts'i.

451. GAYAAKW, GAYAAGW-. *plural of* yaakw.
451.1 gayeekw, gayaagw-. *plural of* yeekw.

452. GAYAK, GAYAG-. *v.i. & n.* grey (colour). [g̣áyakʰ] hb,m.

453. GAYDMSGYEN. *n.* rubber hat. [g̣àydm̩sgʸɛ́n] hb.

454. GAYEXŁ. *plural of* yexł.

455. GAYK, GAYG-, GAGAYKT. *n.* chest (*anat*). [g̣aykʰ] hb,k,pr.
[g̣ag̣áykʰtʰ] k.

456. GAYŁMLÓOP, GAYŁMLÓOB-. *n.* stone mortar. [g̣àyɬm̩lɔ́ʌpʰ] k.

457. GAYNA. *n.* road; trail. [g̣áyna] k,pr.

458. GAYNIIS. *n.* chum salmon; dog salmon. [g̣ayní·s] hb,k.
458.1 gaynis. [g̣áynis] pr.

459. GAYOO. *n.* gable; house front. [g̣ayo·] hb.

460. GEEŁ. *v.t.* drag. [g̣e·ɬ] pr.

461. GEESK, GEESG-. *n.* anal fin. [gɛ·skʰ] hb.

462. GIDIGANIITSK, GIDIGANIITSG-. *n.* northwest wind; the Tlingit.
[gìdig̣aní·cʰkʰ] hb.
462.1 gyidaganiidz. [gʸìdag̣aní·ʒ] pr.
462.2 gyidiganiis. [gʸìdig̣àní·s] hb.
462.3 gyitiganiis. [gʸìtig̣aní·s] hb.

463. GIDZA- almost, just about. [giʒa] hb.
463.1 gyiidz. *adv.* almost. [gʸi·ʒ].

464. GILAAN. *n.* stern (*naut*). [gɩlá·n] hb.
464.1 gyilan. [gʸɩlán] k.

465. GIMGMDZIWS. *n.* sun. [gìmgm̩ʒíws] pr.
465.1 gyemgmdziws. [gʸɛ̀mgm̩ʒíws] hb.
465.2 gyemgmdziwst, gyemgmdziwsd-. [gʸɛ̀mgm̩ʒíwstʰ] pr.

466. GINADZÍIGA. *v.i.* be grounded at low tide. [gìnaʒí·ʌg̣a] m,pr.

467. GINAMANŁ. *v.i.* be left over (of food). [gɩnamánɬ] k,m.

468. GISAGWLGWAALK, GISAGWLGWAALG-. *n.* northern lights; aurora borealis.
[gìsag̣ʷl̩gʷá·lkʰ] hb.
468.1 gisügwülgweelk, gisügwülgweelg-. [gìsɨgʷɨlgʷɛ́·lkʰ] hb.

469. GITS'OOYAX. *n.* bow (*naut*). [gɩcʔɔ́·yʌx̣] hb.
469.1 gyits'oyax. [gʸɩcʔóyʌx̣] pr.
469.2 gyits.oyx. [gʸɩcʔóyx̣] k.

470. GIẄKŁ. *v.t.* & *v.i.* paddle (e.g., a canoe). [giÿkɬ] hb.

471. GNSMHOON, LUUNÜKSMHOON. *n.* dried fish. [gn̩sm̩hɔ́·n] k. [lù·nɨksm̩hɔ́·n] k.
471.1 güünksmhon. [gɨ̂·nksm̩hɔ́n] pr.
471.2 güünsmoon. [gɨ̂·nsm̩ɔ́·n] k.

472. GOK, GOG-. *n.* small berry basket. [g̣ɔkʰ] pr.

473. GOK'OŁ. *plural of* k'oɬ.

474. GOL, GALGOL. *v.t.* empty; spill. [g̣ɔl] pr. [g̣ɑlg̣ɔ́l] pr. (Note: object must be a dry, particulate substance such as sugar, flour, or sand).
474.1 gol. *plural of* baah.

475. GOMSM. *n.* Winter. [g̣ómsm̩] k.
475.1 goomsm. [g̣ó·msm̩] hb,k,pr.

476. GOO. *interr. pron.* what? [go·] k,pr.

477. GOOL, GOOL. *n.* loon. [g̣ɔ́·l] k. [g̣ɔ́·l] k.

478. GOOŁK'UWAALT, GOOŁK'UWAALD-. *v.i.* actually be; certainly be; be in reality.

479. GOOM, GOOM. *n.* ashes. [go·m], [gɔ·m] hb,k,m,pr. [g̣o·m] k.
479.1 goom, gakgom. *n.* ashes; gunpowder. [g̣o·m] k. [g̣ɑkg̣óm] k.

480. GOOP, GOOB-. *n.* wave. [g̣ɔ·pʰ] pr.
480.1 góop, góob-. [g̣oʌpʰ] k.
480.2 góopn. *n.* fish heart; soft palate (*hum. anat.*). [g̣ɔ́·ʌpn̩] pr.

481. GÓOPSXN. *num.* two (of long objects). [g̣ɔ́ʌpsx̣n̩] hb.
481.1 *see* k'oopsxn.

482. GOOS. *v.i.* jump. [g̣ɔ·s] k.

483. GOOS. *n.* basket. [g̣ɔ·s] hb.

484. GO'OSGAN. *n.* woodpecker. [g̣ɔ̀ʔɔsg̣ɑ́n] hb.

485. GOOT, GOOD-, GOGOOT. *n.* heart. [g̣ɔ·tʰ] k. [g̣ɔg̣ɔ́·tʰ] k.
485.1 góot. [g̣ɔʌtʰ] k.

486. GOOXS. *n.* willow tree (Note: used for making spoons). [g̣ɔ·x̣s] pr.

487. GOOYM. *n.* Spring (*season*). [go·ym̩] hb.

487.1 goyim. [góyɩm] pr.
487.2 goyim. [góyɩm] k.

488. GOOYPAH. *v.i.* bright. *n.* moon. [gó·ypʰah] hb.
488.1 goyb. [goyb] pr.
488.2 goyp, goyb-. [goypʰ] pr.
488.3 goy'pa. *n.* daylight. [góyʔpʼɑ] m,pr.

489. GOX. *v.t.* & *v.i.* peck. [gɔx̣] pr.

490. GOYDIKS. *v.i.* arrive; come. [góydɩks] hb.
490.1 goy'diks. [góyʔdɩks] hb.

491. GUGWEELAKS. *v.i.* polished; shiny. [gugʷɛ́·lʌks] pr.

492. GUKK'A'W'TS, GUKK'A'W'DZ-. *plural of* k'aw'ts.

493. GUKPTS'IH. *plural of* pts'ih.

494. GUKWDUS. *plural of* kwdus.

495. GÜKSHÜÜSK, GÜKSHÜÜSG-. *plural of* kshüüsk.

496. GULAPDAAT, GULADAAD-. *num.* two (of persons aboard any conveyance). [gùlʌpdá·tʰ] pr.
496.1 gulipdaat, gulipdaad-. [gùlɩpdá·tʰ] hb.
496.2 gulpdaat, gulpdaad-. [gùl̩pdá·tʰ] pr.

497. GUHXBAA'LAXS. *n.* nightmare. [guɬx̣bá·ʔlɑx̣s] hb.

498. GU'PL. *num.* two (of abstract objects; of round objects). [gúʔpʼl̩] hb.
498.1 guu'pl [gú·ʔpʼl̩] pr.

499. GUPL'ON. *num.* two (of fathoms; of measures) [gùpl̩ʔɔ́n] pr.

500. GÜSGÜÜTS, GÜSGÜÜDZ-. *n.* wren. [gɨsgɨ̀·cʰ] m.

501. GUU. *v.t.* hit; shoot; strike [gu·] pr.
501.1 gúuk, gúug-, guhguuk, gwuguyt. *v.t.* kill; shoot. [guʌkʰ] k,m. [guhgú·kʰ] k. [gʷugúytʰ] k.

502. GUUMAA. *n.* "angel fish"; chimara; rat fish (*spec. Chimaera affinis* and *Hydrolagus colliei*). [gu·má·] hb.

503. GÜGÜÜL. *v.t.* search for (note: inanimate object). [gɨgɨ́·l] pr.
503.1 gyügüül. [gʸɨgɨ́·l] pr.

504. GÜSGÜÜTS, GÜSGÜÜDZ-. *n.* sparrow. [gɨsgɨ́·cʰ] pr.
504.1 gyüsgüüts, gyüsgüüdz-. [gʸɨsgɨ̀·cʰ] pr.

505. GÜÜDAX, GÜTGÜÜDAX. *v.t.* ask. [gɨ́·dax̣] pr. [gɨtgɨ́·dax̣] pr.
505.1 güüdax, gügiidax. [gɨ́·dʌx̣] hb. [gɨgɨ́·dʌx̣] hb.
505.2 güüdisk, güüdisg-. *v.t.* gather up. [gɨ́·dɩskʰ] pr.

505.3 güüks. *v.i.* search. [gĭ·ks] hb.
505.4 güütks. [gĭ·tʰks] pr.
505.5 güül. *v.t. and v.i.* harvest; pick (e.g., berries, seaweed). [gĭ·l] pr.
505.6 güülks. [gĭ·lks] hb.
505.7 güülka. *v.i.* westerly. *n.* West; west wind. [gĭ́·lkʰɑ] hb,m,pr.

506. GÜÜNAKS. *v.i.* be dry. [gĭ́·nʌks] m.
506.1 güünks, lúunaks, lúunks. [gĭ·nks] k. [lúʌnʌks] k. [luʌnks] k.

507. GWAALTK, GWAALTG-. *v.i.* lost. [gʷɔ·ltʰkʰ] k.
507.1 gwatk, gwatg-, gwatgwatk. [gʷatʰkʰ] k. [gʷʌtgʷátʰkʰ] k.
507.2 *see* k'waatk.
507.3 gweetk, gweetg-. *v.i.* disappear. [gʷɛ́·tʰkʰ] pr.

508. GWAANAKS. *v.i.* cooked; done; faded, pale, light (of colour, i.e., decreased chroma with increased value). [qʷá·nʌks] pr.
508.1 gwaanks. [gʷa·nks] hb,k.

509. GWAANTK, GWAANTG-. *v.t.* touch. [gʷa·ntʰkʰ] k.
509.1 gwantk, gwantg-, gwitgwantk. [gʷantʰkʰ] k. [gʷɩtgʷʌ́ntʰkʰ] k.

510. GWAASK, GWAASG-. *v.t.* borrow. [gʷa·skʰ] pr.
510.1 gwask, gwasg-, gwasgwaask. [gʷaskʰ] k. [gʷʌsgʷá·skʰ] k.

511. GWAK, GWAG-. *n.* lip; upper lip. [gʷɑqʰ] m.
511.1 gwax, gwag-. [gʷʌx̣] pr.

512. GWALAK, GWALAG-. *v.i.* burn. [gʷálʌkʰ] hb.
512.1 gwelik, gwelig-. [gʷɛ́lɩkʰ] pr.
512.2 gweelg. *v.i.* burned; burnt; hot. [gʷɛ·lg] pr.
512.3 gwe'lgn. *v.t.* burn. [gʷɛ́ʔlgn̩] pr.
512.4 gwelk, gwelg-, gwilagwéelk. *v.t.* make burn. [gʷɛlkʰ] k. [gʷɩ̀lʌgʷɛ́ʌlkʰ] k.

513. GWALA'MAXS. *n.* Native tea. [gʷɑ̀lɑʔmáx̣s] k,m.

514. GWAŁWOO. *n.* hunter. [gʷʌɬwó·] k,m.
514.1 gwałwóo. *v.t. & v.i.* hunt. [gʷʌɬwóʌ] k,m.

515. GWAN. *num.* three (of flat objects). [gʷʌn] hb.

516. GWANI'TS, GWANI'DZ-. *v.t.* show. [gʷʌníʔc̓] pr.

517. GWANÜKS. *n.* spring (of water). [gʷánɨks] k.
517.1 gwinüks. [gʷɩ́nɨks] pr.

518. GWAT, GWAD-. *n.* father; uncle (reference; F, FB). [gʷatʰ] k.

519. GWATK, GWATG-, LAXGWATKS, LAXGWIIDAKS. *v.i.* be cold; have a cold. [gʷat̄ʰkʰ], [gʷʌt̄ʰkʰ] hb,k,m,pr. [laxˌgʷʌ́tʰks] k. [laxˌqʷí·dʌks] hb.

520. GWE'A. *v.i.* poor. [gʷéʔa] hb.
520.1 gwee. [gʷe·] m,pr.
520.2 gwee'a. [gʷé·ʔa] k,m.

521. GWE'Aɬ. *n.* gunny sack; scrotum. [gʷɛ́ʔaɬ] m,pr.
521.1 gwe'iɬ. [gʷɛ́ʔɩɬ] m.

522. GWESGA. *demons. pron.* that. [gʷɛ́sga] pr.

523. GWEXGOOMSMT, GWEXGOOMSMD-. *n.* winter food. [gʷɛx̣gó·msm̩tʰ] pr.

524. GWIDAA'TS, GWIDAA'DZ-. *n.* coat. [gʷɩdá·ʔc˃] k.
524.1 gwidets, gwidedz-. [gʷɩdɛ́cʰ] pr.
524.2 gwüdaats, gwüdaadz-, gukgwüdaats. *n.* jacket. [gʷɨdá·cʰ] hb. [gùkgʷɨdá·cʰ] hb.

525. GWÍIK, GWÍIG-. *n.* ground hog; marmot; woodchuck. [gʷi·ʌkʰ] m.
525.1 gwiikw, gwiigw-. [gʷi·kʷʰ] hb,pr.
525.2 gwíikw, gwíigw-. [gʷi·ʌkʷʰ] hb.

526. GWILO'K, GWILO'G-. *v.i.* industrious. [gʷɩlóʔk˃] hb.

527. GWILXT'UUS. *v.t.* push (human object). [gʷɩlx̣tʔú·s] k,m.
527.1 gwiɬt'uus. [gʷɩɬtʔú·s] k,m.

528. GWIɬ'AAX, GWIɬ'AAG-. *n.* lip. [gʷɩɬʔá·x̣] pr.
528.1 gwüɬ'aax, gwüɬ'aag. [gʷɨɬʔá·x̣] pr.

529. GWIɬWOH. *v.i.* get out. [gʷɩɬwóh] hb.

530. GWINDAALPK, GWINDAALPG-. *v.t. & v.i.* close [gʷɩndá·lpʰkʰ] k.
530.1 gwindaalapk, gwindaalapg-. [gʷɩndá·lʌpʰkʰ] k.

531. GWINDAAT, GWINDAAD-. *num.* three (of persons aboard a conveyance).

532. GWINSE'IK, GWINSE'IG-. *v.t.* pull (non-human object). [gʷɩnsɛ́ʔikʰ] k,m.

533. GWINSPIIL. *v.t.* pull (human object). [gʷinspɩ́·l] k,m.

534. GWISGAN. *n.* coat; raincoat. [gʷɩsgán] m,pr.
534.1 gwüsgan. *n.* cedar bark; mat coat; raincoat. [gʷɨsgán] hb.
534.2 gwüsxan. [gʷɨsx̣án] hb.

535. GWISGWAS. *plural of* k'was.

536. GWISGWAASK, GWISGWAASG-. *v.i.* blue (colour). [gʷɩsgʷá·skʰ] hb,k.
536.1 gwüsgwaask, gwüsgwaasg-. [gʷɨsgʷá·skʰ] pr.
536.2 gwüsgwaas. *n.* blue jay. [gʷɨsgʷá·s] hb.

536.3 gwüsgwaast, gwüsgwaasd-. [gʷɨsgʷá·stʰ] k.

537. GWIS'NABA'ALA, GUKGWIS'NABA'ALA. *n.* button blanket. [gʷìsnabáʔala] k. [gukgʷìsʔnabáʔala] k.
537.1 gwüsnap'a'la. [gʷɨsnapʔáʔla] hb.

538. GUKGWIS'NABA'ALA. *plural of* gwis'naba'ala.

539. GWISTS'ÍIK, GWISTS'ÍIG-. *n.* fawn. [gʷɩscʔíʌkʰ] k,m.
539.1 gwüssiik, gwüssiig-. [gʷɨssí·kʰ] m,pr.

540. GWITGWAATK' GWITGWAATG-. *plural of* sadziwb. *plural of* sagwaatk.

541. GWITGWINÍIKS. *n.* owl. [gʷɩtgʷɩní·ʌks] k,m.

542. GWÜDATSMSGYEN. *n.* rubber coat. [gʷɨdáchm̩sgʸɛ́n] hb.

543. GWÜLDMMEELSK, GWÜLDMMEELSG-. *v.t.* & *v.i.* foretell; prophesy. [gʷɨldm̩mɛ́·lskʰ] pr.

544. GWÜLDM'NIIDZ. *v.t.* foresee. *v.i.* foresee the future. [gʷɨldm̩ʔní·ʒ] pr.

545. GWÜLII. *num.* three (of round and abstract objects). [gʷɨlí·] hb.

546. GWÜLOON. *num.* three (of humans). [gʷɨlɔ́·n] pr.

547. GWÜN. *num.* three (of flat objects). [gʷɨn] pr.

548. GWÜNNÍIDZN. *v.t.* show. [gʷɨnníʌʒn̩] m,pr.
548.1 gwünníitsn. [gʷɨnníʌchn̩] m,pr.

549. GWÜNU. *v.t.* ask for; demand; express a desire for. [gʷɨnú] k,m,pr.
549.1 gwünuu, gagwünuu. *v.t.* ask for. [gʷɨnú·] hb. [gagʷɨnú·] hb.

550. GWÜSDZÍIK, GWÜSDZÍIG-. *n.* fawn. [gʷɨsʒíʌkʰ] hb.

551. GWÜSGWASM'AN'ON. *n.* ring. [gʷɨsgʷásm̩ʔanʔɔ́n] hb.

552. GWÜSHALAAYT, GWÜSHALAAYD-. *n.* cape; robe. [gʷɨshalá·ytʰ] hb.

553. GWÜSLIGYIYAA. *n.* travelling clothes. [gʷɨsligʸiyá·] m,pr.

554. GWÜSMATI. *n.* mountain goat skin coat. [gʷɨsmátʰi] hb.

555. GWÜSNAYGMGYAAMK, GWÜSNAYGMGYAAMG-. *n.* Chilkat blanket. [gʷɨsnáygm̩gʸá·mkʰ] hb.

556. GWÜS'OL. *n.* bearskin coat. [gʷɨsʔɔ́l] hb.

557. GYAA, DOX. *v.t.* take. [gʸa·] m,pr. [dɔx̣] m,pr.

558. GYA'AGLT, GYA'AGLD-. *v.t.* & *v.i.* roll. [gʸáʔʌgl̩tʰ] pr.

559. GYAAKS. *n.* (way out on) the ocean. [g^{y}a·ks] k.

560. GYAANMX. *n.* Nass-Gitksan language. [g^{y}a·nṃx̣] hb,m.

561. GYAD. *v.t.* hold. [g^{y}ad] pr.

562. GYALX. *n.* the outside, i.e., the open sea. [g^{y}alx̣] k,m.

563. GYA'TS, GYA'DZ-. *n.* down below, i.e., to the South (not underneath). [g^{y}aʔc̓] hb.

564. GYA'WN. *adv.* at this moment; now; right now. [g^{y}áʔwṇ] hb.
564.1 gye'awin. [g^{y}έʔʌwɩn] pr.

565. GYEB, LAPƚ. *v.i.* dip water; draw water. [g^{y}εb] pr. [lapɬ] k.
565.1 gyep, gyeb-. [g^{y}εp^{h}] k,pr.
565.2 gyebn. *v.i.* come out of the water. [g^{y}έbṇ] pr.

566. GEYDMGALDO. *n.* one who lives out in a camp, i.e., a person who takes no care of himself (an insulting expression). [g^{y}ὲdṃgɑldó] hb.

567. GYEDMƚ. *n.* (Western black) oyster catcher; oyster cutter (*orn.*). [g^{y}έdṃɬ] hb,m.

568. GYE'ETS, GYE'EDZ-. *n.* down below, i.e., the South; over away; down river. [g^{y}έʔεc^{h}] k,pr.

569. GYÉEKA. *n.* (down on) the beach. [g^{y}έʌk^{h}ɑ] hb.
569.1 gyíika. [g^{y}íʌk^{h}ɑ] k.

570. GYELAG. *n.* outside (See 562). [g^{y}έlʌg] pr.
570.1 gyelk, gyelg-. [g^{y}έlq^{h}] pr.

571. GYELS. *n.* (blue) mussel. [g^{y}εls] hb,k,m.

572. GYELÜKS, GYILGYALKS. *v.i.* feel (as in 'feel ill'). [g^{y}έlɨks] pr. [g^{y}ɩlg^{y}álks] pr.

573. GYEƚK, GYEƚG-, GYIƚGYEƚK. *v.t.* stab. *n.* spear. [g^{y}εɬk^{h}] m,pr. [g^{y}ɩɬg^{y}έɬk^{h}] m,pr.
573.1 gyiƚk, gyiƚg-. [g^{y}ɩɬk^{h}] pr.

574. GYEM. *n.* Saskatoon berries; serviceberry (*Amelanchier alnifolia*). [g^{y}εm] hb,m,pr.

575. GYEMGAT, GYEMGAD-. *n.* astronomer (specifically, a moon reader, a person who can predict the food seasons). [g^{y}έmgʌt^{h}] m,pr.

576. GYEMGMÁATK, GYEMGMÁATG-. *n.* moon. [g^{y}ὲmgṃáʌt^{h}k^{h}] hb.
576.1 gyemgm'aatk, gyemgm'aatg-. [g^{y}ὲmgṃʔá·t^{h}k^{h}] pr.

577. GYEMK, GYEMG-, GYIKGYEMK. *v.i.* hot; warm. *n.* heat; month; moon; sun. [g^{y}εmk^{h}] hb,k,m,pr. [g^{y}ɩkg^{y}έmk^{h}] k.

578. GYENITGN. *v.t.* wake up. [gʸɛnítgn̩] k.

579. GYENTI. *n.* sea cucumber. [gʸɛ́ntʰi] hb.

580. GYEPS. *v.i.* high. [gʸɛps] m,pr.
580.1 gyips. [gʸɩps] m,pr.

581. GYET, GYED-, GYET *or* GYIKGYET. *n.* human being; man; person. [gʸɛtʰ] k. [gʸɩkgʸɛ́tʰ] k.
581.1 gyit, gyid- [gʸɩtʰ] hb.

582. GYI'AÞ. *n.* male sockeye salmon in red phase. [gʸíʔʌɬ] m,pr.
582.1 gyíiɫ. [gʸiʌɬ] m,pr.
582.2 gyi'i'tɫ. [gʸíʔiʔtɬ̓] hb.
582.3 gyi'tɫ. [gʸiʔtɬ̓] hb.

583. GYIBAAW. *n.* wolf; coyote (by extension). [gʸɩbá·w] m,pr.
583.1 gyibaw. [gʸɩbáw] hb.
583.2 gyibaw. [gʸɩbɑ́w] k.

584. GYIBAWMTS'M'AKS. *n.* wolf eel; wolf fish (not *Anarchichas lupus*, but a local common name for the eel). [gʸibáwmcʔm̩ʔáks] hb.

585. GYIDZ. *v.t.* miss. [gʸiʒ] pr.

586. GYIGYAANI. *n.* up above, i.e., the interior; upriver. [gʸɩgʸá·ni] m,pr.

587. GYIGYIINGYAÞ. *v.t. & v.i.* pray. [gʸɩgʸí·ngʷɑɬ] pr.

588. GYIGYI'OOSK, GYIGYI'OOSG-. *v.i.* stubborn. [gʸɩgʸiʔó·skʰ] hb.

589. GYIGYOOKS' LLÓOKS. *v.i.* float. [gʸigʸɔ́·ks] m,pr. [l̥lɔ́ʌks] k,m,pr.
589.1 gyigyóoks. [gʸigʸóʌks] k.

590. GYIGYOOTK, GYIGYOOTG-. *n.* (European) axe (hb,pr); hatchet (m). [gʸigʸɔ́·tʰkʰ] hb,m,pr.

591. GYÍIGM'ÜÜK, GYÍIGM'ÜÜG-. *n.* coho fly; horse fly. [gʸɩʌgm̩ʔɨ́·qʰ] hb,m.

592. GYIIK, GYIIG-. *n.* fly; mosquito. [gʸi·kʰ] hb.
592.1 gyíik, gyíig-, gyikgyíik. [gʸiʌkʰ] hb,k,m. [gʸikgʸíʌkʰ] k.

593. GYÍIK, GYÍIG-. *v.t.* buy. [gʸiʌkʰ] hb.

594. GYIIMKÞ. *v.t.* wipe. [gʸi·mkɬ] pr.
594.1 gyimɫ, siguunaks. [gʸɩmɬ] k. [sɩgú·nʌks] k.
594.2 gyiims. *n.* diapers; shredded cedar bark. [gʸi·ms] hb,k.

595. GYIINÞ. *v.i.* give food. [gʸi·nɬ] pr.

596. GYÍISK, GYÍISG-, GYISGYÍISK. *v.t.* miss (meeting someone). [gʸi·ʌskʰ] pr. [gʸɩsgyí·ʌskʰ] pr.

597. GYIITK, GYIITG-, GYITGYIITK. *v.i.* flood, swell (k,pr); swollen (hb). [gʸi·tʰkʰ] hb,k,pr. [gʸɩtgʸí·tʰkʰ] pr.
597.1 gyíitk, gyíitg-, gyitgyíitk. *v.i.* flood; swell. [gʸiʌtʰkʰ] k. [gʸɩtgʸíʌtʰkʰ] k. Note: plural denotes repeated activity, i.e. swelling up or flooding.

598. GYÍI'TSN̲. *v.t.* point out. [gʸí·ʌʔcʼṇ] pr.

599. GYIK- again.

600. GYIK̲'ÁAK, GYIK̲'ÁAG-, K̲'A̲YGYIK̲'A̲K. *n.* hip; waist. [gʸiqʔá·kʰ] k. [qʔàygʸiqʔákʰ] k.

601. GYIKGYEMK. *plural of* gyemk. *adv.* more than a month past; more than a month from now.'

602. GYIKGYET, GYIKGYED-. *plural of* gyet.

603. GYIK'OOŁ. *plural of* k'ooɬ. *adv.* years ago; long ago.

604. GYIKSUUNT, GYIKSUUND-. *plural of* suunt.

605. GYIKSÚUT, GYIKSÚUD-. *plural of* ksúut.

606. GYIKSXA̲YTK, GYIKSXA̲YTG-. *plural of* sxa̲ytk.

607. GYIK'WAH. *v.i.* do (something) again. *interj.* Again! Once again! [gʸɩkʔwáh] pr.

608. GYILA̲GYOO. *n.* robin (orn.). [gʸɩlagʸɔ́·] pr.
608.1 gyila̲kyoo. [gʸɩlakʸó·] hb.

609. GYILAKST, GYILAKSD-. *v.t.* give a drink of water to. [gʸɩlákstʰ] pr.

610. GYILATS'I'I'TS, GYILATS'I'I'DZ. *n.* dragonfly. [gʸɩlacʔíʔiʔcʼ] hb.

611. GYILHA̲WLI. *n.* forest; woods. [gʸɩlháwli] pr.

612. GYI'LIILPK, GYI'LIILPG-. *n.* (the place) behind one. [gʸɩʔli·lpʰkʰ] m.

613. GYILOO. *v.t.* & *v.i.* stop. [gʸɩló·] k.

614. GYIŁGYA̲Ł. *v.t.* spear. [gʸɩɬgʸʌ́ɬ] pr.

615. GYIŁ'ON. *n.* tattoo. [gʸɩɬʔɔ́n] hb.

616. GYIŁTS'A̲X. *n.* nose ring. [gʸɩɬcʔáx̣] hb.

617. GYIŁWEENTK, GYIŁWEENTG-. *n.* woodpecker. [gʸɩɬwɛ́·ntʰkʰ] k,m.

618. GYIMST, GYIMSD-. *n.* a match (made of cedar bark).

619. GYINAAS. *n.* boy. [gʸɩná·s] pr.

620. GYINAMAAN. *v.i.* left over (of anything except food). [gʸɩnamá·n] k,m.

621. GYINESKU. *v.t.* leave. [gʸɩnɛskú] k.

622. GYINÍITX. *v.i.* rise. [gʸɩní·ʌtx] pr.

623. GYIPAAYK, GYIPAAYG-, LAPAAYK. *v.i.* fly. [gʸipá·ykʰ] k. [lɑpá·ykʰ] k.
623.1 gyipayk, gyipayg-, lipayk. [gʸɩpáykʰ] pr. [lɩpáykʰ] pr.

624. GYIPAYGMDESX. *n.* (Northern) flying squirrel (*Glaucomys sabrinus*). [gʸɩpáygm̩dɛ́sx̣] hb.

625. GYIS. *v.t.* miss (as a target). [gʸis] pr.

626. GYISDAWŁ. *v.i.* go away; leave. [gʸɩsdáwɨ] k.
626.1 gyisidaawɨ. *n.* downstream. [gʸɩsidá·wɨ] pr.

627. GYISGO. *v.i.* go to another place. [gʸɩsgó] k,m.

628. GYISIHAWAASK, GYISIHAWAASG-. *n.* Northeast wind. [gʸɩ̀sihawá·skʰ] hb.
628.1 gyisihaywas. *n.* a northeaster. [gʸɩ̀sihaywás] hb.

629. GYISIYAASK, GYISIYAASG-. *n.* North. [gʸɩ̀siyá·skʰ] hb,pr.
629.1 gyisiyaask, gyisiyaasg-. *n.* North wind. [gʸɩ̀siyá·skʰ] hb.
629.2 gyisiyáask, gyisiyáasg-. *n.* North. [gʸɩ̀siyá·ʌskʰ] m.

630. GYISŁAAŁ. *v.t.* move (inanimate object). [gʸɩsɨá·ɨ] k,m.

631. GYISTXALT'MTK, GYISTXALT'MTG-. *n.* design; pattern; picture. [g̅ʸɩst̅x̣alt?m̩tʰkʰ] m.

632. GYITS'ÍIPTA. *n.* yesterday. [gʸɩc?í·ʌpʰtʰa] m,pr.
632.1 gyits'iip'ta'a. [gʸɩc?í·p?t'ɑ?ɑ] k.

633. GYITS'OON. *n.* corner (in a house, of a room). [gʸɩc?ɔ́·n] m,pr.
633.1 gyits'óon. *n.* attic; back room; bedroom; kitchen; store room; upper room. [gʸɩc?ɔ́·ʌn] hb. *n.* cave; corner (of a room); hole; the inside. [gʸɩc?ɔ́ʌn] pr.

634. GYITWAALGIT, GYITWAALGID-. *v.t. & v.i.* get revenge (on). [gʸɩtwá·lgɩtʰ] hb.
634.1 gyitwaalgyit, gyitwaalgyid-. *n.* raiders. [gʸɩtwá·lgʸɩtʰ] hb.
634.2 gyitwaaltk, gyitwaaltg-. *v.t. & v.i.* attack; charge. [gʸɩtwá·ltʰkʰ] pr.
634.3 gyitweeltk, gyitweeltg-. *n.* enemy; war. [gʸɩtwɛ́·ltʰkʰ] k,m.

635. GYITXAAWTK, GYITXAAWTG-. *n.* some time ago; the season just past, e.g., summer, if it is now fall. [gʸɩtx̣a·wtʰkʰ] pr.

636. GYIWAɬGN. *n.* ship worms. [g^{y}iwʌ́ɬgn] hb. See also k'yiwaɬgn.

637. GYOOS. *n.* algae; grinnella. [g^{y}o·s] hb.

638. GYUDAN. *n.* horse. [g^{y}udán] pr.
638.1 gyiwdn. [g^{y}iwdń̩] hb.

639. GYÜK, GYÜG-. *n.* hemlock. [g^{y}ɨ̆k^{h}] hb.

H

640. HA. *n.* air. [ha] k.

641. HA'A, HA'A. *n.* goose. [háʔa] k. [háʔa] k.
641.1 haa'k, haa'g-. [ha·ʔq$^{>}$] k.
641.2 ha'ax, ha'ag-. [háʔax̣] k.

642. HAAK'OTSSEMII. *n.* table knife. [ha·qʔɔ́c^{h}sɛ́mi·] pr.

643. HA'AKS. *n.* dipper. [haʔáks] k,m.

644. HAALMMOOT, HAALMMOOD-. *n.* candlefish; olachen; whitebait smelt; the Saviour, Jesus Christ. [hà·lm̩mó·t^{h}] hb.

645. HAAɬGN. *n.* wall. [há·ɬgn̩] hb.

646. HÁAPS. *n.* lid. [haʌps] k,m.
646.1 haa'ps, hakhaa'ps. *n.* cover; top. [ha·ʔp$^{>}$s] k,m. [hakhá·ʔp$^{>}$s] k.
646.2 ha'ps. [haʔp$^{>}$s] k.

647. HAAS. *n.* fireweed (*Epilobium angustifolium*). [ha·s] hb,k,pr.

648. HÁAS. *n.* soft dorsal fin. [haʌs] m.

649. HÁAS, HASHÁAS. *n.* dog. [haʌs] k,m,pr. [hasháʌs] k,m,pr.

650. HAAT, HAAD-. *n.* brother (address, female speaker; archaic). [ha·t^{h}] k.

651. HAAT, HAAD-. *n.* intestines. [ha·t^{h}] k.

652. HAATS, HAADZ-, HASHAATS. *n.* stump. [ha·c^{h}] k. [hasha·c^{h}] k.

653. HA'AWÍINI. *v.t. & v.i.* not yet be; not yet do. *interj.* Not yet! [hàʔʌwíʌni] k.

654. HAAWK, WAAWG-. *n.* birch tree. [ha·wk^{h}] m.

655. HAAXK, HAAXG-, HAXHAAXK. *v.i.* be in misery (m); over-burdened (m). *n.* a cripple. [ha·x̣k^{h}] k,m. [hax̣há·x̣k^{h}] k.

656. HAAYIMGAN. *n.* a rotten tree. [hà·yɩmgán̩] hb.

657. HA'AYIN. *v.t.* put down (a baby or child). [háʔayɩn] k,m.

658. HAA'YTISK, HAA'YTISG-. *n.* house posts. [há·ʔytɩskʰ] hb.

659. HAAYTK, HAAYTG-. *v.i.* stand; stand up. [ha·ytʰkʰ] k,pr.
659.1 haytk, haytg-. [haytʰkʰ] pr.

660. HAAYUK, HAAYUG-. *n.* soul; spirit. [há·yukʰ] k.

661. HAAYWAAS. *n.* South wind; a southeaster. [ha·ywá·s] k,m.
661.1 haywaas. [haywá·s] pr.
661.2 haywées. [haywɛ́ʌs] k.

662. HABAALT, HABAALD-. *v.i.* despair; give up. [habá·ltʰ] m,pr.

663. HADAAY. *v.t.* steer (a canoe). [hadá·y] k.
663.1 hadaay. *n.* rudder (*naut.*). [hadá·y] hb.
663.2 hadeey. [hadɛ́·y] hb.

664. HADANI. *n.* black cod. [hadaní] k,m.

665. HADIIILTK, HADIIILTG-. *n.* dorsal fin of a cod. [hadí·ltʰkʰ] hb.

666. HADIKS, LAHEEDIKS. *v.i.* swim. [hádɩks] pr. [lahé·dɩks] k,pr.
666.1 ha'tks. [háʔtʼks].

667. HADL. *n.* bastard halibut. [hádl̩] hb.

668. HADM. *n.* brother (reference, female speaker; archaic). [hádm̩] k.

669. HADZANÁAS. *v.i.* have good luck. [hàʒaná·ʌs] k.

670. HADZA'ÜÜLT, HADZA'ÜÜLD-. *n.* snail. [hàʒaʔɨ́·ltʰ] k,m.
670.1 ha'tsi'uul. [hàʔcʼiʔú·l] k.

671. HADZEYX, HADZEYG-. *n.* first finger; index finger. [haʒɛ́yx̣] k.
671.1 hats'éex, hats'éeg-. [hacʔéʌx̣] k,pr. [hacʔé·ʌx̣] k.

672. HADZIIWKWSA. *n.* dipper (used to bail water out of a canoe). [haʒí·wkʷʰsa] m,pr.

673. HAGAGAYTK, HAGAGAYTG-. *n.* scissors. [hàgagáytʰkʰ] hb.

674. HAGAYAAN, HAKHAGAYAAN. *n.* club; war club. [hàgayá·n] k. [hakhàgayá·n] k.
674.1 ha'kayk'an, ha'kha'kayk'an. [hàʔqʼayqʔán] k. [hàʔqʼhaʔqʼayqʔán] k.

675. HAGWILHUU. *n.* line; rope; string. [hàgʷɩlhú·] k.
675.1 hagwilhuu. [hàgʷɩlhú·] pr.

676. HAGWILHUUGADEELPK, HAGWILHUUGADEELPG-. *n.* anchor line. [hàgʷɩlhú·gadɛ́·lpʰkʰ] hb.
676.1 hagwilhuungadeelpk, hagwilhuungadeelpg-.

[hàgʷɩlhú·ŋ̣gadɛ́·lpʰkʰ] m,pr.

677. HAGWILO'K, HAGWILO'G-. *n.* bogey man. [hàgʷɩlóʔkʼ] hb.
677.1 hagwilo'ox, hagwilo'og-, hakhagwilo'ox. *n.* sea monster. [hàgʷɩlɔ́ʔɔx̣] k. [hakhagʷɩlɔ́ʔɔx̣] k.
677.2 ha'kwilo'ox, ha'kwilo'og-. [hàʔkʷʼɩlɔ́ʔɔx̣] m,pr.

678. HAGWN. *n.* (Northern) horse mussel. [hágʷn̩] hb.
678.1 hagwn, hagwn. *n.* oyster. [hágʷn̩] k. [hágʷn̩] k.
678.2 ha'kwn. *n.* (large) mussels. [hʌ̀ʔkʷʼn̩] m.

679. HAGYIŁAAM. *n.* carving knife. [hàgʸiɬá·m] pr.

680. HAGYOOKS. *n.* keel (*naut.*). [hagʸɔ́·ks] hb.

681. HAHAHAW. *n.* treasure; valuable objects; valued property. [hahaháw] k,m.

682. HAHANGOOT, HAHANGOOD-. *v.t.* maliciously destroy. [hahaŋgɔ́·tʰ] k.

683. HAHA'YIN. *plural of* ha'yin.

684. HAHOLTK, HAHOLTG-. *plural of* holtk.

685. HA'ITSMGASK, HA'ITSMGASG-. *v.t.* boss around; order. [hàʔɩcʰm̩gáskʰ] k,m.

686. HA'K, HA'G-. *n.* (Canada) goose. [haʔqʼ] hb.
686.1 ha'x, ha'g-. [haʔx̣] hb.

687. HAK'AŁOO. *plural of* ało.
687.1 hak'ałoom. *plural of* ałoom.
687.2 hakhałoo. *plural of* hałoo.

688. HA'KALAAẄ. *n.* club (for clubbing people). [hàʔqʼalá·ÿ] pr.

689. HAK'AŁOMGYEMK, HAK'AŁOMGYMKG-. *plural of* ałomgyemk.
689.1 hak'ałoomgymek, hak'ałoomgyemg-. *plural of* ałoomgyemk.

690. HAK'AŁOMXSO. *plural of* ałomxso.
690.1 hak'ałoomxso. *plural of* ałoomxso.

691. HA'KAYAAN. *n.* club. [hàʔqʼayá·n] pr.

692. HAK'ÉENTK, HAK'ÉENTKG-. *n.* drill bit. [hakʔéʌntʰkʰ] hb.

693. HAKHAA'PS. *plural of* ha'ps.

694. HAKHAŁABIISK, HAKHAŁABIISG-. *plural of* hałabisk.

695. HAKHAŁE'PA. *plural of* hałe'pa.

696. HAKHAŁGYÍIKA. *plural of* hałgyiika.

697. HAKHAPS. *plural of* ap.

698. HAKHAPSXAWGANGAN. *plural of* apsxawgan.

699. HAKHAXBESX. *plural of* axbesx.

700. HAKHOOYA. *n.* clothing. [hakhó·ya] hb.

701. HAK'OO. *n.* back (*anat.*). [hakʔɔ́·] hb.

702. HAKWDAAK, HAKWDAAG-. *n.* bow (weapon). [hakʷʰda·kʰ] k,m.
702.1 hakwdak, hakwdag-. [hakʷʰdakʰ] hb,k,pr.

703. HAKS, HAKHAS. *v.t.* call names; scold. [haks] k,m. [hakháks] k.

704. HALA'LOX. *n.* sea monster; any monstrous sea animal. [halaʔóx̣] hb.

705. HALAXSA'NAX'NOX. *n.* beach knotwood (*Polygonum paronychia*). [haláx̣saʔnax̣ʔnóx̣] hb.

706. HALDAAW. *v.t.* bewitch; cure. [haldá·w] k.

707. HALDM'OOT, HALDM'OOD-. *n.* oolachen (archaic); the Saviour Jesus Christ. [hàldm̥ʔó·tʰ] hb.

708. HALDMBAA. *v.i.* get up. [hàldm̥bá·] pr.

709. HALEYT, HALEYD-. *n.* shaman dancer; shaman's dance. [haléytʰ] k.

710. HALHAL. *n.* a spinning top (toy). [halhál] k.

711. HALHOLTK, HALHOLTG-. *plural of* holtk. *plural of* hooltk.

712. HA'LIAGOOD. *v.t. & v.i.* guess; think (in the sense of believing or having an opinion. [hàʔliʌgɔ́·d] pr.

713. HA'LIDEL. *n.* battlefield. [hàʔlidɛ́l] m,pr.

714. HA'LIDZOOK, HA'LIDZOOG-. *n.* world; universe. [hàʔliʒó·qʰ] k,m.

715. HA'LIKSALAXLAKA MIYAANM. *n.* Christmas. [hàʔliksʌlax̣láqamiyá·nm̥] m.

716. HA'LIGU'PL. *n.* Tuesday. [hàʔligúʔp'l̥] hb,k,pr.

717. HA'LIK'ÜÜL. *n.* Monday. [hàʔlikʔí·l] hb,k,pr.

718. HA'LIK'WILI. *n.* Wednesday. [hàʔlikʷʔɩlí] hb,k,pr.

719. HA'LIKWSTUUNS. *n.* Friday. [hàʔlikʷʰstú·ns] hb,k,pr.

720. HA'LILAAŁK, HA'LILAAŁG-. *plural of* ha'linook.

721. HA'LILAXDZMDZM. *n.* March; April. [hàʔliláx̣ʒm̥ʒḿ] m.

722. HA'LILAXŁGUMEDMGAGUUM. *n.* May; June [hàʔliláx̣ɬgumɛ́dm̥gagú·m] m.

723. HA'LILA̲XSTM̲HON. *n.* July; August. [hàʔlilɑx̣stm̩hón] m.

724. HA'LILA̲XTS'A̲WAS. *n.* September; October. [hàʔlilɑx̣cʔɑwás] m.

725. HA'LILA̲XXSWAANXS. *n.* April; May. [hàʔlilɑx̣x̣swá·nx̣s] m.

726. HA'LINOOK, HA'LINOOG-, HA'LILAAŁK. *n.* bed. [hàʔlinó·kʰ] hb.
[hàʔlilá·ɬkʰ] hb.

727. HA'LISGWAYT, HA'LISGWAYD-. *n.* Sunday. [hàʔlisgʷaytʰ] hb.
727.1 ha'lisgwaytk, ha'lisgwaytg-. [hàʔlisgʷaytʰkʰ] m.

728. HA'LIT'AH. *n.* chair. [hàʔlitʔáh] hb.

729. HA'LITOO. *n.* chest of drawers; cupboard; dresser. [hàʔlitʰó·] hb.
729.1 ha'lit'oomnooł. [hàʔlitʔó·mnó·ɬ] m.
729.2 ha'lit'oonooł. [hàʔlitʔó·nó·ɬ] hb.

730. HA'LITXAALPX. *n.* Thursday. [hàʔlitx̣a·lpx̣] hb,k,pr.

731. HA'LIWAALXS. *n.* floor. [hàʔliwá·lx̣s] nb.
731.1 haaliwaalxs. [hà·liwá·lx̣s] hb.
731.2 ha'liwaaxs. [hàʔliwá·x̣s] m.
731.3 haliwaaxs. [hàliwá·x̣s] m,pr.

732. HA'LIWILDUULGYIT, HA'LIWILDUULGYID-. *n.* battle ground.
[hàʔliwɩldú·lgʸɩtʰ] hb.

733. HA'LI'XHÓON. *n.* July. [hàʔliʔx̣hóʌn] m.

734. HA'LI'XŁA̲'A̲SK, HA'LI'XŁA̲'A̲SG-. *n.* May. [hàʔliʔx̣ɬɑ́ʔɑskʰ] m.

735. HA'LI'XMAAY. *n.* June. [hàʔliʔx̣má·y] m.

736. HA'LI'XSTM̲ÓON. *n.* July. [hàʔliʔx̣stm̩óʌn] m.

737. HA'LI'X'W̤A̲H. *n.* March. [hàʔliʔx̣ʔÿʌ́h] m.

738. HA'LI'XXSWAANK̲, HA'LI'XXSWAANG̲-. *n.* April. [hàʔliʔx̣x̣swá·nqʰ] m.

739. HA'LIYAAYX. *n.* Saturday. [hàʔliyá·yx̣] hb.

740. HALWAALD. *n.* spear head. [halwá·ld] hb.

741. HAŁ- along the side; along the edge. [haɬ] hb.

742. HAŁAALS. *v.i.* work. [haɬá·ls] m.
742.1 hałał. [haɬáɬ] k.

743. HAŁA'APA̲. *n.* (skin) scraper. [haɬáʔapʰɑ] pr.
743.1 hałe'pa, hakhałe'pa. *n.* knife. [haɬɛ́ʔp̓a] k,m.
[hakhaɬɛ́ʔp̓a] k.

744. HAŁA̲BIISK, HAŁA̲BIISG-, HAKHAŁA̲BIISK. *n.* knife; plane (*carp.*).

[hàɬʌbí·skʰ] pr. [hakhàɬʌbí·skʰ] k.
744.1 haɬabisk, haɬabisg-. [hàɬʌbískʰ] k.
744.2 haɬībiisk, haɬibiisg-. [hàɬɩbí·skʰ] k,m.

745. HAꞭAꞭS. *v.i.* work. *n.* work. [haɬáɬs] pr.

746. HAꞭGYÍIK, HAꞭGYÍIG-. *n.* beach. [haɬgʸíʌkʰ] k,m.
746.1 haɬgyíika, hakhaɬgyíika. *n.* shore. [haɬgʸíʌkʰɑ] k,m. [hakhaɬgʸīʌkʰɑ] k.

747. HAꞭO, HAKHAꞭO. *n.* sail. [haɬɔ́] hb. [hakhaɬɔ́] hb.
747.1 haɬoo. *n.* cloth; sail. [haɬɔ́·] k,m,pr.

748. HAꞭOOMBÓOT, HAꞭOOMBÓOD-. *n.* sail. [haɬó·mbóʌtʰ] m.

749. HAꞭOOMXSO. *n.* sail. [haɬó·mx̣só] m.

750. HAꞭWN. *v.i.* sit in a row. [haɬwń̥] hb.

751. HAMHOM. *n.* ankle; ankle bone. [hamhóm] hb,k,pr.

752. HA'MOOK, HA'MOOG-. *n.* straw. [hʌʔmɔ́·qʰ] m,pr.

753. HAMOOLK, HAMOOLG-. *v.i.* be bothered. *n.* a bothersome thing. [hamɔ́·lkʰ] k,m.

754. HANA'A, HANA'NK. *n.* woman. [hanáʔa] k. [hanáʔnqʰ] k.
754.1 hana'a. [hanáʔɑ] pr.

755. HANA'MWAN. *n.* doe. [hanáʔm̥wʌn] hb.

756. HANA'NK, HANA'NG-. *plural of* hana'a.

757. HANHANI. *n.* temple(s) (*anat.*). [hanháni] pr.

758. HANI. *v.i.* thin. [háni] m,pr.

759. HA'NOO. *n.* kelp cod. [haʔnɔ́·] hb.

760. HAN'WILAAKW, HAN'WILAAGW-. *v.t.* destroy. [hɛ̀nʔwɩlá·kʷʰ] k.

761. HAPSGAAWLK, HAPSGAAWLG-. *n.* a (small) spoon. [hapsgɑ̣́·wlkʰ] k.

762. HASAAKL. *v.t.* desire; want; long for. [hasá·kḷ] k,m.
762.1 hasaax. *v.t.* lack; be lacking. [hasá·x̣] k,m.

763. HASHAATS, HASHAADZ-. *plural of* haats.
763.1 hasháats, hasháadz-. *plural of* háats.

764. HASHAYS. *plural of* hayts.

765. HASHAYTS, HASHAYDZ-. *v.t.* send. [hasháychʰ] m,pr.

766. HASHOOSK, HASHOOSG-. *n.* trouble. [hashɔ́·skʰ] k,m.

767. HASIIPK, HASIIPG-. *n.* sickness. [hasí·pʰkʰ] m,pr.
767.1 hasíipk, hasíipg-. [hasíʌpʰkʰ] k.

768. HASOYX. *n.* bell. [hasóyx̣] k.

769. HASTAALEKS. *n.* third finger; ring finger. [hastá·leks] k.
769.1 hastawiks. [hastáwɩks] k,pr.

770. HAT'ÁAPA. *n.* (stone) pestle. [hatʔáʌpʰɑ] k.

771. HAT'AAXS. *n.* a pole used for pushing a canoe in shallow water. [hatʔá·x̣s] pr.

772. HAT'AL. *n.* cedar bark strips used for making baskets. [hatʔál] k,m.

773. HAT'AXGMSIIP, HAT'AXGMSIIB-. *n.* syphillis. [hɑtʔɑ́x̣gm̥sí·pʰ] m.

774. HAT'AXK, HAT'AXG-. *v.i.* bad. [hatʔáx̣kʰ] k.
774.1 hat'axk, hat'axg-. [hatʔɑ́x̣kʰ] hb,m,pr.

775. HATHOTXK, HATHOTXG-. *v.t.* & *v.i.* boil. [hatʰhɔ́tx̣kʰ] m.
775.1 hat'o'aɬk, hat'o'aɬg-. [hatʔɔ́ʔʌɬkʰ] k.
775.2 hato'oxk, hato'oxg-. [hatʰɔ́ʔɔx̣kʰ] hb.

776. HATS'A'AN'ON. *n.* arms (*anat.*). [hàʔc̓ɑʔanʔɔ́n] hb.

777. HATS'AL. *n.* devil fish; octopus; squid. [hacʔál] k,m.
771.1 hats'al. [hɑcʔɑ́l] hb.
777.2 hats'alt, hats'ald-. [hacʔaltʰ] k,m.

778. HATS'ANAASÜÜ. *plural of* hats'anas.

779. HATS'AXɬK, HATS'AXɬG-. *v.i.* (be) in front. [hacʔɑx̣ɬkʰ] m,pr.

780. HATS'IIWKWSA. *n.* bailer (*naut.*). [hacʔí·wkʷʰsa] hb.

781. HATSNAAS. *n.* good luck. [hacʰn̥a·s] hb.

782. HAW. *v.i.* say; talk. [haw] k,pr.

783. HAWAAL. *n.* arrow; spear head. [hawa·l] hb,pr,m.
783.1 hawal. [hawál] k.

784. HA'WEEɬK, HA'WEEɬG-. *v.t.*, *v.i.* & *n.* taboo. [haʔwɛ́·ɬkʰ] k.
784.1 ha'weɬk, ha'weɬg-. [haʔwɛ́ɬkʰ] k.

785. HAWHAW. *n.* a fabuous monster (similar to a panther); an (African) lion. [hawháw] k,pr.
785.1 hawhaw. [hɑwhɑ́w] m.

786. HAWTS, HAWDZ-. *n.* sea loon. [hawcʰ] hb.
786.1 haw'ts, haw'dz-. *n.* (black) cormorant (k,m); bottle-neck duck (m). [hawʔc̓] k,m.
786.2 ha'u'ts, ha'u'dz-. *n.* bottle-neck duck; cormorant. [háʔuʔc̓] m.

787. HAXBAXT, HAXBAXD-. *n.* pocket knife. [hax̣báx̣t^{h}] pr.

788. HAXBEEXS. *n.* hand saw. [hax̣bé·x̣s] m.
 788.1 haxbéexsk, haxbéexsg-. [hax̣bé·ʌx̣sk^{h}] hb.

789. HAYDMX, GAHAYDMX. *n.* language of the Haida. [háydm̩x̣] m.

790. HAYETSK, HAYETSG-. *n.* a copper (potlatch plaque). [hayéc^{h}k^{h}] k.
 790.1 heyatsk, heyatsg-. [hɛyác^{h}k^{h}] k.

791. HAYAAMXS. *v.i.* tricky. [hayá·mx̣s] hb.

792. HAYÁAXK, HAYÁAXG-. *n.* fork. [hayáʌx̣k^{h}] k.
 792.1 hayawxk, hayawxg-. [hayáwx̣k^{h}] k,m.

793. HA'YIN, HAHA'YIN. *v.t.* place upright; set upright; stand up.
 [háʔyɩn] pr. [hahá́ʔyɩn] pr.
 793.1 ha'yn. [háʔyn̩] pr.

794. HAYMAADM. *n.* Northeast wind. [haymá·dm̩] hb.

795. HAYSK, HAYSG-. *v.t.* send. [háysk^{h}] k,m.

796. HAYTKSN, MAXSN. *v.t.* plant; stand up; place upright. [háyt^{h}k^{h}sn̩] pr. [máx̣sn̩] pr.

797. HAYTS. *v.t.* send. [hayts] m,pr.

798. HAYWAAS. *n.* Southeast wind. [haywá·s] hb.

799. HÉEXL. *v.i.* keep trying; never give up. [héʌx̣l̩] m,pr.

800. HELD- many. [hɛld] pr.

801. HIDUU. *n.* fame; good reputation. [hidú·] pr.

802. HMMOOMAX. *v.i.* & *n.* smile. [hm̩mɔ́·max̣] m,pr.

803. HOLTK, HOLTG, HAHOLTK. *v.i.* full. [hɔlt^{h}k^{h}] k,pr. [hahɔ́lt^{h}k^{h}] k.
 803.1 hooltk, hooltg-. [hɔ·lt^{h}k^{h}] k.

804. HON. *n.* fish. [hɔn] hb.
 804.1 hoon. [hɔ·n] k.
 804.2 hóon. [hɔʌn] k.

805. HOOKS. *n.* balsam. [hɔ·ks] hb.

806. HOOKS. *v.i.* come. [hɔ·ks] hb.
 806.1 hooksk, hooksg-. *v.i.* be with. [hɔ·ksk^{h}] pr.
 806.2 hooksn. *v.t.* & *v.i.* put with; be put with. [hɔ́·ksn̩] pr.

807. HOOLTGAGYEMK, HOOLTGAGYEMG-. *n.* full moon. [hɔ́·ltga g^{y}ɛ́ mk^{k}] hb.

808. HOY. *v.t.* use. [hɔy] pr.

809. HOYAX, HOYAG-. *v.i.* correct. [hóyax̣] m,pr.
809.1 hoygyax, hoygyag-. [hóygʸʌx̣] hb,m.

810. HUK'ALAAIS. *plural of* alaais.

811. HUK'AL'ALGYAX, HUK'AL'ALGYAG-. *n.* speaker. [hùkʔalʔalgʸʌx̣] hb.
811.1 huk'algyax, huk'algyag-. [hukʔálgʸʌx̣] hb.

812. HUK'ALASKW, HUK'ALASGW-. *plural of* alaskw.

813. HUKALUK'AŁ. *n.* a fast runner (*plural of* alubaa). [hukàluqʔáɬ] hb.

814. HUKAMADAAL'KASK, HUKAMADAAL'KASG-. *n.* a worshiper (*plural of* amadaalk'ask). [hùkamadaalʔqˀskʰ] hb.

815. HUK'AMADAALX, HUK'AMADAALG-. *plural of* amadaalx.

816. HUK'AT, HUK'AD-. *n.* fisherman. [hukʔátʰ] k,m.

817. HUKBII'K, HUKBII'G-. *n.* a liar. [hukbí·ʔkˀ] hb.

818. HUKDZAP, HUKDZAB-. *n.* jack of all trades. [hukʒʌ́pʰ] hb.
818.1 hukwdzap, hukwdzab-. *n.* skill. [hukʷʰʒapʰ] k,m.

819. HUKHÚUTK, HUKHÚUTG-. *plural of* húutk.

820. HUKKWDEK, HUKKWDEG-. *n.* a good hunter. [hukʰkʷʰdɛ́kʰ] m,pr.

821. HUKWOOMSK, HUKWOOMSG-. *v.i.* always sick; sickly. [hukʰwɔ́·mskʰ] k.
821.1 huk'woomsk, huk'woomsg-. [hukʰʔwɔ́·mskʰ] m.

822. HUM'TSA. *v.t.* kiss. [húmʔcˀa] hb.
822.1 huumpxa. [hú·mpx̣a] k,m.
822.2 hu'umtsax. [húʔumcʰʌx̣] m,pr.

823. HÚUŁNN. *n.* a poisonous root (used for medicine). [huʌɬn̩n̩] m,pr.

824. HUUM. *v.t.* smell. [hu·m] m,pr.
824.1 huumɬ. [hu·mɬ] m,pr.
824.2 huumsk, huumsg-, huumhuumsk. *v.t. & v.i.* sniff; sniffing. [hu·mskʰ] pr. [hu·hu·mskʰ] pr. Note: plural form marks repeated action.

825. HUPL. *n.* dark; evening; night; nighttime. [húpʰl̩] pr.
825.1 hu'pl. [húʔpˀl̩] m.
825.2 huupl. [hú·pʰl̩] pr.
825.3 huu'pl. [hú·ʔpˀl̩] k.
825.4 hu'upl. [húʔupʰl̩] pr.

826. HUUS. *n.* root. [hu·s] k.
826.1 huust, huusd-, gahuust. [hu·stʰ] pr. [g̣ahú·stʰ] pr.

827. HUUT, HUUD-. *v.t. & v.i.* escape. [hu·tʰ] pr.
827.1 huwat, huwad-. [húwatʰ] k.

828. HÚUTK, HÚUTG-, HUKHÚUTK. *v.t.* call; summon. [huʌtʰkʰ] k. [hukhú·ʌtʰkʰ] k.

829. HUWAAL. *plural of* waal.

830. HUWA'A'T, HUWA'A'D-. *plural of* wa'at. *plural of* 'wa'at.

831. HUWAY. *plural of* waay. *plural of* way.

832. HUXGYED. *plural of* xgyet.

I

833. IIM. *n.* porcupine quills. [ʔi·m] k,pr.

834. IIMK, IIMG-. *n.* beard; facial hair; moustache; whiskers. [ʔi·mqʰ] k,pr.
834.1 iimx, iimg, iimx. [ʔi·mx̣] k,pr. [ʔi·mx̣] k.

835. IIS, IIS. *n.* yeast. [ʔi·s] k. [ʔi·s] k.

836. IKSALDAMTK, IKSALDAMTG-. *n.* design; pattern; picture (Note: an idea put onto paper or into a carving, etc., i.e., the concrete representation of an abstraction). [ʔìksaldʌ́mtʰkʰ] m,pr. *See also* gyistxalt'mtk.

837. IŁÉE. *n.* blood. [ʔiłé·ʌ] hb,k,m.

838. IŁEEMTS'AX. *n.* bleeding hearts; western columbine (*Aquilegia formosa*). [ʔiłé·mcʔáx̣] hb.

839. INÁAŁK, INÁAŁG-. *n.* lullaby. [ʔinaʌłkʰ] k.

840. INTANOOŁ. *n.* cupboards for dishes. [ʔìntʰanɔ́·ł] hb.

841. IS. *v.t.* smell like. [ʔis] k.

842. IWKŁA'ALDAAT, IWKŁA'ALDAAD-. *num.* eight (of humans aboard a conveyance). [ʔiwkłáʔaldá·tʰ] hb,pr.

843. IWKŁA'ADOOL. *num.* eight (of humans). [ʔiwkłáʔadɔ́·l] hb,pr. *See also* yukwła'adool.

844. IWKŁA'AL'ON. *num.* eight (of measures); eight fathoms. [ʔiwkłáʔʌlʔɔ́n] pr. *See also* yukła'al'on.

845. IWKŁA'ATK, IWKŁA'ATG-. *num.* eight (of canoes). [ʔiwkłáʔatʰkʰ] hb,pr. *See also* yukła'atk.

846. IWKŁEETSXN. *num.* eight (of long objects). [ʔiwkłɛ́cʰx̣n̥] hb,pr. *See also* yukwłeetsxn.

K

847. K'ÁA. *n.* cut; wound. [qʔaʌ] k,m.
 847.1 k'ah, k'ak'aah. [qʔah] k,m. [qʔaqʔá·h] k.

848. K'AALG. *v.t. & v.i.* steal. [qʔɑ·lg] pr.
 848.1 k'aalk, k'aalg-. *v.t. & v.i.* steal. *n.* thief. [qʔɑlk^{h}] m.
 848.2 k'aa'lk, k'aa'lg-, gak'aa'lk. *v.t. & v.i.* steal. [kʔa·ʔlk^{h}] k. [gɑkʔá·ʔlk^{h}] k.
 848.3 k'aa'lk, k'aa'lg-, wuk'ak'aa'lk. *n.* thief. [kʔa·ʔlk^{h}] k. [wuqʔàqʔá·ʔlk^{h}] k.
 848.4 k'a'almx. *v.t. & v.i.* steal for. [qʔáʔʌlm̥x̣] pr.

849. K'A'ANA. *n.* mast. [qʔáʔanɑ] k,m.

850. K'A'APAYTK, K'A'APAYTG-. *v.i.* fall down (patient subject). [kʔàʔap^{h}áyt^{h}k^{h}] k,m. *See also* ga'apaytk *and* k'ya'apayk.

851. K'AAS. *v.t. & v.i.* have sexual intercourse (with). *n.* sexual intercourse. [qʔa·s] m.

852. K'AAS, MUKMOOLSK. *v.i.* sour. [qʔa·s] k,m. [mukmó·lsk^{h}] k.

853. K'A'AT, K'A'AD-. *n.* cane.

854. K'AAWTS, K'AAWDZ-. *n.* labret (Note: worn by chief's wife or sister and by warriors). [qʔa·wc^{h}] pr.
 854.1 k'awts, k'awdz-. [qʔɑwc^{h}] hb.
 854.2 k'aawtsx. *n.* gills. [qʔa·wc^{h}x̣] m.
 854.3 k'awtsx. [qʔawc^{h}x̣] hb.
 854.4 k'awsł. [qʔɑwsł] k.

855. K'AAX. *v.t. & v.i.* hollow; open. [qʔɑ·x̣] k,m.
 855.1 k'ax. [qʔɑx̣] pr.

856. K'AAYAAN. *v.t.* club. [qʔa·yá·n] pr.

857. K'ABAA. *v.i.* lame. [qʔɑbá·] pr.

858. K'ABATGÜÜŁK, K'ABATGÜÜŁG-. *n.* children. [kʔʌ̀bʌtgɨ́·łk^{h}] hb,pr.

859. K'ADÍISK, K'ADÍISG-. *v.i.* braid one's hair to one side and in one braid. *n.* braid. [qʔɑdí·ʌsk^{h}] m.

860. K'ADZAA. *v.t.* swallow. [qʔɑʒá·] pr.
 860.1 k'adzaał. *v.i.* swallow. [qʔɑʒá·ł] pr. *See also* gats'ał.

861. K'AGAA. *n.* (Harlequin) duck (*Histrionicus histrionicus*). [qʔag̣a·] pr.

862. K'AGAW'TK, K'AGAW'TG-. *v.i.* howl. [kʔɑgáwʔtʾk^{h}] k.

863. K'AH. *v.i.* come. [qʔah] pr.

864. K'AK'AY. *n.* wing. [qʔaqʔáy] k.

865. K'AK'O. *plural of* k'o.

866. K'AK'WÍIKWS. *n.* dried fish belly. [qʔakʷʔí·ʌkʷʰs] m.

867. K'ALA'AKS. *n.* river; upstream; the upper part of a river. [qʔàlaʔáks] k,m.

868. K'ALAAMS. *n.* clustered wild rose (*Rosa pisocarpa*); dwarf woodland rose (*Rosa gymnocarpa*). [qʔalá·ms] hb.
868.1 k'alaamst, k'alaamsd-. *n.* hawberry. [qʔalá·mstʰ] pr.

869. K'ALBIIN. *n.* beetle. [qʔalbí·n] hb.

870. K'ALGYIGYET, K'ALGYIGYED-. *n.* commoner. [qʔàlgʸigɛ́tʰ] hb.

871. K'ALISYETS, K'ALISYEDZ-. *v.t.* club. [kʔʌlɩsyɛ́cʰ] pr.

872. K'ALK'AYS. *n.* knee (*anat.*). [qʔalqʔáys] pr.

873. K'ALMOOSGMLAXSGA'NIIS. *n.* spider crab, [qʔalmɔ́·sgm̩làx̣sgaʔní·s] hb.

874. K'AŁ'AN. *n.* scallops. [kʔaɬʔán] hb.
874.1 k'ał'on. [kʔaɬʔɔ́n] hb.
874.2 k'ał'on. [qʔaɬʔɔ́n] hb.

875. K'AŁAW. *v.t. & v.i.* choke. [kʔaɬáw] k.

876. K'AMEET, K'AMEED-. *num.* one (canoe). [qʔamé·tʰ] pr.

877. K'AMTSN. *adv.* secretly. [qʔámcʰn̩] pr.

878. K'ANDAH. *n.* ray (*ichth.*); skate (*ichth.*). [qʔandáh] hb.

879. K'ANDOOLD. *num.* eight (of flat objects). [qʔandɔ́·ld], [qʔʌndɔ́·ld] pr.

880. K'A'OOTK, K'A'OOTG-. *n.* baby seal. [kʔaʔɔ́·tʰkʰ] hb.

881. K'APK'OOP, K'APK'OOB-. *n.* bunch berries; dwarf dogwood; pigeon berries; *Cornus canadensis*. [qʔapqʔɔ́·pʰ] hb.
881.1 k'apk'oopk, k'apk'oopg-. *v.i.* red hot. *n.* lava. [qʔapqʔɔ̄́·pʰkʰ] pr.

882. K'ASGI. *v.i.* unripe. [qʔʌ́sgi] m.
882.1 k'awsk, k'awsg-. [qʔawskʰ] k.

883. K'ASÍIPSL. *v.i.* wink. [qʔasɩ́ʌpsl̩] k. *See also* gapsl.

884. K'ASK'ADZN. *n.* ants. [qʔasqʔáʒn̩] m. *See also* gasgadzn.

885. K'ASK'AWSK, K'ASK'AWSG-. *plural of* k'awsk.

886. K'ASKOOS, K'ASKOOS. *n.* (sandhill) crane (*Grus canadensis*). [qʔasq^{h}ɔ̄·s] k. [qʔasq^{h}ɔ́·s] k.
886.1 k'awsk'oos. [kʔawskʔó·s] hb.

887. K'ATSIWÉELT, K'ATSIWÉELD-, GAKK'ATSIWELT. *n.* finger. [qʔàc^{h}ɩwɛ̄ʌlt^{h}] k. [g̣akqʔāc^{h}ɩwɛ́lt^{h}] k.

888. K'AWN, GAGAWN. *v.t.* & *v.i.* chew. [qʔawn] k. [g̣ag̣áwn] k.

889. K'AWSK, K'AWSG-, K'ASK'WSK. *v.i.* unripe. [qʔawsk^{h}] k. [qʔāsqʔáwsk^{h}] k.

890. K'AWTS, K'AWDZ-. *n.* grey cod. [qʔawc^{h}] hb.
890.1 k'aw'ts, k'aw'dz-. *n.* tommy cod (*Microgadus proximus*); a little girl. [qʔawʔc$^{>}$] k,m.
890.2 k'a'wts, k'a'wdz-, gukk'a'w'ts. *n.* chin. [qʔaʔwc^{h}] k,pr. [g̣uk^{h}qʔaʔwʔc$^{>}$] k.

891. K'AWTSGN. *num.* one (long). [qʔáwc^{h}gṇ] hb.
891.1 k'awtsxn. [qʔáwc^{h}x̣ṇ] pr.

892. K'AWTSI. *n.* grease; oil. [qʔáwc^{h}i] m,pr.

893. K'AY. *v.t.* bite. [qʔay] pr.

894. K'AYADZEN. *n.* grey snapper (*ichth.*). [kʔàyaʒɛ́n] hb.

895. K'AYEET, K'AYEED-. *n.* bullhead (*ichth*); cabezon; sculpin; sea raven; muddler (*ichth*). Note: not *Ictalarus*, but *Hemitripterus americanus*, *Myoxocephalus octodecemspinosus*, *Scorpaenichthys marmoratus*, and *Cottus bairdi*. [qʔayɛ́·t^{h}] hb.
895.1 kayeyt, k'ayeyd-. [qʔayɛ́yt^{h}] k.

896. K'AYGYIK'AK, K'AYGYIK'AG-. *plural of* gyik'áak.

897. K'AYM. *adv.* almost.

898. KBALDAAT, KBALDAAD-. *num.* ten (humans aboard a conveyance). [k^{h}bʌldā·t^{h}] pr.

899. KBAL'ON. *num.* ten (measures); ten fathoms. [k^{h}bʌlʔɔ́n] pr.

900. KBIDAXS. *n.* starry flounder (*ichth*). [k^{h}bidáx̣s] hb. *See also* xbidaxs.

901. KBIILDIK'AWTSXN. *num.* eleven (of long objects). [kbí·ldiqʔáwc^{h}x̣ṇ] pr.

902. KBIITSXN. *num.* ten (of long objects). [k^{h}bí·c^{h}x̣ṇ] pr.

903. KBOOL. *num.* ten (of humans). [k^{h}bɔ·l] pr.

904. K'ILIILP, K'ILIILB-. *n.* hip (of a roof, i.e., the beam along the hip). [kʔɩlí·lp^{h}] hb. *See also* galiilp.

905. KLAGYET, KLAGYED-. *v.i.* be born (of humans). [klag^{y}ɛ́t^h] k,m.

906. K'LK'OOL. *plural of* k'oolax. *plural of* k'oolx. *plural of* k'oylk.

907. KLUSMS. *n.* Nass River. [klúsm̩s] pr.

908. KŁGUM'OL. *n.* bear cub. [kɨgumʔɔ́l] pr.

909. KŁGÜÜ. *n.* little one(s); young one(s). [kɨgɨ̈·] pr.

910. K'ŁIK'AGUN. *v.t.* crush. [kʔɨiqʔágun] k,m.

911. KŁ'ÜÜNGYAXS. *v.t.* stomp on; trample. [kɨʔɨ̈́·ng^{y}axs] pr.

912. K'MGOOT, K'MGOOD-. *v.i.* kind. [qʔm̩gó·t^h] hb. *See also* gamgoot.

913. K'O, K'AK'O. *n.* back (*anat*). [qʔɔ] k.
913.1 k'oo. [qʔɔ·] hb.

914. K'O'AL. *v.t.* forget. [qʔɔ́ʔʌl] pr.

915. K'ODZ, K'ODZK'ODZ. *v.t., v.i. & n.* cut. [qʔɔʒ] hb,m. [qʔɔʒqʔɔ́ʒ] m,pr. Note: plural marks repeated action, i.e., slice; cut fish or flesh.
915.1 k'os. [qʔɔs] m,pr.
915.2 k'ots, k'odz-. [qʔɔc^h] m,pr.

916. K'OL. *plural of* baa.

917. K'OLDAAT, K'OLDAAD-. *num.* six (humans aboard a conveyance). [qʔɔldá·t^h] pr.

918. K'OLSXN. *num.* six (of long objects). [qʔɔ́lsx̣n̩] hb.

919. K'OŁ, GOK'OŁ. *n.* year. [kʔɔɨ] k. [gɔkʔɔɨ] k.
919.1 k'ooł. [kʔo·ɨ] pr.

920. K'OMAGOOT, K'OMAGOOD-. *v.i.* selfish. *n.* a selfish person. [qʔɔmagɔ́·t^h] hb.
920.1 k'omgoot, k'omgood-. *v.i.* hopeful. [qʔɔmgɔ·t^h] hb.

921. K'OO. *n.* back bone. [kʔo·] hb.

922. K'OODZAX. *v.t.* break (a string or line); *v.i.* die (of humans only). [qʔɔ́ʒʌx̣] pr.

923. K'OOK, K'OOG-. *n.* basket. [kʔo·k^h] hb.

924. K'OOL- alone. [kʔɔ·l] k. *See also* k'yaal-.

925. K'OOL. *num.* one (of humans). [kʔɔ·l] pr.

926. K'OOL. *num.* six (of abstract, flat, and round objects). [qʔo·l] hb.

927. K'OOLAX. *v.i.* dull; warm one's back by the fire. [qʔɔ́·lʌx̣] pr.

927.1 k'oolx, k'lk'ool. *num.* dull. [qʔo·lx̣] hb. [qʔl̩kʔó·l] hb.

928. K'OOLD. *num.* six (of abstract, flat, and round objects). [qʔɔ·ld] pr.
928.1 k'oolt, k'oold-. [qʔɔ·ltʰ] pr.

929. K'OOLDA'ON. *num.* six (of measures); six fathoms. [qʔɔ́·ldʌʔɔ́n] pr.

930. K'OOLDOOL. *num.* six (of humans). [qʔɔ·ldɔ́·l] pr.

931. K'O'OLDZAX. *v.t.* carry on one's shoulder. [qʔɔ́ʔɔlʒʌx̣] pr.

932. K'OOLI. *n.* scalp. [qʔɔ́·li] pr.

933. K'OOLTK, K'OOLTG-. *num.* six (of canoes). [qʔɔ·ltʰkʰ] pr.

934. K'OOLTSXN. *num.* six (of long objects). [qʔɔ́·lcʰx̣n̩] pr.

935. K'OOLX. *v.i.* dull. [qʔɔ·lx̣] k.
935.1 k'oylk, k'oylg-, galgolik. [qʔɔylqʰ] k. [galɡ̣ɔ́lɩqʰ] k.

936. K'OOŁKS. *n.* sister-in-law (reference and address; man speaking; BW, WZ, FBSW). [kʔɔ·łks] pr.
936.1 k'otks. [kʔotʰks] k.

937. K'OOMTK, K'OOMTG-. *v.t.* desire; wish (pr). *n.* hope (hb). [qʔɔ·mtʰkʰ] hb,pr.
937.1 k'oomtk, k'oomtg-, gaxgoomtk. *v.t. & v.i.* hope. [qʔo·mtʰkʰ] k,m. [gax̣ɡ̣o·mtʰkʰ] k.

938. K'OON. *n.* (Northern) fur seal; Alaska fur seal; *Callorhinus ursinus*. [qʔɔ·n] hb,k,m,pr.

939. K'OOPSXN. *num.* two (of long objects). [qʔɔ́·psx̣n̩] pr.

940. K'OOS. *n.* bushes. [qʔɔ·s] m,pr.

941. K'OOXS. *n.* maple tree. [qʔo·x̣s] m.

942. K'OS, GASGOS. *v.t. & v.i.* shoot (pr). *v.i.* jump (k). [qʔɔs] k,pr. [qʔos] k. [gasɡ̣ɔ́s] k.

943. K'OTS, K'ODZ-. *v.t.* chop down. [qʔɔcʰ] pr.

944. K'OX. *v.t.* pluck; pull out. [qʔɔx̣] pr.

945. K'OXŁ. *n.* red cedar softened by steaming and used to mend canoes, etc. [qʔɔx̣ł] pr.

946. KPAAẄ. *n.* chin; jaw. [kʰpa·ÿ] hb,pr.
946.1 kpal, gakpal. [kʰpal] k. [gakpʰal] k.

947. KPIIL. *num.* ten (of abstract and round objects). [kʰpi·l] pr.

948. KP'I'NSXN. *num.* ten (of long objects). [kʰpʔíʔn̩sx̣n̩] hb.

949. KSAA, GAKSAA. *n.* shark (esp. blue and hammerhead). [ksa·] k. [gaksá·] k.
949.1 ksah. [ksah] hb.

950. KSA'AAMKS. *n.* clear water. [ksʌʔá·mks] m,pr.

951. KSABUU. *v.i.* blow. [ksabú·] hb.

952. KSAK'O'OŁ. *v.t. & v.i.* forget. [ksakʔɔ́ʔʌɬ] k,m.

953. KSAKWŁEEL. *v.i.* be born (of animals). [ksʌkʷʰɬɛ́·l] m,pr.

954. KSALAKLAK, KSALAKLAG-. *v.i.* fall down; fall out a window; be born. [ksʌláqʰlaqʰ] pr.
954.1 ksalaxlax, ksalaxlag-. [ksaláx̣lax̣] pr.

955. KSAŁOO. *v.i.* swim out (of a fish). [ksʌɬɔ́·] pr.

956. KSAM'ESK, KSAM'ESG-. *n.* (mother's) milk. [ksʌmʔɛ́skʰ] pr.

957. KSAMAXS. *n.* dirt; black (colour; a neologism). [ksamáx̣s] hb.

958. KSAP'E'AL. *v.t.* tear out. [ksʌpʔɛ́ʔʌl] pr.

959. KSATS'ÍIBA. *v.i.* tie one's hair in a coil on top of one's head (Note: signifies a warrior and a brave man). [ksʌcʔí·ʌba] pr.

960. KSAWAXŁAAS. *n.* pink (colour: the colour of huckleberries just before they turn red). [ksʌwʌx̣ɬá·s] hb. *See also* xswaxɬaas.

961. KSA'WOOX. *v.t. & v.i.* dream. [ksʌʔwɔ́·x̣] pr.

962. KSDAMOOLSAL'ON. *num.* nine (of measures); nine fathoms. [ksdʌmɔ́·lsʌlʔɔ́n] pr.

963. KSIBUHBUU'AKS. *v.t. & v.i.* splash. [ksɩbùhbu·ʔáks] hb. *See also* buhbuu'aks.

964. KSIGWAANTK, KSIGWAANTG-. *v.i.* rise (of the sun). [ksɩgʷá·ntʰkʰ] m.
964.1 ksüügwaantk, ksüügwaantg-. [ksɨ̈·gʷá·ntʰkʰ] pr.

965. KSIHOON. *n.* coho salmon (turned red). [ksɩhó·n] hb.

966. KSIIL, GAKSÍILT. *n.* tear, i.e., a teardrop. [ksi·l] k, [gaksíʌltʰ] k.
966.1 ksil. [ksil] k,pr.

967. KSIIŁ. *n.* lizard; newt; salamander. [ksi·ɬ] hb,
967.1 ksiiɬk, ksiiɬg-. [ksi·ɬkʰ] m,pr.
967.2 ksiɬ. [ksiɬ] m,pr.

968. KSIIW' KSUKSIIW. *n.* scraper. [ksi·w] k,m. [ksuksí·w] k.

969. KSIMAŁIITK, KSIMAŁIITG. *n.* (light) green; liquid green (colour).

[ksimaɬí·tʰkʰ] hb.

970. KSIN'AK̲, KSIN'AG̲-. *n.* middle finger; second finger. [ksɩnʔáqʰ] pr.

971. KSINAAŁ. *v.i.* breathe. [ksɩna·ɬ] pr.
971.1 ksinaaɬk, ksinaaɬg-, lusanaaɬk. [ksɩná·ɬkʰ] hb,m,pr.
Note: plural form also means: *n.* miracle; wonder.
971.2 ksinaaɬkw, ksinaaɬgw-. [ksɩná·ɬkʷʰ] pr.

972. KSITS'A̲L. *n.* tears (teardrops); half-dried salmon. [ksɩcʔál] m,pr.

973. KSIIW. *n.* inner bark of the hemlock (Note: a food, the inner bark is scraped off and the scrapings are soaked in olachen grease, drained, cooked, and sweetened with sugar). [ksiw] hb,m,pr.

974. KSŁÜÜDAT, KSŁÜÜDAD-. *n.* down below; the bottom one. [ksɬɨ́·datʰ] m.

975. KSŁÜÜSGM̲NOO. *n.* night gown. [ksɬɨ́·sgm̩nó·] hb.

976. KSŁÜÜSK, KSŁÜÜSG-, GÜKSŁÜÜSK. *n.* shirt. [ksɬɨ̆·skʰ] hb.
[g̣ɨksɬɨ̆·skʰ] hb.

977. KSOOX, KSOOG̲-. *plural of* ksüü.

978. KSOOG̲M̲LA̲XA̲'YENS. *n.* frost. [ksò·gm̩laxaʔyɛ́ns] hb.

979. KSTA̲MASCOOL. *num.* nine (of humans). [kstʌmasɔ́·l] pr.

980. KSTA̲MOOS. *num.* nine (of abstract, flat, and round objects).
[kstʌmɔ́·s] pr.
980.1 kstimoos. [kstɩmɔ́·s] hb.

981. KSTA̲MOOSK, KSTA̲MOOSG-. *num.* nine (of canoes). [kstʌmɔ́·skʰ] pr.
981.1 kstm̲oosk, kstm̲oosg-. [kstm̩ɔ́·skʰ] pr.

982. KSTIMOOSDAAT, KSTIMOOSDAAD-. *num.* nine (humans aboard a conveyance).
[kstɩmɔ́·sdá·tʰ] pr.

983. KSTIMOOTSX̲N̲. *num.* nine (of long objects). [kstɩmɔ́·cʰx̣n̩] pr.
983.1 kstümoosx̲n̲. [kstɨmɔ́·sx̣n̩] hb.

984. KSTN̲SOOL. *num.* five (of humans). [kstn̩sɔ́·l] pr.

985. KSTÚUNS. *num.* five (of flat objects). [kstu·ʌns] hb.

986. KSTÚUNSX̲N̲. *num.* five (of long objects). [kstú·ʌnsx̣n̩] hb.

987. KSUKSIIW. *plural of* ksiiw.

988. KSUUD. *n.* autumn; fall. [ksu·d] pr.
988.1 ksuut, ksuud-, gyiksúut. *n.* autumn, fall (hb,k); winter (hb). [ksu·tʰ] hb,k. [gʸɩksúʌtʰ] k.
988.2 kwsúut, kwsúud-. *n.* autumn; fall. [kʷʰsuʌtʰ] pr.

989. KSÜÜ, KSOOX. *v.i.* go out (exit). [ksɪ̈·] hb,pr. [ksɔ·x̣] hb,pr.

990. KSÜÜHUUTK' KSÜÜHUUTG-, KSÜÜHUHUUTK. *v.i.* call out.
[ksɪ̈·hú·tʰkʰ] pr. [ksɪ̈̀·hɨhú·tʰkʰ] pr.

991. KSÜÜLG. *n.* middle. [ksɪ̈·lg] pr.

992. KSÜÜŁÓOTK, KSÜÜŁÓOTG-. *v.i.* crawl out. [ksɪ̈·ɬɔ́ʌtʰkʰ] m,pr.
922.1 ksüüło'otk, ksüüło'otg-. [ksɪ̈·ɬɔ́ʔɔtʰkʰ] m,pr.

993. KTS'OKS. *n.* flooring inside the hatch (*naut*). [kʰcʔɔks] hb.
993.1 kts'ooks. *n.* boards in the bottom of a canoe.
[kʰcʔɔ·ks] pr.

994. K'UL'ON. *num.* three (of measures); three fathoms. [kʔulʔɔ́n] pr.

995. K'UTK'WA'AD. *plural of* k'wa'ad.

996. KUTKWÁATK, KUTKWÁATG-. *plural of* kwáatk. *plural of* gweetk.

997. K'ÜÜDET, K'ÜÜDED-. *adv.* seldom ever; a few days ago. [kʔɪ̈·dɛ́tʰ] pr.

998. K'ÚU'K, K'ÚU'G-. *v.t., v.i. & n.* have sexual intercourse (with);
sexual intercourse. [qʔu·ʌʔq˃] m.

999. K'ÜÜL. *num.* one (of abstract and round objects). [kʔɪ̈·l] hb,pr.

1000. K'ÜÜLDA'ON. *num.* one (of measures). *n.* one fathom. [kʔɪ̈̀·ldʌʔɔ́n] pr.
1000.1 k'üül'on. [kʔɪ̈̀·lʔɔ́n] pr.

1001. K'ÜÜLDMGAAY. *num.* one (of measures). *n.* one fathom.
[qʔɪ̈·ldm̩gạ́·y] hb.

1002. K'ÜÜLGAYŁ. *v.i.* act as one (in unison); go as one. [kʔɪ̈̀·lgạyɬ] m,pr.

1003. K'ÜÜTI. *n.* a box for picking berries. [kʔɪ̈́·tʰi] pr.

1004. K'WAADAMŁK, K'WAADAMŁG-. *v.i.* pregnant. [kʷʔá·dʌmɬkʰ] pr.

1005. K'WA'ADIS. *v.t.* miss. [kʷʔáʔadɩs] k.

1006. K'WAAS. *v.t.* break. *v.i.* break; be broken. [kʷʔa·s] k.
1006.1 k'waas. [kʷʔɑ·s] k.
1006.2 k'was. [kʷʔas] k.
1006.3 k'was, gwisgwas. [kʷʔʌs] k,pr. [qʷɩsgʷʌ́s] k.

1007. K'WAA'TIS. *v.i.* be lost. [kʷʔá·ʔt˃ɩs] k.
1007.1 k'wa'a'tis. [kʷʔáʔaʔt˃ɩs] k.
1007.2 k'waatk, k'waatg-. *v.i.* be lost; be missed.
[kʷʔá·tʰkʰ] m,pr.

1008. KWDAXS, KWDAAŁAXS. *v.t.* leave. [kʷʰdɑx̣s] hb. [kʷʰdá·ɬʌxs] hb.
1008.1 kwtaaxs, kwtaałaxs. [kʷʰta·x̣s] pr. [kʷʰtá·ɬʌxs] hb.
1008.2 kwtaxs. [kʷʰtax̣s] pr.

1008.3 kwtaxs. [kʷʰtax̣s] hb.

1009. KWDEK, KWDEG-. *v.t.* shoot. [kʷʰdɛkʰ] m,pr.

1010. KWDII, LAKWDIIDI. *v.i.* hungry. [kʷʰdi·] k. [lʌkʷʰdí·di] k.
1010.1 kwtii, lukwtidi. [kʷʰti·] pr. [lukʷʰtídi] pr.

1011. KWDUS' GUKWDUS. *n.* knife; woman's knife. [kʷʰdus] k. [g̣ukʷʰdús] k.
1011.1 kwduus. [kʷʰdu·s] k.
1011.2 kwtuus. [kʷʰtu·s] m,pr.

1012. K'WIDAAT, K'WIDAAD-. *num.* one (of humans aboard a conveyance). [kʷʔidá·tʰ] hb,pr.

1013. K'WÍINTI. *n.* salmon stomach. [kʷʔí·ʌntʰi] m.

1014. K'WILI. *num.* three (of abstract and round objects). [kʷʔɩlí] pr.

1015. KWLAXSƚA'T, KWLAXSƚA'D-. *n.* football. [kʷʰlax̣sɬáʔt˃] hb.

1016. KWLIGUKWLAXS. *v.t.* utterly destroy by kicking (Note: *a plural form of* kwɬaxs). [kʷʰlìgukʷʰláx̣s] hb.
1016.1 kwlikwlaxs. [kʷʰlikʷʰláx̣s] hb.

1017. KWƚAASK, KWƚAASG-, NUKWƚAASK. *v.t.* kick. [kʷʰɬa·skʰ] k. [nukʷʰɬá·skʰ] k.
1017.1 kwɬaxs. [kʷʰɬax̣s] m,pr.

1018. KWƚEEL. *v.i.* fall. [kʷʰɬɛ·l] m,pr.

1019. KWƚIWAALXS. *plural of* kwɬiyáa.

1020. KWƚNA'ANAX. *v.i.* broken. [kʷʰɬnáʔʌnʌx̣] m,pr.
1020.1 kwɬnaa'naxt, kwɬnaa'naxd-. *v.t.* break into pieces. [kʷʰɬná·ʔnʌx̣tʰ] m,pr.

1021. KWƚWOO. *n.* hunter. [kʷʰɬwɔ·] pr.
1021.1 kwɬwo'o. *v.t. & v.i.* hunt. [kʷʰɬwɔ́ʔɔ] pr.

1022. KWƚIYÁA, KWƚIWAALXS. *v.i.* walk across. [kʷʰɬiyá·ʌ] m.

1023. KWƚIYEETSK, KWƚIYEETSG-. *v.t.* pound. [kʷʰɬiyɛ́·cʰkʰ] k,m.

1024. KWSK'AY. *n.* fourth finger; little finger. [kʷʰsqʔáy] pr.

1025. KWSTU'ANSXN. *num.* five (of canoes and long objects). [kʷʰstúʔʌnsx̣n̩] pr.

1026. KWSTUNS. *num.* five (of abstract, round, and flat objects). [kʷʰstuns] pr.

1027. KWSTUNSAL'ON. *num.* five (of measures). *n.* five fathoms. [kʷʰstúnsʌlʔɔ́n] pr.

1028. KWSTUNSDAAT, KWSTUNSDAAD-. *num.* five (of humans aboard a conveyance). [kʷʰstúndá·tʰ] pr.

1029. KWSTUUNS. *num.* five (of abstract and round objects). [kʷʰstu·ns] hb.

1030. KWTSIILTK, KWTSIILTG-. *v.i.* tremble. [kʷʰci·ltʰkʰ] m,pr.

1031. K'WÜLA'MAXS. *n.* Hudson Bay tea (m); Indian tea (hb); pink rhododendron (*Rhododendron macrophyllum*). [kʷʔɨ̀laʔmáx̣s] hb,m.

1032. K'WÜSK'WAASL. *v.t.* break up. [kʷʔɨskʷʔá·sl̥] pr.

1033. KXAA'O. *n.* female sockeye salmon. [qx̣á·ʔo] hb.

1034. K'YAAK, K'YAAG-. *num.* one (of flat objects). [kʸʔa·kʰ] hb,pr.

1035. K'YAAL. *v.i.* alone. [kʸʔa·l] k.
1035.1 k'yaal- alone. [kʸʔa·l] k. *See also* k'ool-.

1036. K'YAA'LK, K'YAA'LG-. *v.t.* steal. [kʸʔa·lkʰ] k.

1037. K'YAALS, K'YAALS. *n.* a block of dried cocles. [kʸʔa·ls] k,m. [kʸʔa·ls] k.

1038. K'YA'APAYK, K'YA'APAYG-. *v.i.* drop down; fall down (agent subject). [kʸʔàʔapʰáykʰ] k,m.

1039. K'YAAPN. *v.t.* scrape. *v.i.* scraped. [kʸʔá·pʰn̥] k. *See also* gaa'pn.

1040. K'YABAA. *v.i.* lame. [kʸʔabá·] k.
1040.1 k'obaa. [kʔɔbá·] k.

1041. K'YABEELDA, K'YIGAXBEELDA. *n.* cliff. [kʸʔabɛ́·ldʌ] k,m. [kʸʔɩgax̣bɛ́·ldʌ] k,m.

1042. K'YAG. *v.i.* choke. [kʸʔag] pr.
1042.1 k'yak, k'yag-, k'yikk'yak. [kʸʔakʰ] pr. [kʸɩkʰkʸʔákʰ] pr.

1043. K'YAP, K'YAB_. *num.* ten (of flat objects). [kʸʔapʰ] hb.
1043.1 k'yep, k'yeb-. [kʸʔɛpʰ] pr.
1043.2 k'yep, k'yeb-. *num.* ten (of round and abstract objects). [kʸʔɛpʰ] hb.

1044. K'YEEXK, K'YEEXG-, HUUT. *v.i.* escape; flee; run away. [kʸʔɛ·x̣kʰ] k. [hu·tʰ] k.
1044.1 k'yéexk, k'yéexg-. [kʸʔe·ʌx̣kʰ] pr.
1044.2 k'yeexkw, k'yeexgw. [kʸʔɛ·x̣kʷʰ] k.

1045. K'YEPDIK'YAAK, K'YEPDIK'YAAG-. *num.* eleven (of flat objects). [kʸʔɛ̀pʰdikʸʔá·kʰ] pr.

1046. K'YEPDIT'APXAAT, K'YEPDIT'APXAAD-. *num.* twelve (of flat objects). [kʸʔɛ̄pditʔʌpx̣á·tʰ] pr.

1047. K'YEPSK' K'YEPSG-. *num.* ten (of canoes). [kʸʔɛpskʰ] pr.

1048. KYI'AK'AKSM MAADM. *n.* sleet. [kʸiʔakʔáksm̩ma·dm̩] hb.

1049. K'YIDAWɬ. *v.i.* sink. [kʸʔidáwɬ] k,m. *See also* tkyidawɬ.

1050. K'YIDEH. *n.* herring rake. [kʸɩdɛ́h] pr.

1051. K'YIDOS. *v.t.* submerge. [kʸʔɩdós] k,m. *See also* tgyit'úus.

1052. K'YIGAXBEELDA. *plural of* k'yabeelda.

1053. K'YÍIDZXAN. *v.t.* point out. [kʸʔí·ʌʒx̣an] pr.

1054. K'YILAA. *n.* palm of hand; bear paw. [kʸʔɩlá·] pr.

1055. K'ILAM. *v.t.* give. [kʔɩlám] k.
 1055.1 k'yilaam. [kʸʔɩʌ́·m] k.
 1055.2 k'yi'nam, k'yilk'yinam. [kʸʔɩʔnʌ́m] pr. [kʸʔɩ̀lkʸʔɩnám] pr.

1056. K'YI'OKS. *v.i.* fall on. [kʸʔiʔɔ́ks] k.

1057. K'YIPKEP, K'YIPKEB-. *num.* twenty (of flat objects). [kʸʔɩpʰkʰɛ́pʰ] pr.

1058. K'YIWAɬGN. *n.* shipworms. [kʸʔiwʌ́ɬgn̩] hb.

1059. KYOOXT, KYOOXD-. *n.* grass. [kʸʰɔ·x̣tʰ] pr.

L

1060. LAA. *v.i.* go (Note: plural subject). [la·] pr.

1061. LA'A. *v.t.* bite. [láʔa] m.

1062. LA'ABAL, LAKLA'ABAL. *v.i.* hurry; do something hastily; twinkle (of stars). [láʔabʌl] pr. [lʌkláʔabʌl] pr.

1063. LA'AGWIL. *v.t.* wrap up. [láʔagʷɩl] pr.
 1063.1 la'akwil. *v.t.* cover, wrap. [láʔakʷʰɩl] k,m.
 1063.2 láawil. [láʌwɩl] k,m.

1064. LA'AKS. *v.i.* drink (note: plural subject; *see* aks). [laʔáks] pr.

1065. LAAKWS, LAKLAKWS. *v.t.*, *v.i.*, & *n.* light. [la·kʷʰs] k. [lʌklákʷʰs] k.
 1065.1 lakws. [lakʷʰs] pr.

1066. LAALT, LAALD-. *n.* worm. [la·ltʰ] hb,m,pr.
 1066.1 láalt, láald-. [la·ʌltʰ] m,pr.
 1066.2 laaltk, laaltg-. *v.i.* slow. [la·ltʰkʰ] pr.
 1066.3 láaltk, láaltg-, galáaltk. [laʌltʰkʰ] k. [g̣aláʌltʰkʰ] k.

1067. ŁÁAŁK, ŁÁAŁG-. *plural of* nóok.

1068. LAAM. *n.* whiskey. [la·m] k,m.

1069. LAAMDZAX. *plural of* ts'ii.

1070. LAAN, LAAN. *n.* fish eggs; roe. [la·n] k,pr. [la·n] k.

1071. LAANMHÓON. *n.* female fish. [là·nm̥hɔ́ʌn] hb.

1072. LAAẄ. *n.* trout. [la·ÿ] k,m,pr.
 1072.1 laẅ, laklaẅ. [laÿ] k. [lʌkláÿ] k.

1073. LAAẄMMÜLIIT, LAAẄMMÜLIID-. *n.* steelhead (*ichth*). [là·ÿm̥mɨlí·tʰ] hb,pr.

1074. LABAALD. *v.i.* pay back a debt. [lʌbá·ld] pr.
 1074.1 labaals. [lʌbá·ls] pr.
 1074.2 labaalg. *v.t.* hate. [lʌba·lg] pr.
 1074.3 labaalxk, labaalxg-. *v.t.* detest; hate. [lʌbá·lx̣kʰ] k.

1075. LABA'ON. *n.* arm muscle (biceps). [lʌ̀bʌ·ɔ́n] pr.

1076. LABAXSA 'YAGAGYEMK, LABAXSA 'YAGAGYEMG-. *n.* noon. [lʌbáx̣sʌʔyàgagʸɛ́mkʰ] m.

1077. LABN. *v.i.* come to the surface; surface; emerge. [lʌ́bn̩] pr.

1078. LAGALÓOP, LAGALÓOB-. *n.* brown; rust (colour). [làgʌlóʌpʰ] hb,k,m.

1079. LAGAX'AGM GYIGYOOTK, LAGAX'AGM GYIGYOOTG-. *n.* double-headed axe. [làgax̣ʔágm̩gʸigʸó·tʰkʰ] hb.

1080. LAGAX'ALGYAX. *n.* linguist. [lagax̣ʔalgʸʌx̣] hb.

1081. LAGAXNIITSK, LAGAXNIITSG-. *n.* one who has "eyes in the back of his head." [làgax̣ní·cʰkʰ] hb.

1082. LAGAXTS'AP, LAGAXTS'AB-. *n.* a dying person who has begun talking to the dead, i.e., who is "in both houses." [làgax̣cʔápʰ] hb.

1083. LAGUULA. *v.t.* burn. [lʌgú·la] pr.
 1083.1 laguulaẅ. [lʌgú·lʌÿ] pr.
 1083.2 lagúulgit. *v.t.* burn the possessions of a dead person. *n.* the burnt possessions of a dead person. [lʌgúʌlgɩtʰ] m.

1084. LAGÜÜNSK, LAGÜÜNSG-. *v.i.* be together (of humans only). *n.* one family; one group (of people). [lʌgɨ̈·nskʰ] pr.

1085. LAGYIIL. *n.* eyebrow. [lʌgʸí·l] pr.

1086. LAHAADIKS. *plural of* hadiks.
 1086.1 laheediks.

1087. LAHAAL. *n.* stick game. [lahá·l] pr.

1088. LAHAYTK, LAHAYTG-. *v.i.* be unable (to); have bad luck. [laháyt^{h}k^{h}] pr.

1089. LAHÉEDIKS. *plural of* hadiks.

1090. LAK, LAC-, LAK. *n.* fire; firewood; fuel; anything burning. [lak^{h}] pr.
1090.1 lek, leg-. [lɛk^{h}] pr.
1090.2 lak, lag-. *n.* wood. [lʌk^{h}] pr.
1090.3 lēk, lēg-. [lɛk^{h}] pr.

1091. LAKWDIIDI. *plural of* kwdii.

1092. LAŁK, LAŁG-. *plural of* sgüü.

1093. LAMDZAX. *plural of* ts'ii.

1094. LAMK, LAMG-. *plural of* gyamk. *plural of* gyemk. *plural of* gyimk.
1094.1 lamk, lamg-.

1095. LA'NIIDZ. *v.i.* have a feeling things aren't right, a foreboding. [laʔní·ʒ] pr.

1096. LAPAAYK, LAPAAYG-. *plural of* gyipaayk.
1096.1 lipayk, lipayg-. *plural of* gyipayk.
1096.2 lipayuk, lipayug-.

1097. LAPLA'PGN. *v.t.* mix up; turn over (plural object); *v.i.* overturn everything. [lʌplʌʔp̓gn̩] pr.

1098. LAPŁ. *plural of* gyep.

1099. LAT, LAD-. *v.i.* have diarrhoea. *n.* diarrhoea. [lʌt^{h}] pr.

1100. LA'WEEL, LÚUWAL. *v.i.* drip. [lʌʔwɛ́·l] k. [lu·ʌwál] k.

1101. 'LAX, 'LAG-, LILAK. *n.* needle (both sewing and from a coniferous tree). [ʔlax̣] k. [lɩláq^{h}] k.
1101.1 'laxs. [ʔlax̣s] k.

1102. LAXA. *n.* heaven; sky; storm. [lax̣á] k,m,pr.

1103. LAXDII, DIDII. *n.* hill. [lax̣dí·] m,pr. [didí·] m,pr.

1104. LAXGAYNA. *n.* street. [lax̣gáyna] pr.

1105. LAXGWATKS. *plural of* gwatk.

1106. LAXGWIIDAKS. *plural of* gwatk.

1107. LAXGWIIKW, LAXGWIIGW-. *n.* springtime. [lax̣g^{w}í·k^{wh}] m.

1108. LAXHA. *n.* in the air (*See* laxa). [laxhá] pr.

1109. LAXHALHAL. *n.* upstairs. [làxhalhál] pr.

1110. LAXHUU. *n.* sandbar. [laxhú·] hb.

1111. LAXLAGMKS. *n.* calm, spec. the calm before the tide shifts. [laxlágmks] m.

1112. LAXLAX. *plural of* k'ya'apayk.

1113. LAYMIDÍIK, LAXMIDÍIG-. *n.* springtime. [làxmɩdí·kʰ] m.

1114. LAX'NAKS. *n.* a woman who has two husbands (*plural of* 'naks). [lax?náks] hb.

1115. LAXNAP'AA. *n.* a high meadow. [làxnʌp?á·] m.
1115.1 laxnap'aal. *n.* cottonwood grove. [làxnʌp?á·l] m,pr.

1116. LAX'OH. *n.* the top (m); a patch of moss (pr). [lax?ɔ́h] m,pr.
1116.1 laxoh. *n.* on top. [laxɔ́h] pr.

1117. LAX'OOL. *n.* eyelids. [lax?ɔ́·l] pr.

1118. LAX'OO WAAP. LAX'OO WAAB-. *n.* roof. [lax?ɔ́·wá·pʰ] hb.

1119. LAXS. *v.i.* bathe. [laxs] k,pr.

1120. LAXSÍIT, LAXSÍID-. *plural of* xsíit.

1121. LAXS'NEEXS. *n.* top of foot. [laxs?nɛ́·xs] pr.

1122. LAXSNIIL. *n.* back of hand. [laxsní·l] pr.
1122.1 laxs'niild. [laxs?ní·ld] pr.

1123. LAXST'ÓOGA. *plural of* xst'ook.
1123.1 laxxst'ooyga.
1123.2 laxstox. *plural of* stox.

1124. LAXST'ÚU'PL. *n.* platform; stage. [laxst?ú·ʌ?p'l̩] hb.

1125. LAXSÜÜLDA. *n.* ocean. [laxsɨ́·lda] m,pr.

1126. LAXSUUMAAY. *n.* month of picking berries (last part of June); summertime. [laxsú·má·y] m.

1127. LAXSÜ'YENS. *n.* springtime. [làxsɨ?yɛ́ns] m.

1130. LAXT'AA. *n.* lake. [laxt?á·] k,m,pr.

1131. LAXTS'A'ADZAKS. *n.* field; garden. [laxc?á?aʒʌks] m,pr.

1132. LAXWIIHÓON. *n.* month when the salmon starts to run; July; summertime. [laxwí·hɔ́ʌn] m.

1133. LA̲XYUUP, LA̲XYUUB-. *n.* earth; ground. [lɑx̣yú·pʰ] m.

1134. LAYOON. *n.* Indian celery, spec. the female plant (*Heracleum lanatum*); cow parsnips. [layɔ́·n] hb.
1134.1 leyoon. [lɛyɔ́·n] m.

1135. LEEKS'AAKS. *n.* flood tide; rising tide. [lɛ·ksʔá·ks] pr.

1136. LEGI. *n.* algae (chordaria). [lɛ́gi] hb.

1137. LEHEELD. *v.t.* forbid; stop. [lɛhɛ́·ld] pr.

1138. LEŁG. *plural of* 'nóok.
1138.1 leɫk, leɫg-.

1139. LI'A̲'PL̲. *v.t.* tear up. [líʔʌʔp̓l] pr.

1140. LIBAAS. *plural of* baas.
1140.1 libas.

1141. LIBETS'AẄ, LAKLOBITS'AẄ. *n.* kidney. [lɩbɛcʔáÿ] k,pr.
[lʌklòbīcʔáÿ] k.

1142. LIBILTWALTK, LIBILTWALTG-. *n.* enemy. [lɩbɩltʰwáltʰkʰ] pr.

1143. LIDZÓOX. *plural of* dzóox.

1144. LIGYI'ALA̲X. *v.i.* leave in anger. [ligʸiʔálɑx̣] hb.

1145. LIGYIDNAA. *pron.* anybody; anyone; anything; somebody; someone; something. [lɩgʸɩdná·] pr.
1145.1 ligyitnaa. [ligʸitná·] pr.

1146. LIGYIGYAKSK, LIGYIGYAKSG-. *v.t.* push down into the water; submerge. [ligʸigʸa·kskʰ] pr.

1147. LIGYIMTI. *n.* cotton; flannel; wool. [ligʸɩ́mtʰi] hb.

1148. LIGYINDAH. *adv.* anyplace; anywhere; wherever. [ligʸindáh] pr.
1148.1 ligyindeh. [lɩgʸɩndɛ́h] pr.

1149. LII, LII. *n.* (body) hair; fur; feather; pubic hair (m: if speaking of a human being and if not modified by a body part). [li·] k,m,pr. [li·] k.
1149.1 liy, liy. [liy] k. [liy] k.

1150. LII. *v.i.* take cooked food out of the fire (archaic). [li·] pr.

1151. LIIDA̲KSK, LIIDA̲KSG-. *plural of* gaksk. *plural of* gyaksk.

1152. LÍIDZXK, LÍIDZXG-. *v.t.* & *v.i.* count; read. [liʌʒx̣kʰ] hb,m,pr.
1152.1 líisk, líisg-. [liʌskʰ] k.

1153. LIIŁ. *v.t.* watch for, guard. *v.i.* wait. [li·ɫ] pr.

1154. LIIMETI. *n.* wool. [lì·mέtʰi] pr.

1155. LÍIMG. *plural of* gyiimkł

1156. LIIMI. *v.t.* & *v.i.* sing. *n.* song. [lí·mi] pr.

1157. LIIMK'OY. *n.* funeral song; mourning song. [li·mkʔɔ́y] k,m.
1157.1 limxk'oy. [lɩmx̣kʔóy] k,m.

1158. LIIMTS'U'UTS, LIIMTS'U'UDZ-. *n.* feathers. [lì·mcʔúʔucʰ] pr.

1159. LIIMYE'TSISK, LIIMYE'TSISG-. *n.* fur. [lì·myέʔcˀɩskʰ] pr.

1160. LIISGÜÜ. *v.t.* put on (e.g. clothes). [lì·sgɨ́·] hb.

1161. LIITSK, LIITSG-. *n.* mountain grouse; spruce grouse. [li·cʰkʰ] hb.

1162. LIITSX. *v.t.* & *v.i.* count; read. *n.* numbers; reading material. [li·cʰx̣] hb.

1163. LIIWÁA'PAH. *n.* cabin (of a boat). [li·waʌ́ʔpˀah] hb.

1164. LIK'AGYET, LIK'AGYED-. *n.* nobleman. [lɩqʔagʸέtʰ] pr.
1164.1 lik'agyigyet, lik'agyigyed-. *n.* commoners. [lɩqʔàgʸigʸέtʰ] hb,m.

1165. LIKSGYEDMGYET, LIKSGYEDMGYED-. *n.* a different person; someone else. [lɩksgʸὲdm̩gʸέtʰ] hb.
1165.1 liksgyet, liksgyed-. *n.* a different thing; something else. [lɩksgʸέtʰ] hb.

1166. LIKSGOOT, LIKSGOOD-. *v.i.* crazy. [lɩksg̣ɔ́·tʰ] hb. *See also* lüksgoot.

1167. LIKSOOG-. *n.* door. [lɩksɔ́·γ̣] pr.
1167.1 liksoox, liksoog-. [lɩksɔ́·x̣] pr.
1167.2 likxsook, likxsoog-. [lɩkx̣sɔ́·kʰ] pr.

1168. LIKSWAAS. *n.* wind change at the end of a heavy rain. [lɩkswá·s] hb.

1169. LILT'IILDISM. *plural of* t'ilt.

1170. LILT'USK, LILT'USG-. *plural of* t'usk.

1171. LISGÜÜ. *v.i.* be on; be lying on. [lisgɨ́·] m.

1172. LISGWAYT, LISGWAYD-. *plural of* sgwaytk.

1173. LIWDSK, LIWDSG-. *plural of* gaksk.

1174. LIYAAK, LIYAAG-. *v.t.* follow. [liyá·kʰ] pr.

1175. LLOOKS. *plural of* gyigyooks.

1176. LLOOKSMGANGAN. *n.* driftwood. [l̥lɔ̀·ksm̩gaŋán] hb.

1177. LOGAGADEELPK, LOGAGADEELPG-. *v.t.* anchor on both ends. [lɔ̀g̣ag̣àdɛ́·lpʰkʰ] m.

1178. LOGALOOP, LOGALOOB-. *n.* brown (colour). [lɔgaló·pʰ] hb.

1179. LOGMBAA. *v.i.* step into. [lɔg̣m̥bá·] pr.

1180. LOGMT'AA. *v.i.* sit near. [lɔg̣m̥tʔá·] pr.

1181. LOGOXTXANAAẄ. *n.* landing places or moorings on both sides of a point of land. [lɔ̀gɔx̣tx̣àná·ÿ] m.

1182. LOGASK, LOGASG-, LOOLGASK. *v.i.* wet. [lɔ́g̣askʰ] pr. [lɔ́·lg̣askʰ] pr.
1182.1 logsk, logsg-. [lɔg̣skʰ] pr.

1183. LOK, LOG-. *v.i.* rotten. [lɔqʰ] m.
1183.1 loox, loog-. [lo·x̣], [lɔ·x̣] k,pr.
1183.2 lox, log-, lóolt. [lox̣] k. [loʌltʰ] k.

1184. LO'K, LO'G-. *n.* eel. [lɔʔq̓] hb.

1185. LÓO. *n.* fish spawn; fish sperm. [lo·ʌ] hb.

1186. LÓOGAWDI. *v.i.* be empty. [lɔʌg̣áwdi] k.

1187. LO'OKY, LO'OGY-. *n.* mud. [lɔ́ʔɔkʸʰ] pr.

1188. LOOMHÓON. *n.* male fish. [lò·mhɔ́ʌn] hb.

1189. LOON. *n.* horse clam(s). [lo·n] hb,k.
1189.1 lóon. [lɔʌn] hb,m.

1190. LOOP, LOOB-, LÜPLOOP. *n.* rock; stone; cement. [lɔ·pʰ] k,pr. [lɨplɔ́·pʰ] k.
1190.1 loob. [lɔ·b] pr.
1190.2 lóop, lóob-. [lɔʌpʰ] k,pr.
1190.3 lo'op, lo'ob-. [lɔ́ʔɔpʰ] m.
1190.4 lop, lob-. [lɔpʰ] hb,pr.
1190.5 lóo'pis. *n.* testes. [lɔ́·ʌʔp̓is] m.

1191. LO'OTS, LO'ODZ-, LO'OTS. *n.* elderberry. [lóʔocʰ] k. [lóʔocʰ] k.
1191.1 lu'uts, lu'udz-, lu'uts. [lúʔucʰ] k. [lúʔucʰ] k.

1192. LO'OX, LO'OX. *n.* eel. [lóʔox̣] k,m. [lóʔox̣] k.

1193. LOOYG. *v.i.* move camp. [lɔ·yg] pr.
1193.1 looyk, looyg-, laklooyk. [lɔ·ykʰ] pr. [lʌklɔ́·ykʰ] pr.

1194. LU'ALM TSM'AKS. *n.* living things in the water; water life. [luʔə̄lm̥cʰm̥ʔáks] hb.

1195. LU'AN'ON. *n.* the person who pays for the burial of a dead person.

[luʔanʔɔ́n] pr.

1196. LU'APÜS. *v.t. & v.i.* sew. *n.* thread. [luʔʌpɨs] pr.

1197. LÜBAAS. *plural of* baas.
1197.1 lübáas. *plural of* báas.

1198. LUBAASK, LUBAASG-. *n.* a southeaster. [luba·sk^h] hb.

1199. LUDAALTK, LUDAALTG-. *v.t.* meet. [luda·lt^{h}k^h] k,m.

1200. LUDAWŁDAGYEMK, LUDAWŁDAGYEMG-. *n.* afternoon. [ludáwɨdag^{y}ɛ́mk^h] m,pr.

1201. LUDEP, LUDEB-. *v.t.* try on for size. [ludɛ́p^h] m,pr.

1202. LUDMDAM. *v.t.* crush; hug; squeeze. [ludm̩dám] m.
1202.1 ludmis. *n.* crush; hug; squeeze. [ludḿ̩is] m.

1203. LUGAWSGA'AAKS. *n.* zero tide. [lugàwsgaʔá·ks] k,m.
1203.1 luk'awska'aks. [lukʔàwskàʔáks] k,m.
1203.2 lugawsga'aks. *n.* low water. [lugàwsgaʔáks] hb.
1203.4 luugawsga'aks. [lu·gàwsgaʔáks] m.

1204. LÜGOOKS. *n.* charcoal; anything charred. [lɨgɔ́·ks] pr.

1205. LUGÜÜNKSAX. *v.i.* thirsty. [lugɨ́·nksax̣] pr.

1206. LUGWNDAAT, LUGWNDAAD-. *num.* three (of humans aboard a conveyance). [lùg^{w}n̩dá·t^h] hb.

1207. LUGYÍIS, LUGYISGYÍIS. *v.i.* be wrong; make a mistake. [lug^{y}íʌs] k,m. [lùg^{y}ɩsg^{y}íʌs] k.

1208. LUHO'NŁ. *v.t.* fill. [luhɔ́ʔn̩ɨ] m,pr.

1209. LUK'AHGYET, LUK'AHGYED-. *n.* the dead (*lit.* open people). [luqʔáhg^{y}ɛ̄t^h] m,pr.

1210. LUKDÍI. *plural of* kwdii.
1210.1 lukwtida.
1210.2 lukwtidi.

1211. LUKŁIHOOYA. *n.* underclothes. [lukɨihó·ya] pr.

1212. LUKŁIWAAP, LUKŁIWAAB-. *n.* under the house. [lukɨiwá·p^h] pr.

1213. LUK'OL, LUK'OLK'OL. *v.i.* alone. [lukʔɔ́l] k. [lukʔɔlkʔɔ́l] k.

1214. LUK'OOLDAAT, LUK'OOLDAAD-. *num.* six (of humans aboard a conveyance). [luqʔɔ́·lda·t^h] hb.

1215. LÜKSGÓOD. *v.i.* crazy; not concentrating; wander (of the mind). [lɨksgɔ́ʌd] hb.
1215.1 lüksgoot, lüksgood-. [lɨksgɔ́·t^h] hb.

1215.2 lüksgoot, lüksgood-. *v.i.* crazy; stubborn; grief-stricken; insane with grief; strange. [lɨksgɔ́·tʰ] m,pr.
1215.3 luksgoyt, luksgoyd-. *v.i.* foolish. [luksgóytʰ] k,m.

1216. LÜKSGYIGYET, LÜKSGYIGYED-. *n.* different kinds of things. [lɨksgʸigʸɛ́tʰ] pr.

1217. LÜKSO'AK. *n.* doorway. [lɨksɔ́ʔaqʰ] m.
1217.1 lüksóox, lüksóog-. *n.* door. [lɨksɔ́ʌx̣] k.

1218. LÜKSTAA. *n.* island. [lɨkstʰá·] k,m.

1219. LÜKSTS'AP, LÜKSTS'AB-. *n.* stranger(s) (*lit.* from another village). [lɨkscʔʌpʰ] hb.

1220. LUKSTUNSODAAT, LUKSTUNSODAAD-. *num.* five (of humans aboard a conveyance). [lukstúnsodá·tʰ] hb.

1221. LUKSÜÜLK, LUKSÜÜLG-. *n.* right in the middle. [luksɨ́·lkʰ] pr.

1222. LÜKSWAAS. *n.* a sudden rain when the sun is shining. [lɨkswá·s] hb.

1223. LÜKS'YENS. *n.* weeds. [lɨksʔyɛ́ns] hb.

1224. LUGWIL. *v.i. & pron.* many. *adv.* reality; very. [lúgʷɩl] pr.
1224.1 lu'kwil. [lúʔkʷ̓ɩl] pr.
1224.2 lu'wil. [lúʔwɩl] pr.

1225. LU'GWILGYEMK, LU'GWILGYEMG-. *v.i.* red hot; very hot. [luʔgʷɩlgʸɛ́mkʰ] pr.
1225.1 lu'kwilgyemk, lu'kwilgyemg-. [lùʔkʷɩlgʸɛ́mkʰ] pr.
1225.2 lu'wilgyemk, lu'wilgyemg-. [lùʔwɩlgʸɛ́mkʰ] pr.

1226. LU'KWIL WIIHELT' LU'KWIL WIIHELD-. *v.i* very many. [lùʔkʷɩlwi·hɛ́ltʰ] pr.
1226.1 lu'wil wiihelt, lu'wil wiiheld-. [lùʔwɩlwi·hɛ́ltʰ] pr.

1227. LUKWŁIKSŁÜÜSK, LUKWŁIKSŁÜÜSG-. *n.* undershirt. [lùkʷɬɩksɬɨ́·skʰ] hb.

1228. LUKWŁIP'AXS. *n.* underpants. [lùkʷɬɩpʔáx̣s] hb.

1229. LUŁAP, LUŁAB-, LUŁAPŁAP. *n.* a deep hole. [luɬʌ́pʰ] pr. [lùɬʌpɬʌpʰ] pr.

1230. LUŁEPŁEP, LUŁEPŁEB-. *plural of* łep.

1231. LUŁGUUL. *v.i.* narrow. [luɬqu·l] k,pr.

1232. LUMAAKS. *v.t. & v.i.* wash (clothes). [lumá·ks] m,pr.
1232.1 lumáaksn. [lumáʌksn̩] k.

1233. LÜMOOTK, LÜMOOTG-. *plural of* mootk.

1234. LUNIGYÍISN. *v.t. & v.i.* trade. [lunigʸíʌsn̩] k,m.

1235. LU'NÍITSK, LU'NÍITSG-. *v.t. & v.i.* stare (at) (Note: *a plural form of* 'niits. [luʔní·ʌcʰkʰ] m.

1236. LU'OOKS. *v.i.* wide. [luʔɔ́·ks] m,pr.

1237. LÜPLEET, LÜPLEED-. *n.* minister; pastor; preacher; priest. [lɨplɛ́·tʰ] m,pr.

1238. LÜSA'AAXS. *plural of* süs'aaxs.

1239. LÜSAAẅSK, LÜSAAẅSG-. *v.i.* talk together. [lisa·ÿskʰ] pr.

1240. LUSANAAŁK, LUSANAAŁG-. *n.* miracle; wonder (Note: *plural of* ksinaałk.

1241. LUSBAGA DIŁ . . . between here and . . . [lusbága dɩɬ] pr.

1242. LUSGA'AGYEE. *n.* partitions. [lusgàʔayé·] hb.
1242.1 lusga'ayée. *n.* bulkhead (*naut*). [lusgàʔayé·ʌ] hb.
1242.2 lusga'o'yáa. [lusgàʔoʔyá·ʌ] m.

1243. LÜSIIN. *v.i.* be drunk (inebriated). [lɨsí·n] m,pr.

1244. LUSISGUUM. *v.i.* pregnant. [lusisgú·m] m.

1245. LÜSYEN. *n.* (blue) mink; platinum mink. [lɨsyɛ́n] hb.

1246. LUTGYIŁOO. *v.t. & v.i.* push into. *v.i.* cave in; fall into. [lutgʸɩɬɔ́·] m,pr.

1247. LUTSIK'AAX. *v.t.* bury. *v.t. & v.i.* dig. [lucʰiqʔá·x̣] k,m.

1248. LUTXAPXOLDAAT, LUTXAPXOLDAAD-. *num.* seven (of humans aboard a conveyance). [lutx̣ px̣óldá·tʰ] hb.

1249. LUTXASGÜÜ. *v.t.* put in sideways. [lutx̣asgɨ́·] hb.

1250. LUUDAGWN. *v.i.* drown. [lu·dágʷn̩] k.
1250.1 luudakʷɬn. [lu·dákʷʰɬn̩] m.

1251. LUUDISK, LUUDISG-. *v.i.* learn; store up food and wood for the winter. [lú·diskʰ] pr.

1252. LÚULGYIT, LÚULGYID-. *n.* feast. [lúʌlgʸɩtʰ] hb,k,pr.

1253. LUULP, LUULB-, TS'MLUULP. *n.* fish trap; horseshoe rock trap (used to catch fish in the falling tide); fish pond. [lu·l̩pʰ] hb. [cʔm̩lú·l̩pʰ] hb.

1254. LUUŁK, LUULŁG-. *n.* nest. [lu·ɬkʰ] hb.

1255. LUUNA. *v.i.* dry (not stative). [lú·na] pr.
1255.1 luunu. [lú·nu] pr.
1255.2 luunks. *plural of* güünks.
1255.3 lúunks.

1256. LUUNÜKSMHOON. *plural of* güünksmhon. *plural of* güünsmoon. *plural of* gnsmoon.

1257. LUUPK, LUUPG-. *v.t. & v.i.* sew. [lu·pkʰ] pr.

1258. LUSANAAŁK, LUSANAAŁG. *v.i.* be surprised (Note: a profound emotional response, not superficial in the sense of "be delighted"). [lusaná·ɬkʰ] pr.

1259. LUUT, LUUD-, LAKLUUT. *n.* wedge. [lu·tʰ] k. [lʌklú·tʰ] k.
1259.1 lúut, lúud-. [lu·ʌtʰ] k.

1260. LUUYEELTK, LUUYEELTG-. *v.i.* return. [lu·yɛ́·ltʰkʰ] pr.
1260.1 luyaaltk, luyaaltg-. [luyá·ltʰkʰ] k.

1261. LUWAAKS. *plural of* waaks.

1262. LU'WAL, LAKLU'WEL. *v.i.* drip. *n.* a drop. [lúʔwʌl] pr. [lʌklúʔwɛl] pr.
1262.1 lu'wel. [lúʔwɛl] pr.

1263. LUWANTGMGOOD. *v.i.* be worried. [luwʌ̀ntgmgɔ́·d] pr.

1264. LUWANTK, LUWANTG-. *v.i.* worry. [luwʌ́ntʰkʰ] pr.

1265. LUWAY. *plural of* duway.

1266. LUWI. *n.* alder tree. [lúwi] hb,m,pr.

1267. LUYELTK, LUYELTG-. *v.i.* turn back. [luyɛ́ltʰkʰ] k,m.

Ł

1268. ŁA'AGY. *n.* scar. [ɬáʔagʸ] pr.
1268.1 ła'aky, ła'agy-. *v.i.* be glued on; stick. [ɬáʔakʸʰ] pr.
1268.2 Ałga ła'akył gyet. *No one was there.*
1268.3 ła'agynsk, ła'agynsg-. *n.* glue (Note: made from boiled whole fish). [ɬáʔagʸn̩skʰ] pr.

1269. ŁAALB. *v.t.* plane. [ɬaalb] pr.

1270. ŁA'AL. *v.t.* move. [ɬáʔal] pr.
1270.1 ła'ald. [ɬáʔald] pr.

1271. ŁAANTGA'AKS. *n.* flood. [ɬá·ntʰgaʔáks] pr.

1272. ŁAANTK, ŁAANTG-. *v.i.* come up; rise (of water). [ɬa·ntʰkʰ] pr.

1273. ŁA'ASK, ŁA'ASG-, ŁA'ASK. *n.* seaweed; algae (enteromorpha). [ɬáʔaskʰ] hb,k,m. [ɬáʔaskʰ] k.

1274. ŁÁATS, ŁÁADZ-, ŁAKŁATS. *n.* scraper. [ɬaʌcʰ] k. [ɬʌkɬácʰ] k.
1274.1 łaatsx. *n.* salmon tails, split and smoked (archaic). [ɬa·cʰx̣] pr.

1275. ŁA'AX. *v.t. & v.i.* bite. [łá?ax̣] pr.

1276. ŁA'AYASK, ŁA'AYASG-, ŁALŁA'AYASK. *v.t. & v.i.* climb. [łá?ayʌskʰ] pr. [łʌlłá?ayʌskʰ] pr.
1276.1 łe'yaxsk, łe'yaxsg-. [łé?yʌxskʰ] hb. [łɛ́?yʌx̣skʰ] hb.

1277. ŁABIISK, ŁABIISG-. *v.t. & v.i.* whittle. [łʌbí·skʰ] pr.

1278. ŁAGYIGYET, ŁAGYIGYED-. *n.* the olden times; the old people; tradition. [łàgʸigʸɛ́tʰ] hb,k,pr.
1278.1 łałagyigyet, łałagyitgyed-. [łałàgʸigʸɛ́tʰ] k.

1279. ŁA'GYIN. *v.t.* bend. [łá?gʸɩn] pr.
1279.1 ła'kyn. [ła?kʸ'n̩] hb.
1279.2 łe'ign. *v.t.* bend; make crooked. [łɛ́?ɩgn̩] hb.
1279.3 łeky, łegy-. *v.t.* bend (pr). *v.i.* bent; crooked; twisted. [łɛkʸʰ] hb,k,pr.
1279.4 łek, łeg-, łiłük. *v.i.* bent; crooked; twisted. [łɛkʰ] k. [łíłɨkʰ] k.
1279.5 łiłük, łiłüg-. *v.i.* undo; untie (Note: *plural form of* łek). [łíłɨkʰ] k.
1279.6 łe'lk, łe'lg-. *v.i.* crooked. [łɛ́?l̩kʰ] hb.
1279.7 łe'ik, łe'ig-. [łɛ́?ɩkʰ] hb.
1279.8 łíiłak, łíiłag-. [łíʌłʌkʰ] hb.

1280. ŁAK'AW. *v.t. & v.i.* bite. [łaq?áw] k.

1281. ŁAKŁGUKSN. *plural of* łguksn.

1282. ŁAKŁGWT'IINA. *plural of* łgwt'iin.

1283. ŁAKŁPUN. *plural of* łpun.

1284. ŁAK'OOTS, ŁAK'OODZ-. *n.* rhubarb. [łʌq?ɔ́·cʰ] pr.

1285. ŁAKŁAKWS. *v.i.* shake oneself. [łʌkłákʷʰs] hb,pr.

1286. ŁAKYIYAASAH. *n.* dusk (just before dark). [łakʸiyá·sáh] hb.
1286.1 łatyiyaasah. [łatʰyiyá·sáh] m.

1287. ŁAŁÚUNGYIT, ŁAŁÚUNGYID-. *n.* slave. [łʌłú·ʌngʸɩtʰ] pr.

1288. ŁAMAXSK, ŁAMAXSG-. *plural of* batsk.

1289. ŁAN. *v.i.* darker; stronger (Note: when referring to colour, increased chroma and decreased value). [łan] hb.

1290. ŁA'NAAK, ŁA'NAAG-. *adv.* a long time. [ła?ná·kʰ] k.

1291. ŁAP, ŁAB-. *v.i.* deep. [łapʰ] k.
1291.1 łep, łeb-, lułepłep. [łɛpʰ] k. [lùłɛpłɛ́pʰ] k.
1291.2 łap, łab-. *v.i.* deep. *n.* hole. [łʌpʰ] pr.

1292. ŁA'T, ŁA'D-, ŁIKŁA'T. *n.* ball. [ła?t'] k. [łɩkłá?t'] k.

1293. ƚAXS, ƚIKƚAXS. *n.* claws; nails; finger nails; toe nails. [ɬax̣s] k,m,pr. [ɬɩkɬax̣s] k.

1294. ƚAXSMSII. *n.* toe nail. [ɬàx̣sm̩sí·] pr.

1295. ƚBUUN. *n.* whale; lots; plenty. [ɬbu·n] pr.
1295.1 'Wii ɬbuun waald. *They've got everything* (hb).
1295.2 ɬpun, ɬakɬpun. [ɬpun] k. [ɬʌkɬpún] k.
1295.3 ɬpuun. [ɬpu·n] hb,k,pr.
1295.4 ɬpúun. [ɬpuʌn] hb.

1296. ƚÉETX. *n.* slime; slobbers; spit. [ɬɛ·ʌtx̣] pr.

1297. ƚEEXK, ƚEEXG-. *v.i.* stop; get control of oneself (esp. when crying on talking uncontrollably fast or loud). [ɬɛ·x̣kʰ] m.

1298. ƚEƚAP, ƚEƚAB-. *v.t.* cut smooth; make smooth; plane; smooth. [ɬέɬʌpʰ] pr.

1299. ƚEMS. *n.* affine; in-law; son-in-law (reference and address); daughter-in-law (reference and address); father-in-law (reference and address); mother-in-law (reference and address); cousin's wife (reference and address: MZSW). [ɬɛms] k.

1300. ƚGAAWK' ƚGAAWG-. *n.* sister (female speaker; reference and address: ♀Z, ♀FBD, ♀MZD; also ♂MZD). [ɬga·wkʰ] k.
1300.1 ɬgaawlk, ɬgaawlg-. [ɬga·wlkʰ] k.

1301. ƚGU'AƚAAN. *n.* brother-in-law (male speaking; address and reference: WB). [ɬguʔʌɬá·n] pr.

1302. ƚGÜDELPK, ƚGÜDELPG-. *v.i.* very short. [ɬgɨdέlpʰkʰ] m,pr.

1303. ƚGUƚ. *n.* nephew; niece (address and reference: ♂B(W)Ch, ♀Z(H)Ch, HBCh, HZCh, WBCh, WZCh). [ɬguɬ] k.
1303.1 ɬguɬk, ɬguɬg-. *v.i.* little; small. *n.* child (in general and as relative term of address: S, D). [ɬguɬkʰ] k.
1303.2 ɬguɬgmt'a'a. *n.* term of reference for a deceased child. [ɬgúɬgm̩tʔáʔa] k.

1304. ƚGUƚGMHANA'A. *n.* girl; daughter. [ɬgúɬgm̩hanáʔa] k.

1305. ƚGUƚGMHANA'A ƚGÜLIS. *n.* sister's greatgrandchildren (address and reference). [ɬgúɬgm̩hanáʔaɬgɨlís] k.

1306. ƚGUƚGMHANA'IT'A'A. *n.* deceased daughter (reference). [ɬgúɬgm̩hanáʔitʔáʔa] k.

1307. ƚGUƚGMƚGWÜSLIS. *n.* grand nephew; grand niece. [ɬgúɬgm̩ɬgʷɨslís] k.

1308. ƚGUƚGM'YU. *n.* boy; son. [ɬgúɬgm̩ʔyú] k.

1309. ƚGUƚGMYUƚGÜLIS. *n.* brother's greatgrandchildren (address and reference). [ɬgúɬgm̩yúɬgɨlís] k.

1310. ŁGUŁGMYUWIT'A'A. *n.* deceased son (reference). [ɫgúɫgm̩yúwitʔáʔa] k.

1311. ŁGUK'OOŁKS. *n.* brother-in-law (woman speaking: HB). [ɫgukʔɔ́·ɫks] pr.

1312. ŁGUŁ ŁGWISLIS. *n.* nephew; niece (man speaking; address: ♂BS, ♂BD). [ɫgúɫɫgʷɩslís] k.

1313. ŁGUMET, ŁGUMED-. *n.* egg. [ɫgumɛ́tʰ] hb,k,pr.
1313.1 ɫgümet, ɫgümed-. [ɫgɨmɛ́tʰ] hb,k,pr.

1314. ŁGÜMIIK, ŁGÜMIIG-. *n.* sawbill duck; hooded merganser; red breasted merganser. [ɫgɨmí·kʰ] hb.

1315. ŁGUM'YEE, GAKŁGUM'YEE. n. old dog (chum, keta) salmon. [ɫgumʔyɛ́·] k. [gakɫgumʔyɛ́·] k.

1316. ŁGUTS'UUSK, ŁGUTS'UUSG-. *v.i.* little. [ɫgucʔú·skʰ] pr.

1317. ŁGÜÜŁK, ŁGÜÜŁG-. *n.* a young one. [ɫgɪ̈·ɫkʰ] k.

1318. ŁGUUKSN. *v.i.* unable. [ɫgú·ksn̩] pr.

1319. ŁGUWAALKS. *n.* prince. [ɫguwá·lks] k.
1319.1 ɫguwaaliksik, ɫguwaaliksig-. [ɫguwá·lɩksɩkʰ] pr.

1320. ŁGUWOOMŁK, ŁGUWOOMŁG-. *n.* child; infant. [ɫguwɔ́·mɫkʰ] k,pr.

1321. ŁGWIDUULS. *n.* sister-in-law (woman speaking; address and reference: BW, HZ, FBSW). [ɫgʷɩdú·ls] k.
1321.1 ɫgwidzuu. [ɫgʷɩʒú·] k.
1321.2 ɫgwiduulsit'a'a. *n.* deceased sister-in-law (reference). [ɫgʷɩdú·lsitʔáʔa]k.

1322. ŁGWITA'O. *n.* (cross) cousin (reference: FZCh, MBCh, FZSW, FZDH). [ɫgʷɩtʰaʔó] k.
1322.1 ɫgwüta'o. [ɫgʷɨtʰɑʔɔ́] k.

1323. ŁGWT'IIN, ŁAKŁGWT'IINA. *n.* steep valley. [ɫgʷtʔí·n] pr. [ɫʌkɫgʷtʔí·nɑ] pr.

1324. ŁGWÜDZÚUS. *n.* sister-in-law (woman speaking; *see also* ɫgwiduuls). [ɫgʷɨʒúʌs] k.

1325. ŁGWÜŁUUGYIT, ŁGWÜŁUUGYID-. *n.* plug (*naut*). [ɫgʷɨɫú·gʸɩtʰ] hb.

1326. ŁGWÜSGAAY. *n.* little finger. [ɫgʷɨsgá·y] pr.

1327. ŁGWÜSGÜÜ. *v.i.* glad; happy; joyful. [ɫgʷɨsgɪ̈́·] k,m,pr.

1328. ŁGWÜSLIS. *n.* nephew; niece (address and reference). [ɫgʷɨlís] k.
1328.1 ɫgwüslisk, ɫgwüslisg-. [ɫgʷɨslískʰ] k.

1329. ŁI'AWIN. *n.* brant. [ɫíʔʌwɩn] pr.

1329.1 ƚi'win. *n.* American goose. [ɬí?wɩn] hb.

1330. ȽIISK' ȽIISG-. *v.t. & v.i.* stop. [ɬi·skʰ] pr.

1331. ȽIITK, ȽIITG-. *v.i.* move down. [ɬi·tʰkʰ] pr.

1332. ȽIK, ȽIG-, GAȽIK. *v.i.* explode. [ɬikʰ] k. [ga̤ɬíkʰ] k.

1333. ȽIKȽÚUNTI. *plural of* ƚúunti.

1334. ȽIKWT'AA'YNMGYET, ȽIKWT'AA'YNMGYED-. *n.* grandson (address and reference: DS, SS, FBSS, FBSDS, FBSSS, MZSS). [ɬɩkʷʰt?á·?ynm̥gʸɛ́tʰ] k.

1335. ȽIKWT'AA'YNMHANA'A. *n.* granddaughter (address and reference: DD, SD, FBSD, FBSDD, FBSSD, MZSD). [ɬɩkʷʰt?á·?ynm̥haná?a] k.

1336. ȽIȽUUNGIT. *n.* slave. [ɬɩɬú·ngɩtʰ] pr.

1337. ȽINGIITX, GAȽINGIITX. *n.* Tlingit language; Tlingit dialect. [ɬɩngí·tx̣] m. [ga̤ɬɩngí·tx̣] m.

1338. ȽIOON. *n.* elk; wapiti. [ɬió·n] hb.
1338.1 ƚiyüün. [ɬiyɨ́·n] pr.

1339. ȽIOON. *n.* bannock bread. [ɬiɔ́·n] hb.

1340. ȽM'AN'ON. *n.* wrist. [ɬm̥?an?ɔ́n] pr.

1341. ȽMKTII. *n.* brother; sister (address and reference: ♀B, ♀FBS, ♀MZS, ♂Z, ♂FBD, ♂MZD). [ɬm̥kʰtʰí·] k.
1341.1 ƚmktíi. [ɬm̥kʰtʰí·ʌ] k.

1342. ȽMOOM. *v.t.* help. [ɬmɔ·m] pr.
1342.1 ƚümoom. [ɬimɔ́·m] k,pr.

1343. ȽO. *v.t.* honour; respect. [ɬɔ] m.
1343.1 ƚoot. [ɬɔ·tʰ] pr.
1343.2 ƚootk, ƚootg-. *v.i.* crawl; slither. [ɬɔ·tʰkʰ] pr.

1344. ȽO'A'TAXK, ȽO'A'TAXG-. *v.t.* swallow up. [ɬɔ́?ʌ?tʼʌx̣kʰ] pr.
1344.1 ƚootx. *v.i.* slurp food. [ɬɔ·tx̣] pr.

1345. ȽOGA. *plural of* yaa. *plural of* yáa. *plural of* yee.

1346. ȽOO. *v.i.* drift; swim (of fish) (pr). *n.* landslide (hb,m). [ɬɔ·] hb,m,pr.
1346.1 ƚóol. *v.t.* push in the water (*not into the water*). [ɬɔ·ʌl] pr.
1346.2 ƚoowl. [ɬɔ́·wl̥] pr.
1346.3 ƚo'otk, ƚo'otg-. *n.* clouds. [lɔ́?ɔtʰkʰ] pr.

1347. ȽU'ADÜÜ. *v.t.* keep; preserve. [ɬu?ʌdɨ́·] pr.

1348. ƚUK'OOTKS. *n.* brother-in-law (address and reference: ZH, HB, WB, FBDH). [ɨuqʔɔ́·tʰks] k.
1348.1 ɨuk'otksit'a'a. *n.* deceased brother-in-law. [ɨuqʔótʰksɪtʔáʔa] k.
1348.2 ɨuk'óotks. *n.* brother-in-law. [ɨuqʔɔ́ʌtʰks] k.

1349. ƚUKT'A'YIN. *n.* grandchild (address and reference: ChCh, FBSCh, FBSChCh, MZChCh). [ɨuktʔáʔyɪn] k.

1350. ƚUKWT'A'ANM NAGWAT. *n.* father's grandchild (reference: FBDCh). [ɨukʷʰtʔáʔanm̩nʌgʷátʰ] k.
1350.1 ɨukwt'a'anm nügwet. [ɨukʷʰtʔáʔanm̩nɨgʷɛ́tʰ] k.

1351. ƚULUU. *v.t.* shake out (a flat object); untie. [ɨu·lú·] pr.
1351.1 ɨuuɨuu. *v.i.* shake oneself. [ɨu·ɨú·] pr.

1352. ƚÜÜLSK, ƚÜÜLSG-, GAKƚÜÜSK. *n.* shirt. [ɨɨ̈·lskʰ] k. [gɑkɨɨ̈·lskʰ] k.

1353. ƚÚUNTI, ƚIKƚÚUNTI *and* ƚÜKƚÚUNTI. *v.i.* angry. [ɨú·ʌntʰi] hb,m,pr. [ɨɪkɨúʌntʰi] m. [ɨɨkɨú·ʌntʰi] hb.

1354. ƚUUT, ƚUUD-. *n.* wedge. [ɨu·tʰ] m.
1354.1 ɨúut, ɨúud-. [ɨuʌtʰ] hb.

1355. ƚÜÜWAAP, ƚÜÜWAAB-. *n.* under the house. [ɨɨ̈·wá·pʰ] hb.

1356. ƚ'WA'IL. *v.t.* mix up; stir. [ɨʔwáʔɪl] pr.
1356.1 ɨ'wa'ayil. [ɨʔwáʔʌyɪl] pr.

M

1357. MAADM. *n.* (falling) snow; snowflakes. [má·dm̩] hb,k,pr.

1358. MAADMGYEKS. *n.* the calm following a northeast wind and during which large, wet snowflakes fall slowly. [mà·dm̩gʸɛ́ks] hb.

1359. MÁALK, MÁALG. *v.t.* & *v.i.* burn. [maʌlkʰ] pr.

1360. MAALSK, MAALSG-. *v.t.* & *v.i.* narrate; relate; tell. [ma·lskʰ] pr.
1360.1 meɨ. [mɛɨ] k.

1361. MÁAN. *v.i.* leave food; be left; be left over. [ma·ʌn] m,pr.

1362. MÁANWINEEYA. *n.* food left-overs. [má·ʌnwɪné·yɑ] k.

1363. MÁAS, MÁAS. *n.* (tree) bark. [ma·ʌs] hb,k,m,pr. [ma·ʌs] k.

1364. MÁASAGAN. *n.* tree bark. [má·ʌsɑgɑ́n] hb.

1365. MAASGMGAWS. *v.i.* red headed. *n.* red hair; a red headed person. [má·sgm̩gáws] hb.

1366. MAATG, MATMATG. *v.i.* dirty; slimy. [ma·tʰg] pr. [mʌtmátʰg] pr.

1367. MA'AWLK, MA'AWLG-. *n.* anchor line. [maʔáwlkʰ] hb.

1368. MAAXAY. *n.* rainbow. [má·x̣ay] hb.
  1368.1 máaxay. [máʌx̣ay] k.

1369. MAAY, MAAY. *n.* berry; huckleberry; great grandmother. [ma·y] hb,k,pr. [ma·y] k.

1370. MAAYAGALIPLIIP, MAAYAGALIPLIIB-. *n.* thunder berries; twisted stalk (*Streptopus amplexifolius*); small twisted stalk (*S. streptopoides*). [má·yagalɩplí·pʰ] hb.

1371. MAAYA'OL. *n.* bear berry (*Arctostaphylos media*). [má·ycʔɔ́l] hb.

1372. MAAYHAGWILHUU. *n.* rope berry; Himalayan blackberry (*Rubus procerus*); traililing blackberry (*R. ursinus*). [má·yhagʷɩlhú·] hb,m,pr.

1373. MA'AKWS. *n.* herring spawn. [máʔakʷʰs] k,m.

1374. MAGAAYT, MAGAAYD-. *n.* nightmare. [magá·ytʰ] m.
  1374.1 magayk, magayg-. *n.* sleep [magáykʰ] hb.

1375. MAGAK'OXS. *plural of* mak'oxs.

1376. MAGON. *v.t. & v.i.* explain. [mʌg̣ɔ́n] k,pr.

1377. 'MAGON. *v.i.* troll. [ʔmag̣ɔ́n] k.

1378. MAGOON. *n.* head of a river. [mʌg̣ɔ́·n] pr.

1379. MAGOOXS. *n.* salmon berries (*Rubus spectabilis*). [magɔ́·x̣s] hb,pr.
  1379.1 magoxst, magoxsd-. [magɔ́x̣stʰ] pr.
  1379.2 mak'oxs, mak'oxs. [maqʔɔ́x̣s] k. [maqʔɔ́xs] k.

1380. MAGUUL. *n.* strawberries. [magú·l] pr,m.

1381. MAGWA'LAH. *n.* deep winter. [magʷáʔlah] hb.
  1381.1 magwa'lü. [magʷáʔlɪ̈] m.
  1381.2 magwe'elü. [magʷέʔεlɪ̈] hb,k,m.

1382. MAHAAG. *n.* moss. [mahá·g] pr.
  1382.1 mahaak, mahaag-. [mahá·qʰ] pr.

1383. MAHANA'A. *v.i.* effeminate. *n.* effeminate man. [mahanáʔa] m.

1384. 'MAK, 'MAG-. *v.i.* catch fish; fish. [ʔmaqʰ] k,pr.

1385. MAKSIIŁ. *n.* weasel. [mʌksí·ɬ] hb,k,m.
  1385.1 müksiił. [mɨksí·ɬ] k,m.

1386. MAKWS. *n.* blizzard; dry snow; powder snow. [makʷʰs] hb.
  1386.1 'makws. *n.* snowstorm with a northwest wind and powder snow. [ʔmakʷʰs] hb.

1387. MAŁIITK, MAŁIITG-. *n.* green; blue green; yellow green (colour). [maɫí·tʰkʰ] hb. *See also* xsmaɫiitk.
1387.1 maɫíitk, maɫíitg-. [maɫí·ʌtʰkʰ] hb,k,pr.
1387.2 müɫíitk, müɫíitg-. [mɨɫí·ʌtʰkʰ] hb,k,pr.

1388. MAŁIŁK, MAŁIŁG-, MAKMAAŁIŁK. *v.i.* tell. [máɫɩɫkʰ] k.
1388.1 meɫiɫ. [mɛ́lɩl] k.

1389. MAN- up. [man] hb.

1390. 'MAN. *v.t.* anoint; rub with oil. *v.i.* masturbate. *n.* massage; rubdown. [ʔmʌn] k,m,pr.

1391. MA'NAXK, MA'NAXG-. *v.i.* high; reach the top. [maʔnáx̣kʰ] k,m.

1392. MANBULASK, MANBULASG-. *v.i.* erupt (of a geyser). [manbúlaskʰ] hb.
1392.1 manbu'nsk, manbu'nsg-. [manbúʔn̥skʰ] hb.

1393. MANGYA'AGLT, MANGYA'AGLD-. *v.t.* roll up. [mangʸáʔʌgl̥tʰ] pr.

1394. MANHAKHAKWŁA. *n.* shoestring. [manhakhákʷʰɫa] hb.

1395. MANLIKLOOYG. *v.i.* be frightened; get excited. [manlɩkló·yg] pr.

1396. MANLOOYG, GULAGAMINLOOYG. *v.i.* move up. [manló·yg] pr. [gùlagamɩ̄nló·yg] pr.

1397. 'MANWAALXS. *plural of* münyáa.
1397.1 münwaalxs. [mɨnwa·lx̣s] m,pr.

1398. MA'OL. *n.* an epilectic (*lit*: like a bear). [mʌʔɔ́l] pr.

1399. MA'ON. *n.* chamber pot; elbow (*anat*); elbow bone. [maʔɔ́n] hb.

1400. MAS'AWS. *n.* rouge; bridal shower (formerly a dressing up of a bride for her wedding and done by her future mother-in-law). [mʌsʔáws] hb.
1400.1 müs'aws. *n.* ochre. [mɨsʔáws] k.

1401. MASGM'IŁEE, MÜSMASGMGA'IŁEE. *n.* blood red (colour). [mʌ̀sgm̥ʔiɫé·] pr. [mɨsmʌ̀sgm̥gaʔiɫé·] pr.

1402. MASGM'OL. *n.* brown bear. [màsgm̥ʔɔ́l] hb.

1403. MASK, MASG-, MISMASKT. *n.* red; red orange (colour). [maskʰ] hb. [mɩsmásktʰ] k.
1403.1 mask, masg-. [mʌskʰ] pr.
1403.2 mesk, mesg-. [mɛskʰ] k.
1403.3 masx. *n.* breast. [mʌsx̣] pr.

1404. MASXAYLÓOP, MASXAYLÓOB-. *n.* metridium anemone. [mʌsx̣ayló ʌpʰ] hb.

1405. MATI. *n.* mountain goat; mountain sheep (bighorn sheep); domestic sheep. [mátʰi] hb,k,pr.

1406. MAT'IIBN. *n.* a person with webbed fingers. [mat?í·bn̩] hb.

1407. MATXALAALT, MATXALAALD-. *n.* snake. [matx̣alá·lt^h] hb.

1408. MATXAW. *n.* a person with a nervous tic. [matxáw] hb.

1409. MAXLAGALGALIIS. *n.* Audobon's warbler. [mʌ̀x̣lagàlgalí·s] hb.

1410. MAXŁ. *v.i.* climb a mountain. [max̣ɬ] pr.

1411. MAXŁYE'TSÜ. *v.t.* try to outdo with a potlatch. *v.i.* give a great potlatch. [max̣ɬyɛ́?c̓ɨ] pr.

1412. MAXMÉE. *n.* grouse; partridge; pheasant. [mʌx̣mé·ʌ] pr.
 1412.1 maxmeex. [max̣mɛ́·x̣] hb.

1413. MAXS. *plural of* betsk. *plural of* haaytk. *plural of* haytk.
 1413.1 maxsn. *plural of* betsgn. *plural of* haytksn.

1414. MAXS. *plural of* p'as.

1415. MAXSGAPTS'AN. *plural of* pts'an.

1416. MÉEK, MÉEG-. *n.* pine cone; pine nut. [mɛ·ʌq^h] pr.
 1416.1 méex, méeg-, méex. [mɛ·ʌx̣] k. [mɛ·ʌx̣] k.

1417. MELA. *v.i.* be in a hurry. [mɛ́la] pr.

1418. MELIIT, MELIID-. *n.* rainbow trout; steelhead. [mɛlí·t^h] hb.
 1418.1 miliit, miliid-. [mɩlí·t^h] k,m,pr.

1419. MEŁÜÜ. *n.* pillow. [mɛɬɨ·] pr.

1420. METXALAALT, METXALAALD-. *n.* snake. [mɛtx̣alá·lt^h] pr. *See also* matxalaalt.

1421. MIDÍIK, MIDÍIG-. *n.* grizzly bear; (African) lion. [mɩdíʌk^h] hb.
 1421.1 müdíik, müdíig-. [mɨdí·ʌk^h] hb,m,pr.

1422. MIHAAŁ. *n.* dwarf blueberry (*Vaccinium caespitosum*). [mihá·ɬ] hb.

1423. MIHOOKS, MÜKMIHOOKS. *v.i.* smell good; be fragrant. [mihɔ́·ks] m,pr. [mɨkmihɔ́·ks] pr.

1424. MÍIK, MÍIG-, ÜM'AM. *v.i.* ripe. [mi·ʌk^h] k,pr. [?ɨm?ám] k.
 1424.1 míik, míig-, míik. *n.* rain cloud; storm cloud; sawbill duck (merganser: *see also* ɬgümíik). [mi·ʌk^h] k,pr. [mi·ʌk^h] k.

1425. MÍILK, MÍILG-, MAKMÍILK. *v.i.* dance. [mi·ʌlk^h] k,pr. [mʌkmí·ʌlk^h] k.
 1425.1 míiɬk, míiɬg-. [mi·ʌɬk^h] k,pr.

1426. MIINS. *n.* wood used for carving. [mi·ns] hb.

1427. MISMUUS. *n.* cow; cattle. [mɩsmú·s] hb.
1427.1 müsmúus. [mɨsmú·ʌs] hb,pr.

1428. MISÜÜ. *n.* grey hair. [mɩsɨ́·] hb.

1429. MIYAAN. *n.* base of a tree; master; lord. [miyá·n] pr.

1430. MIYOOP, MIYOOB-. *n.* rice. [miyɔ́·pʰ] hb,k.
1430.1 miyuup, miyuub-. [miyú·pʰ] hb,k.

1431. MIYUUBMGYET, MIYUUBMGYED-. *n.* Northern rice root; chocolate lily; Chinese rice; Indian rice; Kamchatka fritillary (*Fritillaria camschatcensis* and *F. lanceolata*). [miyú·bm̩gʸɛ́tʰ] hb.
1431.1 miyuu'mgyet, miyuu'mgyed-. [miyú·ʔm̩gʸɛ́tʰ] hb.

1432. MI'YÚUTA. *v.i.* mannish. *n.* a mannish woman. [mɩʔyú·ʌtʰɑ] m.

1433. MMAH. *v.t.* kiss (esp. a child). [m̩máh] hb.

1434. MMO, GAMO. *n.* milk; a suckling baby. [m̩mɔ́] k. [gɑmɔ́] k.
1434.1 mmoo. [m̩mɔ́·] m.

1435. MO'AN. *v.t.* put aboard. [mɔ́ʔʌn] pr.
1435.1 mo'kan. [mɔʔqʼʌn] pr.

1436. MOK, MOG-. *n.* kelp. [mɔqʰ] k,m,pr.
1436.1 mox, mog-. [mɔx̣] k,m,pr.

1437. MOKS. *n.* white (colour). [mɔks] hb.
1437.1 moksk, moksg-. [mɔkskʰ] hb.
1437.2 mooks, mooks. *n.* snow (on ground). [mɔ·ks] k,pr. [mɔ·ks] k.
1437.3 mooksk, mooksg-, mookmoosk. *n.* white (colour). [mɔ·kskʰ] k,pr. [mɔ·kskʰ] hb.

1438. MOKSA. *v.i.* sour. [mɔksa] hb.

1439. MOKSGM'OL. *n.* cinnamon bear, white bear (*Euarctos americanus kermodei*), Kermodes bear, Island white bear (hb); polar bear (m,pr). [mɔ̀ksgm̩ʔɔ́l] hb,m,pr.

1440. MO'MX, MO'MG-, GAMO'MG. *v.i.* smile. [mɔʔmx̣] k. [gɑmɔʔmg̣] k.
1440.1 moo'mx. [mɔ·ʔmx̣] k.
1440.2 muu'mk, muu'mg-. [mu·ʔmqʰ] k.

1441. MOOK, MOOG-. *n.* kelp. [mɔ·qʰ] hb.
1441.1 moox, moog-. [mɔ·x̣] hb.

1442. MOOKSGMGAWS. *n.* blond hair; a blond person. [mɔ̀·ksgm̩gáws] hb.

1443. MOOLK, MOOLG-. *v.i.* nervous; sick of something; irritated; uneasy; irritated by a noise. [mɔ·lkʰ] m,pr.
1443.1 moolks. *n.* crabapple. [mɔ·lks] pr.
1443.2 moolksx, mukmoolsk. *v.i.* sour. [mɔ·lksx̣] m,pr. [mukmɔ́·lskʰ] pr.

1444. MOOMS. *v.i.* crippled; mentally ill; left handed. *n.* a habit; birth defect. [mɔ·ms] hb.
1444.1 móoms. *v.i.* crazy. [mɔ·ʌms] m.

1445. MÓON, MÓON. *n.* salt water; sea. [mɔʌn] k,pr. [mɔʌn] k.

1446. MOOS, MOOS. *n.* thumb. [mɔ·s] hb,k,pr. [mɔ·s] k.
1446.1 'moosx. *n.* chewed fat (Note: the fat is prepared by chewing; it is eaten by heating it and licking it). [ʔmɔ·sx̣] pr.

1447. MOOTK, MOOTG-. *v.i.* safe; saved. [mɔ·tʰkʰ] pr.

1448. MOXK, MOXG-. *v.t.* & *v.i.* go aboard. [mɔx̣kʰ] pr.

1449. MUK, MUG-, GAMÚUKT. *n.* ear (*anat*). [mukʰ] k. [gạmúʌkʰtʰ] k.
1449.1 muu. [mu·] hb,k,pr.
1449.2 múu. *n.* earrings [mu·ʌ] hb,k,m.

1450. MÚUMS. *v.i.* stubborn; obstinant; self-willed; head-strong. [mu·ʌms] m,pr.

1451. MÜDZAGALE. *n.* flowers. [mɨʒʌgalé] hb.
1451.1 müdzagalee. *n.* flowers; houseplants. [mɨʒagạlé·] hb,k,m,pr.

1452. MÜLA- both. [mɨla] pr.

1453. MÜNLII. *n.* chest hair. [mɨnlí·] pr.

1454. MÜNYÁA, MÜNWAALXS. *v.i.* ascend; go up; walk up. [mɨnyá·ʌ] m,pr. [mɨnwá·lx̣s] m,pr.

1455. MÜSÍIN. *n.* copper. [mɨsí·ʌn] pr.

1456. MÜSOO. *n.* sockeye salmon; blueback salmon; red salmon. [mɨsɔ́·] hb,k,m,pr.

1457. MÜS'OL. *n.* cinnamon bear (Note: local common name for *Euarctos americanus kermodei*, the Kermodes bear or island white bear, found on Cribbel Island). [mɨsʔɔ́l] hb,k,m,pr. *See also* moksgm'ol.

1458. MÜTKYA'WN. *n.* left hand. [mɨtʰkʰyáʔwn̥] k,pr.

1459. MÜ'WATSA. *v.i.* act crazy (*lit*: like an otter). *n.* a crazy person. [mɨʔwácʰa] k.

1460. MUUS. *n.* moose. [mu·s] hb.

N

1461. NAA. *pron.* who. [na·] m,pr.
1461.1 náa. [na·ʌ] m,pr.

1462. NAA, NE'NAA. *n.* snowshoes. [na·] hb,pr. [nɛʔná·] k.

1462.1 náa. [naʌ] k.

1463. NAA. *n.* bait. [na·] hb.
1463.1 'naa, 'naa. [ʔna·] k,m,pr. [ʔna·] k.

1464. NA'A, GANAA'NAX. *n.* woman's dress; skirt. [náʔɑ] hb,m. [gɑná·ʔnʌx̣] hb.
1464.1 na'ax, naa'nax. [náʔax̣] k. [ná·ʔnʌx̣] k.
1464.2 na'ga. [náʔgɑ] pr.
1464.3 naa'k, naa'g-. [na·ʔqʼ] k.

1465. NA'AAMG. *v.i.* peaceful. [nʌʔá·mg] pr.
1465.1 n'aamx. [nʔá·mx̣] pr.

1466. NA'AAMSK, NA'AAMSG-. *v.t.* blame. [naʔá·msk^{h}] hb.
1466.1 na'eemsk, na'eemsg-. [naʔɛ́·msk^{h}] hb.

1467. NA'AGOYBA. *v.i.* visible. *n.* a little light; a point of light. [nàʔʌgóybɑ] m,pr.

1468. NAAK'OK, NAAK'OG-. *v.i.* bald. [ná·qʔoq^{h}] m.
1468.1 nagoox, nagoog-. [nɑgó·x̣] hb.
1468.2 'náak'ok, 'náak'og-, 'náak'aak. *v.i.* be cut open; be a hole there. [ʔnaʌqʔɔ́k^{h}] k,m. [ʔnaʌqʔá·k^{h}] k,m.

1469. NAAŁ. *n.* breath. [na·ɬ] pr.
1469.1 naał, ganaał. *v.id* fast (not stative), i.e., go hungry. [na·ɬ] k,pr. [gɑnáɬ] k.
1469.2 naałx. *n.* windpipe; trachea. [na·ɬx̣] pr.

1470. NA'AMADZAPDZAP, NA'AMADZAPDZAB-. *plural of* aamadzap. *plural of* aamdzap.

1471. 'NAAMTXAW. *n.* halibut bait. [ʔná·mtx̣áw] m,pr.

1472. NAASU. *n.* raspberry. [ná·su] m,pr.

1473. NÁAT, NÁAD-, GWÜNÁAT. *n.* sir; "my dear" (respectful address of a male). [naʌt^{h}] k,pr. [g^{w}ɨnáʌt^{h}] k.
1473.1 náatsk, náatsg-. *n.* harpoon point; harpoon barb. [na·ʌc^{h}k^{h}] pr.

1474. 'NAAXŁ, 'NAAXŁ. *n.* blackfish; killer whale; false killer whale. [ʔna·x̣ɬ] k. [ʔna·x̣ɬ] k.
1474.1 neexł. [nɛ·x̣ɬ] hb.

1475. NAAXS. *v.i.* & *n.* plastic. [na·x̣s] hb.
1475.1 nee'k, nee'g-. *n.* anal fin; dorsal fin. [nɛ·ʔqʼ] hb.
1475.2 ne'ix, ne'ig-. [nɛʔɩx̣] hb.
1475.3 ne'k, ne'g-. [nɛʔqʼ] m.

1476. NABAXT, NABAXD-. *v.t.* & *v.i.* wrestle. [nʌbɑ́x̣t^{h}] m,pr.

1477. NADÁAM. *v.t.* & *v.i.* carve. [nadáʌm] k.

1477.1 nat'm. *v.i.* sketch out a pattern or design (Note: using human hair brush and ink made of soot and olachen grease). [natʔḿ̩] m.

1478. NADIST'U'UTSK, NADIST'U'UTSG-. *plural of* t'u'utsk.

1479. NAGADELPK, NAGADELPG-. *n.* an anchorage. [nagadɛ́lpʰkʰ] hb.
1479.1 nagagadeelpk, nagagadeelpg-. *n.* anchor line. [nàgagadɛ́·lpʰkʰ] m,pr.

1480. NAGADZAW. *v.i.* & *n.* a few; several. [nagaʒáw] m,pr.

1481. NAGAGANAW. *n.* (foliose dog) lichen (*lit:* frog's dress). [nàgaganáw] hb,k.

1482. NAGAGOXT, NAGAGOXD-. *n.* dried fish nose. [nagagɔ́x̣tʰ] m.

1483. NAGANDZI'ISK, NAGANDZI'ISG-. *n.* ancestresses; grandmothers. *plural of* nts'íi'ts.
1483.1 naganüts'íi'tsk, naganüts'íi'tsg-.

1484. NAGATS'ÉE. *n.* red fox. [nagacʔɛ́ʌ] hb.
1484.1 nagats'éet, nagats'éed-. [nagacʔɛ́·ʌtʰ] m,pr.

1485. NAGAWEEY. *n.* fish fin. [nagawɛ́·y] pr.

1486. NAGWAAT, NAGWAAD-. *n.* father (reference; deceased or alive; F, FB). [nʌgʷā·tʰ] m.
1486.1 nagwat, nagwad-. [nʌgʷátʰ] k.
1486.2 nügwat, nügwad-. [nɨgʷátʰ] k.
1486.3 ngwadi. *n.* father (address: F, FB). [n̩gʷadi] k.
1486.4 nügwet, nügwed-. [nɨgʷɛ́tʰ] k.

1487. NAHAAPT, NAHAAPD-. *n.* box cover; lid (of a box). [nahá·pʰtʰ] k,m.

1488. NAHOOŁ. *n.* drum. [nahɔ́·ɬ] k,m.
1488.1 nóoł. [nɔ·ʌɬ] m,pr.

1489. NAHÓON. *n.* fishing ground (Note: an owned place for fishing). [nahɔ́ʌn] m,pr.

1490. NAK- direction toward. [nak] m,pr.
1490.1 nakgii. *adv.* here. [nakgí·] m,pr.
1490.2 nakgwii. [nakgʷi·] m,pr.
1490.3 naklax'oot, naklax'ood-. *n.* open top. [naklax̣ʔɔ́·tʰ] m,pr.

1491. 'NAK, 'NAG-, 'NAK'NÚUNG. *v.i.* long. [ʔnʌkʰ] pr. [ʔnʌkʔnúʌng] pr.
1491.1 'naka. *v.i.* reach out with the hand.

1492. NAK'AXBA'ALA. *n.* on the south side. [nàʔqʾax̣báʔala] pr.

1493. NAK'AWST, NAK'AWSD-. *plural of* gaws.

1494. NAK'EEDA. *n.* muskrat. [nak?ɛ́·da] hb.
1494.1 nak'eeda. [naq?é·dʌ] m,pr.

1495. NAKHAAYWAASK, NAKHAAYWAASG-. *n.* northeast. [naqʰha·ywá·skʰ] m,pr.

1496. NAKS. *v.t. & v.i.* marry. [naks] k.
1496.1 'naks, ganiwnaks. [?naks] k. [ganíwnaks] k.
1496.2 naks. *n.* husband; wife; spouse (address and reference). [naks] k.
1496.3 'naks. [?naks] k.
1496.4 'naks, ganiwnskt, lax'naks. (Note: ganiwnskt is a general plural for spouse, while lax'naks refers to the spouses of one person). [?naks] k. [ganíwnskʰtʰ] k. [lax̣?náks] k.
1496.5 'naksit'a'a. *n.* deceased spouse (reference). [?nàksit?á?a] k.

1497. NAKSŁGWÜLIS. *n.* nephew-in-law; niece-in-law (address and reference: BDH, BSW, ZDH, ZSW). [nàksłgʷɨlís] k.

1498. NAKSMYA'WIN. *n.* right hand. [nʌksm̩yá?wɩn] pr. *See also* smya'win.

1499. NAKSUNIISK, NAKSUNIISG-. *n.* mirror; window. [naksuní·skʰ] m,pr.

1500. NAGOOK, NAGOOG-. *n.* in front. [nagɔ́·qʰ] m.
1500.1 nak'oox, nak'oog-. [nàq?ɔ́·x̣] k.

1501. NALÜKSGYIGYIT, NALÜKSGYIGYID-. *n.* quilt. [nalɨksgʸigʸítʰ] m.

1502. NALÚUŁK, NALÚUŁG-, NAKNALUUŁK. *n.* nest. [nʌlúʌłkʰ] k.
[nʌknʌlú·łkʰ] k.

1503. NAŁGUGOTKS. *n.* deceased sister-in-law (reference: ♂BW, HZ, WZ). [nałgugotʰks] k.
1503.1 nałgugotkst'a'a. [nałgugótʰkst?a?a] k.

1504. NAMAASAGYÍIK, NAMAASAGYÍIG-. *n.* hemlock bark. [namá·sʌgʸíʌkʰ] m,pr.

1505. NAMAASALUWI. *n.* alder bark. [namá·sʌlúwi] m,pr.

1506. NAMAASASA'MIN. *n.* spruce bark. [namá·sʌsá?mɩn] m,pr.

1507. NAMAASM'MGAN. *n.* red cedar bark. [namá·sm̩?m̩gán] m,pr.

1508. 'NA'NA. *n.* mallard duck. [?na?ná] hb.
1508.1 'na'naat, 'na'naad- [?na?ná·tʰ] m,pr.

1509. 'NANAK, 'NANAG-. *v.i.* foolish; crazy; disobedient; incorrigible. [?nánakʰ] k,m.

1510. NA'NIITK, NA'NIITG-. *n.* Judgement Day; the resurrection of the dead at the last judgement. [na?ní·tʰkʰ] m,pr.

1511. NAPLANTK, NAPLANTG-. *v.i.* appear. [naplántʰkʰ] m,pr.

1512. NAPŁAXŁ. *v.i.* tall. [nʌpɬáx̣ɬ] pr.

1513. NASGYETK, NASGYETG-. *v.t.* tease; make fun of. [nʌsg^{y}ɛ́t^{h}k^{h}] pr.

1514. NASTOO. *v.i.* & *n.* half. [nast^{h}ɔ́·] m,pr.
1514.1 nast'óoks. *n.* side (of the body). [nastʔɔ́ʌks] k.

1515. NASTOOGYEMK, NASTOOGYEMG-. *n.* half moon. [nʌstó·g^{y}ɛ́mk^{h}] hb.

1516. NASMHAWTKS. *v.t.* promise. *n.* something one believes in. [nʌsm̥háwt^{h}ks] k,m.

1517. NA'TSIKS. *n.* fish tail; caudal fin; tail fin. [nʌ́ʔcˀɩkš] m.
1517.1 na'dzüks. [nʌ́ʔʒɨks] pr.

1518. NAXNOX. *v.i.* supernatural; have supernatural power. *n.* a supernatural being. [nɑx̣nɑ́x̣] hb,k.

1519. NAXNOXMHANA'A. *n.* a cheater woman; a clever woman; a trickster. [nɑx̣nɔ́x̣m̥hanɑ́ʔɑ] m,pr.

1520. NAXNOXM'YUUT, NAXNOXM'YUUD-. *n.* a cheater; a trickster. [nɑx̣nɔ́x̣m̥ʔyū·t^{h}] m,pr.

1521. 'NAX'NUU. *v.t.* & *v.i.* hear. [ʔnɑx̣ʔnú·] pr.

1522. NAX'PIDZUU. *v.t.* fear. *v.i.* be afraid. *n.* a haunted place. [nàx̣ʔpˀiʒú·] pr.

1523. NAXSNÜGWET, NAXSNÜGWED-. *n.* uncle-in-law (reference: MZH). [nɑx̣snɨg^{w}ɛ́t^{h}] k.
1523.1 naxsnügwedit'e'e. *n.* deceased uncle-in-law (reference: MZH). [nɑ́x̣snɨg^{w}ɛ́dɩtʔɛ̀ʔɛ] k.

1524. NAY. *n.* mother (archaic; address; M). [nay] k.

1525. NA'YEEN. *n.* rust. [naʔyɛ́·n] k,m.

1526. NA'YEŁK, NA'YEŁG-. *v.i.* smooth. [naʔyɛ́ɬk^{h}] k,m.

1527. NAYGYEŁXS. *v.t.* & *v.i.* tattoo(k). *n.* a puncture (m). [nayg^{y}ɛ́ɬx̣s] k,m.
1527.1 naygyiłgyełxs. *n.* tattoo. [nayg^{y}ɩɬg^{y}ɛ́ɬx̣s] m.

1528. NDEH. *interr.* where, when, how. *excl.* Get out! Get away! [n̩dɛ́h] pr.
1528.1 ndede. [n̩dɛ́dɛ] pr.

1529. NDO'O. *excl.* Go ahead! Go on! [n̩dɔ́·ɔ] pr.

1530. NDZOK, NDZOG-. *n.* edge. [n̩ʒɔ́q^{h}] m,pr.
1530.1 ndzox, ndzog-. [n̩ʒɔ́x̣] m,pr.

1531. NEE'. *v.i.* confess something; admit doing something. [nɛ·ʔ] m,pr.

1532. NIBAAX. *v.t. & v.i.* wrestle (m). *n.* warrior (k). [nɩbá·x̣] k,m.

1533. NIBIP, NIBIB-. *n.* uncle (address: MB; reference: MB, FZH). [nɩbípʰ] k.
1533.1 nübip, nübib-. [nɨbípʰ] k.

1534. NIGYITYAAKWS. *plural of* yaakw.
1534.1 nigyityeekws. *plural of* yeekw.

1535. 'NÍIDZ, LU'NÍITSK. *v.t. & v.i.* look; see. [ʔni·ʌʒ] k,m,pr. [luʔní·ʌcʰkʰ] m.

1536. NÍITK, NÍITG-. *v.i.* get up. [niʌtʰkʰ] m.

1537. NIIYA. *n.* grandfather (address and reference: FF, MF, FFB, MFB).

1538. NIKT'AA. *n.* aunt (reference: FZ). [nɩktʔá·] k.
1538.1 nükt'aa. [nɨktʔá·] k.

1539. NIP'A'LA. *n.* button. [nɩpʔáʔla] hb,pr.
1539.1 nip'aola. [ntpʔáɔla] pr.

1540. NISAHÓON. *n.* fish trap; weir. [nɩsahɔ́ʌn] hb.

1541. NISGÜÜSK, NISGÜÜSG-. *n.* funeral box. [nɩsgɨ́·skʰ] pr.

1542. 'NISIPSÍIBNSK, 'NISIPSÍIBNSG-. *n.* friend. [ʔnɩsɩpsɩ́ʌbn̥skʰ] k.

1543. NLA'IDA. *n.* light house; sign; signal. [n̥láʔɩda] m,pr.

1544. NLAK, NLAG-. *n.* fireplace. [n̥lákʰ] m,pr.
1544.1 'nlak, 'nlag-. [ʔn̥lákʰ] hb.

1545. NLU'UPIS. *n.* thread. [n̥lúʔupɩs] pr.

1546. NŁANAGN, NŁÜKŁANAGN. *n.* barrel. [n̥ɬanagn̥] k,m. [n̥ɬɨkɬanagn̥] k,m.

1547. 'NŁGABUUS. *n.* scallop (*Chlamys hastata*). [ʔn̥ɬgabú·s] hb.

1548. 'NŁOMSK, 'NŁOMSG-, NIKA'NŁOMSK. *v.t.* respect. *v.i.* sacred. *n.* a sacred person; a respected person. [ʔn̥ɬomskʰ] k. [nɩkʌʔn̥ɬómskʰ] k.
1548.1 'nłoomsk, 'nłoomsg-. [ʔn̥ɬɔ́·mskʰ] k,pr.
1548.2 'nłóomsk, 'nłóomsg-. [ʔn̥ɬɔ́ʌmskʰ] k,m.

1549. 'NŁTS'IIK, 'NŁTS'IIG. *n.* sea shell. [ʔn̥ɬcʔí·kʰ] hb.

1550. NŁÚULK, NŁÚUŁG-. *n.* bird's nest. [n̥ɬúʌɬkʰ] pr. *See also* nalúułk.

1551. NŁÚUT, NŁÚUD-. *v.i.* be under. [n̥ɬúʌtʰ] k,m.

1552. NNAAẄ. *n.* lullaby. [n̥ná·ÿ] m,pr.
1552.1 nnaẅ. [n̥náÿ] hb.

1553. NOŁ. *n.* dishes. [nɔɬ] k.

1554. NOO. *n.* mother (alive or deceased; reference: M, MZ, FBW, MBW). [nɔ·] k,m,pr.
1554.1 no'o. *n.* mother (address: M, MZ, FBW, MBW). [nɔ́ʔɔ] k.

1555. NOOK, NOOG-, LEŁK. *v.i.* lie down (Note: subject must be animate). [no·kʰ], [nɔ·kʰ] pr. [lɛɬkʰ] k.
1555.1 nóok, nóog-, láałk. [nɑʌkʰ] k. [nɔʌkʰ] m. [laʌɬkʰ] pr.
1555.2 'nóok, 'nóog-. [ʔnɔʌkʰ] k.

1556. NOOML. *n.* eyelashes. [nɔ́·ml̩] pr.

1557. NÓOSÜ. *n.* wolverine. [nóʌsɪ̈] hb.
1557.1 noosüü. [nɔ́·sɪ̈·] m,pr.

1558. NOOTS, NOODZ-, GANOODZIT. *n.* homosexual. [nɔ·cʰ] k. [gɑnɔ́·ʒɩtʰ] k.

1559. NT'AA'MA HAK'ÉENTK. *n.* hand drill. [n̩tʔá·ʔmɑ hɑkʔέʌntʰkʰ] hb.

1560. NTAHAWAAL. *n.* quiver. [n̩tʰʌhawá·l] k.
1560.1 ntahaweel. [n̩tʰahawέ·l] pr.

1561. NTS'I'IS, NAGANDZI'ISK. *n.* grandmother (reference) k. [n̩cʔíʔis] k. [nagɑnʒíʔiskʰ] m,pr.
1561.1 nts'íi'ts, nts'íi'dz-. [n̩cʔí·ʌʔcʼ] k.
1561.2 nüts'i'is, naganüts'íi'tsk. [nɨcʔíʔis] k. [nagɑnɨcʔí·ʌʔcʼkʰ] m,pr. (Note: plural form also means ancestresses).
1561.3 nts'i'i'ts, nts'i'i'dz-. *n.* great aunt (address). [n̩cʔíʔiʔcʼ] k.

1562. NTS'AWS, NTS'ÜKTS'AWS. *v.t.* copy; imitate. [n̩cʔáws] m,pr. [n̩cʔɨkcʔáws] m,pr.

1563. NTS'ÓOŁ. *n.* a place between; space between; niche. [n̩cʔɔ́·ʌɬ] m,pr.

1564. NTS'OOŁA'NLAK, NTS'OOŁA'NLAG-. *n.* a place or room behind the fireplace. [n̩cʔɔ́·ɬɑʔn̩lákʰ] hb.
1564.1 nts'óołnlak, nts'óołnlag-. [n̩cʔɔ́·ʌɬn̩lákʰ] m,pr.

1565. NTXALAA. *n.* descendants. [n̩tx̣alá·] m,pr.

1566. NÜKNÚUNGMBUTS, NÜKNÚUNGMBUDZ-. *n.* wading boots. [nɨknú·ʌngm̩búcʰ] hb.

1567. NUKWŁAASK, NUKWŁAASG-. *plural of* kwłaask.

1568. NUU, NUU. *n.* halibut hook. [nu·] k,pr. [nu·] k.

1569. NÚUNGAT, NÚUNGAD-. *v.t.* take hold of. [nú·ʌngʌtʰ] pr.

1570. NUUTK, NUUTG-. *v.t.* & *v.i.* dress. [nu·tʰkʰ] hb,pr.

1571. NÜWA'NA. *n.* seed(s). [nɨwáʔnɑ] pr.

O

1572. OKS, AK'OKS. *v.i.* fall. [ʔɔks] k. [ʔakʔɔ́ks] k.

1573. OL, OL. *n.* (black) bear. [ʔɔl] hb,m,pr. [ʔɔl] k.
1573.1 al. [ʔɑl] hb.

1574. OŁK, OŁG-. *n.* firewood. [ʔɔɬkʰ] k.

1575. ONXŁ, ONXŁ. *n.* water lily. [ʔɔnx̣ɬ] k,m.

1575. OO. *adv.* yes. [ʔɔ·] k.

1576. -OOL. *num. suffix.* of human beings. [-ɔ·l] hb.

1577. OOMLK, OOMLG-. *n.* gun powder. [ʔɔ́·ml̩kʰ] k,m.

1578. O'OS. *n.* cousin (address: FZD, FZDH, FZS, FZSW, MBS, MBD).
[ʔɔ́ʔɔs] k.

1579. O'OS, GAL'O'OS. *n.* stomach. [ʔɔ́ʔɔs] m,pr. [gɑlʔɔ́ʔɔs] m,pr.

1580. OO'TSN. *n.* spirit; nothingness. [ʔɔ́·ʔcʼn̩] m,pr.
1580.1 o'otsn. [ʔɔ́ʔɔcʰn̩] m,pr.

1581. OOY, AY'OOY. *v.t.* throw. [ʔɔ·y] k. [ʔayʔɔ́·y] k.
1581.1 oyɨ. *v.i.* throw. [ʔɔyɨ] pr.

P

1582. P'A'A. *n.* father (neologism; address: F, MZH). [pʔaʔa] k.

1583. P'AALT, P'AALD-. *n.* gloves. [pʔa·ltʰ] hb.
1583.1 p'alt, p'ald-. [pʔaltʰ] m.

1584. P'AALDIHAŁOO. *n.* cotton gloves. [pʔá·ldihaɬɔ́·] hb.

1585. P'AALDITXAH. *n.* leather gloves. [pʔá·ldɪtx̣ɑ́h] hb.

1586. P'AASÜ. *v.i.* fart (Note: a man's word. *See also* wilaan).
[pʔá·sɨ̈] pr.

1587. P'ÁATSAH. *n.* fucus algae. [pʔáʌcʰɑh] hb.

1588. P'ALGYÜXSK, P'ALGYÜXSG-, P'LP'ALGYÜXSK. *v.i.* heavy.
[pʔálgʸɨx̣skʰ] k,m,hb,pr. [pʔl̩pʔálgʸɨx̣skʰ] hb,pr.

1589. P'AŁMUU. *n.* earring. [pʔʌɬmú·] k,m,pr.

1590. P'AS. *v.i.* grow; mature; develop. [pʔas] k.
1590.1 p'as, maxs. [pʔɑs], [pʔʌs] k,m,pr. [mɑx̣s] k.

1591. P'ASAXK, P'ASAYG-, P'ISP'ASAGNT. *v.t. & v.i.* split; separate. [p?ásʌx̣kʰ] k,m,pr. [p?ɩsp?ásʌg̣ṇtʰ] k.

1592. P'ASII. *n.* cloth diapers. [p?ɑsí·] hb.

1593. P'AXS, GAP'AXS, P'ÜXP'AXS. *n.* pants; leggings; trousers. [p?ɑx̣s] hb,k,m,pr. [gɑp?áx̣s] hb. [p?ɨx̣p?áx̣s] hb.

1594. P'AXSÜTS'AALAXS. *n.* long woolen underpant; longjohns. [p?áx̣sɨts?á·lɑx̣s] hb.

1595. P'ÉEGL, P'ÉEGN. *v.t.* tear out and turn over. [p?é·ʌg̣l̩] k,m,pr. [p?é·ʌg̣ṇ] k,m,pr.

1596. P'EEL. *v.t.* sing about in a ridiculing manner; ridicule.

1597. P'IIɫ. *v.t.* peel. [p?i·ɫ] hb.
1597.1 p'iiɫk, p'iiɫg-. *v.i.* mashed. [p?i·ɫkʰ] hb.
1597.2 p'iiɫn. *v.t.* nudge; smash; crush; flatten (Note: using some instrument such as a hammer). [p?í·ɫṇ] hb,k,m,pr.
1597.3 p'iiɫn, p'aɫp'iiɫn. [p?aɫp?í·ɫṇ] hb.

1598. P'I'IɫOSK, P'I'IɫOSG-, P'ÜKP'I'IɫOSK. *n.* a square of dried seaweed. [p?ì?iɫóskʰ] k,m,pr. [p?ɨkp?ì?iɫóskʰ] k.

1599. P'IINS. *n.* Indian celery (male plant); cow parsnips (*Heracleum lanatum*). [p?i·ns] hb,m.

1600. P'IYAAN. *n.* smoke. [p?iyá·n] k,m,pr.

1601. PLAKSK, PLAKSG-, PLIIPLAKSK. *v.i.* exhausted; overworked; beaten up. [plɑkskʰ] hb. [plí·plɑkskʰ] hb.
1601.1 pɫakskw, pɫaksgw-, pɫiipɫakskw. [pɫɑkskʷʰ] k,m. [pɫí·pɫɑkskʷʰ] k,m.
1601.2 pɫakskw, pɫaksgw-. *v.i.* have aching bones from overwork. [pɫákskʷʰ] hb.

1602. PLIYAAẄ. *v.t.* tell. [pliya·ÿ] k,pr.

1603. PɫOON. *n.* sea otter (*Enhydra lutris*). [pɫɔ·n] hb.
1603.1 pɫóon, bapɫóon. [pɫɔʌn] hb,k,m,pr. [bʌpɫɔ́ʌn] k.

1604. P'ÓO. *v.i.* broken. [p?ɔʌ] k,m,pr.
1604.1 p'óok, p'óog-. *n.* snowy owl (*Nyctea scandiaca*). [p?oʌqʰ] hb.

1605. PSAH. *n.* clay. [psah] hb.
1605.1 psah. [psɑh] k,m,pr.

1606. PTAL, BUPTAL. *n.* rib(s) [pʰtal] k,m,pr. [buptál] k.
1606.1 ptel. [pʰtɛl] k.
1606.2 pteeltk, pteeltg-, bupteeltk. *v.t. & v.i.* climb. [pʰtɛ·ltʰkʰ] k,m,pr. [buptɛ́·ltʰkʰ] k,m,pr.
1606.3 pteltk, pteltg-. [pʰtɛltʰkʰ] hb.

1607. PTELDMBÓOT. *n.* ribs (*naut*). [pʰɛldm̩bɔ́ʌtʰ] hb.

1608. PTÓOŁ. *n.* basement; foundation; house platform. [pʰtɔ·ʌɨ] k,m,pr.

1609. PTS'AAN, BUPTS'AAN. *n.* totem pole. [pʰcʔa·n] k,m,pr. [bupcʔá·n] pr.
1609.1 pts'an, maxsgapts'an. [pʰcʔan] k. [màx̣sgʌpcʔán] k.

1610. PTS'IH, BUPTS'IH, GUKPTS'IH. *n.* comb. [pʰcʔih] k,m,pr. [bupcʔíh] pr. [gukpcʔíh] k.

1611. P'UYŁK, P'UYŁG-. *v.i.* get out of the way. [pʔuyɨkʰ] k,m,pr.

1612. PUKSK, PUKSG-. *v.i.* spit. *n* saliva. [pʰukskʰ] k,m,pr.

1613. P'ÚU. *v.i.* scatter. [pʔu·ʌ] k,m,pr.
1613.1 p'úul. *v.t.* scatter. [pʔu·ʌl] k,m,pr.
1613.2 p'úutk, p'úutg-, p'úutk. *v.i.* scattered. *n.* steam. [pʔu·ʌtʰkʰ] k,m,pr. [pʔu·ʌtʰkʰ] k.

1614. P'ÚUN'AKS. *v.t.* & *v.i.* splash. [pʔúʌnʔáks] k,pr.
1614.1 p'úunaks. [pʔúʌnʌks] m.

S

1615. SA'AAWX, GASA'AAWX. *n.* Adam's apple; larynx. [saʔá·wx̣] hb. [gasaʔá·wx̣] hb.

1616. SAALDZIK, SAALDZIG-. *v.i.* groan. [sá·lʒɩkʰ] pr.
1616.1 saldzik, saldzig-. [sálʒɩkʰ] k.

1617. SAALI. *v.t.* invite; talk into going. [sá·li] m,pr.

1618. SAALOGAMGOS. *v.i.* jump into. [sa·lɔ́gʌmgɔ́s] m,pr.

1619. SAALOOKSK, SAALOOKSG-. *plural of* sagyooks. *See also* se'awulksk *and* süawilksk.
1619.1 salilooks.

1620. SA'AŁ. *v.t.* divide. *v.i.* settle an estate. [sáʔaɨ] k.
1620.1 sa'kał. [sáʔqʼaɨ] k.

1621. SAAŁK, SAAŁK-. *v.i.* perishable. [sa·ɨkʰ] pr.

1622. SAANTK, SAANTG-. *plural of* moxk.
1622.1 saantk, saantg-. *v.t.* board; go aboard. *v.i.* board; continue; go aboard; go ahead. [sa·ntʰkʰ] m,pr.

1623. S'AAWG. *n.* throat. [sʔá·wg] pr.

1624. SA'AWAN. *v.t.* put into a box (pr); put more into a box, shake down to make settle in a box (m). [sáʔawʌn] m,pr.
1624.1 sa'awünsk, sa'awünsg-. *n.* book; paper. [sáʔawɨnskʰ] pr.
1624.2 sa'awünsk, sa'awünsg-. [sáʔʌwɨnskʰ] pr.

1624.3 se'wünsk, se'wünsg-. [sɛ́ʔwɨnskʰ] pr.

1625. SADZIWB. *v.i.* disappear; be lost; melt away before one's eyes. [saʒíwb] pr.
1625.1 sagwaatk, sagwaatg-. [sagʷá·tʰkʰ] k,m.

1626. SAGAMGYEMK, SAGAMGYEMG-. *n.* sunshine. [sáɣamgʸɛ́mkʰ] pr.

1627. SAGAWDI. *v.i.* be nothing there. [sagáwdi] pr.

1628. SAGAWHAYTK, SAGAWHAYTG-. *v.i.* stamp on the edge (of); stand near the edge (of). [sàgawháytʰkʰ] pr.

1629. SAGAWSAA. *v.i.* lucky; have good luck. [sàgawsá·] pr.

1630. SAGAYNA. *v.i.* fall down (inanimate subject). [sagáyna] m,pr.

1631. SAGAYTWAAL. *plural of* waal. *plural of* weel.

1632. SAGYAA. *v.t.* take off. [sʌgʸa·] pr.

1633. SAGYOOKS, SAALOOKSK, SALILOOKS. *v.i.* drift away. [sagʸɔ́·ks] pr,m. [sa·lɔ́·kskʰ] pr. [salilɔ́·ks] m.

1634. SAH. *n.* day. [sah] hb.
1634.1 seh. [sɛh] m,pr.

1635. SAHAKWDAK, SAHAKWDAG-. *n.* yew. [sahakʷʰdakʰ] hb.

1636. SAHO'YAGNSK, SAHO'YAGNSG-. *n.* inner bark (Note: used to make stencils for patterns). [sahɔ́ʔyagn̩skʰ] m.

1637. SAK, SAG-, SEESAX. *v.i.* sharp. [saqʰ] hb,m. [sʌqʰ] pr. [sɛ́·sax̣] k.
1637.1 sax, sag-. [sax̣] hb,k. [sʌx̣] k.
1637.2 saxsaasax. *n.* thornbush. [sax̣sá·sax̣] pr.

1638. SA'KALST, SA'KALSD-. *n.* a measure: length of span from thumb to first finger. [sáʔqʼalstʰ] m,pr.

1639. SAKS. *n.* driftwood. [saks] hb.
1639.1 s'hoks. [šʔhɔ́ks] m.

1640. SAKSK, SAKSG-, SAKSAKSK. *v.i.* clean. [sakskʰ] k,m,pr. [sʌksákskʰ] k.
1640.1 seksk, seksg-, sakseksk. [sɛkskʰ] k,pr. [sʌksɛ́kskʰ] k.
1640.2 saksgn. *v.t.* clean. [sáksgn̩] m,pr.

1641. SA'KT, SA'KD-. *v.i.* be split. [saʔqʼtʰ] k.

1642. SA'KY, SA'GY-. *v.t.* pull. [saʔkʸʼ] pr.
1642.1 say'k, say'g-. [sayʔkʼ] pr.

1643. SALAASÜÜ. *n.* canyon; gorge. [sʌlá·sï·] pr.

1644. SAMI. *n.* flesh; meat. [sámi] k,m.
  1644.1 semii. [sέmi·] pr.

1645. SAM'K, SAM'G-. *n.* butter clam. [sʌm?q˃] hb.
  1645.1 sam'x, sam'wx-. [sʌm?x̣] hb.
  1645.2 sem'k, sem'g-. [sɛm?q˃] k,m.
  1645.3 se'mx, sakse'mx. [sɛ?mx̣] k,m. [sʌksέ?mx̣] k.
  1645.4 smk, smg-. *n.* a prepubescent girl. [sḿ̩kʰ] m.

1646. SA'MN. *n.* spruce. [sá?mn̩] hb.

1647. SANAAȽK, SANAAȽG-. *v.i.* be surprised; be astonished. [saná·ɬkʰ] pr.

1648. SA'NIIST, SA'NIISD-. *n.* mountain. [sa?ní·stʰ] k.
  1648.1 sxa'niist, sxa'niisd-. [sx̣a?ni·stʰ] k.

1649. SASOO. *n.* rattle. [sasó·] pr.
  1649.1 sesoo, süksesoo. [sɛsɔ́·] k. [sɨksɛsɔ́·] k.

1650. SAT'UUS. *v.i.* push something. [sat?ú·s] k,m.

1651. SAXDOO. *v.t.* gather. [sax̣dɔ́·] pr,m.

1652. SAXS LABAGAYT SE'KYA. *n.* seine boat. [sáx̣slábagaytʰsέ?kʸʰa] hb.

1653. SAXS UUMTXAW. *n.* halibut boat. [sáx̣s?u·mtx̣áw] hb.

1654. SAXSWOOXSK, SAXSWOOXSG-. *plural of* xswooxsk.

1655. SASYAAMX. *v.t.* imitate. [sayá·mx̣] hb.

1656. SAYP, SAYB-. *n.* bone. [saypʰ] pr.
  1656.1 seeyp, seeyb-. [sɛ·ypʰ] hb.
  1656.2 seyp, seyb-, sikseyp. [sɛypʰ] k. [sɩkséypʰ] k.
  1656.3 saypk, saypg-. *v.i.* hard. [saypʰkʰ] pr.
  1656.4 seypk, seypg-. [sɛypʰkʰ] k.
  1656.5 saypn. *v.t.* harden. [saypʰn̩] pr.

1657. SE'AWULKSK, SE'AWULKSG-. *plural of* sagyooks. [se?awúlkskʰ] k.
  1657.1 süawilksk, süawilksg-. [sɨáwɩlkskʰ] k.

1658. SÉEG. *v.t.* need. [sɛ·ʌg̣] m,pr.

1659. SEGYEKS. *v.i.* be calm. [segʸέks] k,m.

1660. SELAYA. *v.t.* & *v.i.* visit. [sɛláyʌ] k,m.

1661. SE'MN. *n.* spruce. [sέ?mn̩] pr.
  1661.1 se'mün. [sέ?mɨn] pr.

1662. SEYBMK'OO. *n.* backbone. [sèybm̩k?ó·] hb.

1663. SGA- across the way; in the way, i.e., obstructing. [sg̣a] hb.

1664. SGAA. *n.* nurse shark. [sga·] hb.

1665. SGAAG. *v.t.* & *v.i.* refuse. [sg̣a·g̣] pr.

1666. SGAAYKSK, SGAAYKSG-. *v.t.* hurt; wound. *v.i.* be hurt; be wounded. [sga·yk̄skʰ] pr.
1666.1 sxaytsk, sxaytsg-. *v.t.* hurt; wound. [sx̣áycʰkʰ] k,m.

1667. SGABUU. *v.i.* & *n.* a number; a few; some. [sg̣abú·] pr.

1668. SGADAWŁ. *v.i.* go across. [sg̣adáwɨ] m,pr.

1669. SGAN, SIKSXAN. *n.* woven mat; fish scales. [sg̣an] hb,k.
[sɩksx̣ān] k.
1669.1 sxan. [sx̣an] k.

1670. SGANAKT, SGANAKD-. *n.* length (of space); duration (of time). [sg̣anākʰt̄ʰ] m,pr.

1671. SGANHAŁOO. *n.* mast (*naut*). [sg̣anhaɨ́ɔ́·] m.

1672. SGA'NÍIS. *n.* mountain. [sg̣aʔní·ʌs] m.

1673. SGANIS. *n.* elbow; chamber pot; bed pan. [sg̣ánis] pr.

1674. SGANK'YIIN. *n.* harpoon shaft. [sg̣ankʸʔí·n] m,pr.
1674.1 sgank'yíin. *n.* spear handle; spear shaft. [sg̣ankʸʔíʌn] pr.

1675. SGANMOOLKSGM TS'M'AKS. *n.* precious coral; sponges, esp. dead man's fingers (*lit*: crab apple in the water). [sg̣anmɔ́·lksgm̥cʔm̥ʔáks] hb.

1676. SGANSÜXSAASÜX. *n.* thorn bush. [sg̣ànsíx̣sá·sɨx̣] m.

1677. SGATS'ÜÜ, SGATS'ÜTS'ÜÜ. *v.i.* ugly. [sg̣acʔɨ̄·] m,pr.
[sg̣acʔɨcʔɨ̄·] m.
1677.1 sxatsúu. [sx̣acʰú·ʌ] k.

1678. SGAWG. *v.i.* deaf; hard of hearing. [sg̣awg̣] m,pr.

1679. SGA'YA'A. *n.* curtains. [sg̣aʔyáʔa] m,pr.
1679.1 sga'yáak, sga'yáag-. [sg̣aʔyáʌqʰ] hb.
1679.2 sga'ya'ka. [sg̣aʔyáʔq̓a] m.

1680. SGAYTK, SGAYTG-. *n.* dark(ness). [sg̣aytʰkʰ] hb.
1680.1 sgeetk, sgeetg-. [sg̣e·t̄ʰkʰ] pr.
1680.2 sxaytk, sxaytg-, gyiksxaytk. [sx̣aytʰkʰ] k.
[gʸɩksx̣áyt̄ʰkʰ] k.

1681. SGII. *v.t.* put down; place. *v.i.* be lying on. [sgi·] pr.
1681.1 sgüü. [sgɨ̄·] hb,pr.

1681.2 sgüüłagwi. *Put it there.*
1681.3 sgüülagwa'a. *Put it here.*

1682. SGINIIS. *n.* jack pine. [sgɩní·s] hb.
1682.1 sgyiníist, sgyiníisd-. [sg^{y}ɩníʌst^{h}] pr.

1683. SGOKS. *v.i.* lack; miss; stop; leave off; be extended as far as possible; be short of; not to have enough. [sgoks] m.
1683.1 sgoksk, sgoksg-. [sgoksk^{h}] m.
1683.2 sgooksk, sgooksg-. [sgɔ·ksk^{h}] m.
1683.3 sgooksk, sgooksg-. [sgɔ·ksk^{h}] pr.

1684. SGOOX. *v.i.* first. [sgɔ·x̣] pr.

1685. SGÜGAT, SGÜGAD-. *v.i.* interested. *n.* interest. [sgɨgʌt^{h}] hb.

1686. SGÜÜ, LISGÜÜ, DOO, LAŁK. *v.t.* put down; lay down. *v.i.* lie down; be lying down. [sgɨ̆·] pr. [lisgɨ́·] m. [do·] pr. [lałk^{h}] pr.
1686.1 sgüümk, sgüümg-, gasgüümk. *n.* language of the Southern Tsimshians. [sgɨ̆·mq^{h}] m. [gɑsgɨ́·mq^{h}] m.
1686.2 sgüüxs. [sgɨ̆·x̣s] hb.

1687. SGWAYTK, SGWAYTG-, LISGWAYT, SIKSGWAYTK. *v.i.* stop; rest. [sg^{w}ayt^{h}k^{h}] m,pr. [lisg^{w}áyt^{h}] pr. [sɩksg^{w}áyt^{h}k^{h}] pr. Note: lisgwat is plural with human subject, siksgwaytk is plural with non-human subject.

1688. SGYAAMSM. *n.* sparrow hawk. [sg^{y}á·msm̩] pr.

1689. SGYEN, GAXSGYEN. *n.* lead; pitch; gum. [sg^{y}ɛn] k,pr. [gɑx̣sg^{y}ɛ́n] k.
1689.1 sgyin. [sg^{y}ɩn] pr.

1690. SGYEETK, SGYEETG-, SKATKTANIK. *v.i.* easy. [sg^{y}ɛ·t^{h}k^{h}] k.
1690.1 sketk, sketg-. [skɛt^{h}k^{h}] k.

1691. SGYET, SGYED-. *n.* spider. [sg^{y}ɛt^{h}] k,pr.
1691.1 sgyit, sgyid-. [sg^{y}ɩt^{h}] pr.
1691.2 sgyet, sgyed-, siksgyet. [sɩksg^{y}ɛ́t^{h}] k.

1692. SIGOOTK, SIGOOTG-. *v.t.* start thinking about; originate (of an idea). [sɩgɔ́·t^{h}k^{h}] m.
1692.1 sügootk, sügootg-. *v.t.* mind (pr); bring up (e.g., a topic of discussion) (m). [sɨgɔ́·t^{h}k^{h}], [sɨɣɔ́·t^{h}k^{h}] m,pr.

1693. SIGUUNAKS. *plural of* gyimł.

1694. SIGWAAN. *v.t. & v.i.* bake. [sɩg^{w}á·n] k,m.
1694.1 sügwaanał. *v.t. & v.i.* cook. [sɨg^{w}á·nʌł] hb,m.

1695. SIGYEMK, SIGYEMG-. *v.t. & v.i.* heat. [sɩg^{y}ɛ́mk^{h}] k,m.

1696. SIGYIDMHANA'A. *n.* princess; ma'am (polite form of address for any woman of any rank). [sɩg^{y}ìdm̩hánɑʔɑ] pr.

1696.1 sgyidmna'a. [sg^{y}ìdm̩ná?a] pr.

1697. SIGYOOTK, SIGYOOTG-. *plural of* sit'aatk.

1698. SIHÓON, GASIHON. *v.i.* smoke salmon. [sɩhɔ́ʌn] m,pr. [g̣àsɩhɔ́n] m,pr.

1699. SII, GASÜSII. *n.* shin bone; tibia; foot; sun ray. [si·] k. [g̣as+sí·] k.

1700. SIYIN. *n.* a root (Note: medicinal value). [sɩyɩ́n] pr.

1701. SIIBIBAN. *n.* Audobon's warbler. [si·bíbʌn] hb.

1702. SIIDZMWAS. *n.* flannel blanket; sheet. [sì·ʒm̩wʌ́s] m,pr.

1703. SIILGIT. *n.* the eldest one. [sí·lgɩt^{h}] m,pr.

1704. SIIN. *v.i.* dizzy. [si·n] pr.
1704.1 lüsiin. *v.i.* drunk. [l+sí·n] pr.

1705. SIIPGMGYIMK, SIIPGMGYIMG-. *v.i.* menstruate; have one's period. *n.* menstruation. [sí·pgm̩g^{y}ɩ́mk^{h}] m.

1706. SÍIPK, SÍIPG-, SISIIPK. *v.i.* sick. [siʌp^{h}k^{h}] k. [sɩsí·p^{h}k^{h}] hb,k.
1706.1 síi'pn. *v.t. & v.i.* love. [síʌ?p'n̩] pr.
1706.2 síi'pnsk, síi'pnsg-. *n.* friend. [síʌ?p'n̩sk^{h}] pr.

1707. SILAHANA'A. *n.* sister-in-law (address and reference: ♂BW if she is also his WZ). [sɩlahaná?a] k,m.

1708. SILAH'YU. *n.* brother-in-law (address and reference: ♀ZH if he is also her HB). [sɩlàh?yú] k,m.
1708.1 sila'yu. [sɩlà?yú] k.

1709. SILMDA'AXK, SILMDA'AXG-. *v.t.* get back. [sɩlm̩da?áx̣k^{h}] pr.

1710. SILMDOOX. *v.t.* take back. [sɩ̀lm̩dɔ́·x̣] pr.

1711. SILMYULAL. *v.i.* homesick. [sɩ̀lm̩yulál] k,m.

1712. SILUAAM. *v.t.* make happy. [sɩluá·m] k,m.

1713. SILUAMGÓOT, SILUAMGÓOD-. *v.i.* be happy (m); be surprised (k). [sɩluamg̣ɔ́ʌt^{h}] k,m.

1714. SI'NAA. *v.t.* bait. [sɩ?ná·] pr.

1715. SI'NAWOOX. *v.t.* admonish; warn. [sɩ̀?nʌwɔ́·x̣] k,m.

1716. SI'NDOONIK, SI'NDOONIG-. *n.* garden. [sɩ̀?n̩dɔ́·nɩk^{h}] pr.
1716.1 sndooyntk, sndooyntg-. [sn̩dɔ́·ynt^{h}k^{h}] k.

1717. SISDZOOXS. *v.i.* cohabit; play house. [sɩsʒɔ́·x̣s] pr,m.

1718. SISGWANGAATKS. *v.t.* implore. [sìsgʷʌngá·tʰks] m,pr.

1719. SISUUS. *plural of* ts'uusk.

1720. SIT'ÁA. *v.t. & v.i.* begin. [sɩtʔáʌ] m.
1720.1 sit'a'm. [sɩtʔáʔm] k.
1720.2 sit'aatk, sit'aatg-, sigyootk. *v.i.* start off (e.g., in a canoe or on skiis). [sɩtʔá·tʰkʰ] m,pr. [sɩgʸɔ́·tʰkʰ] pr.

1721. SITYAAWD. *v.t.* exchange; pay back; return. *v.i.* exchange; reciprocate. [sɩtʰyá·wd] m,pr.

1722. SITIYAWKSA. *v.t.* rinse out. [sɩtʰiyawksʌ] k.
1722.1 sityóoks. [sɩtʰyɔ́ʌks] m.

1723. SI'TSIL'UUMDEE. *n.* provisions; supplies. [sìʔcʼɩlʔú·mdɛ·] m,pr.

1724. SITYA'MSK, SITYA'MSG-. *v.t. & v.i.* dress. [sɨtʰyáʔmskʰ] k,m.

1725. SKAH. *n.* (Pacific) herring; American shad; alewife (*ichth*). [skʌh] hb,pr. *See also* tskah.

1726. SK'ÚUNSK, SK'ÚUNSG-, GASK'U'UNSK, SIKSKU'UNSK. *v.i.* teach. *n.* teacher. [skʔúʌnskʰ] k,m.
[gaskʔúʔunskʰ] (plural for noun and for subject of intransitive verb) k.
[sɩkskúʔunskʰ] (plural deleted object) k.
1726.1 sk'u'unt, sk'u'und-, siksk'u'nt. *v.t.* teach. [skʔúʔuntʰ] k. [sɩkskʔúʔuntʰ] k.

1727. SM'ALGYAX. *n.* language of the Coast Tsimshian. [sm̥ʔálgʸʌx̣] hb. Also used to refer to the old parent language of the three Tsimshianian languages, i.e., to proto-Tsimshian.

1728. SM'ALWILU. *n.* gunny sack; burlap. [sm̥ʔàlwɩlú] k,m,pr.
1728.1 smhagwilhuu. [sm̥hágʷɩlhú·] k,m,pr.

1729. SM'EESK, SM'EESG-. *n.* home brew; homemade berry wine. [sm̥ʔɛ́·skʰ] pr.

1730. SMGAN. *n.* cedar. [sm̥gạ́n] hb.

1731. SMGYIGYET, SMGYIGYED-. *n.* chief (address form); the nobility; councillors; talking chiefs; *plural of* sm'oogyit.

1732. SMGYIIK, SMGYIIG-. *n.* woodpecker. [sm̥gʸi·kʰ] pr.

1733. SMHAW. *v.i.* be sure. [sm̥háw] m,pr.
1733.1 smhawksn. *v.t.* believe. [sm̥háwksn̥] hb.

1734. SMHAWNAKS. *v.i.* be married. [sm̥hawnạ́ks] pr.

1735. SMHAYWAS. *n.* southeaster. [sm̥haywas] hb.

1736. SMHU'ADZAX. *n.* a brook. [sm̥huʔʌʒʌx̣] m,pr.

1737. SMII'KASK, SMII'KASG-. *n.* song sparrow. [sm̩í·ʔkʼaskʰ] hb.

1738. SMK'AWTSI. *n.* olachen grease. [sm̩qʔáwcʰi] pr.

1739. SMKSIIYATS, SMKSIIYADZ-. *v.t.* chop out. [sm̩ksi·yácʰ] m,pr.
 1739.1 smksiyets, smksiyedz-. [sm̩ksiyɛ́cʰ] m.
 1739.2 smksüüyats, smksüüyadz-. [sm̩ksɨ·yácʰ] pr.
 1739.3 smksüyets, smksüyedz-. [sm̩ksɨyɛ́cʰ] m.

1740. SMLAK, SMLAG-. *n.* open fire. [sm̩lʌ́kʰ] m,pr.

1741. SMMAY. *n.* (oval leaf) blueberry (*Vaccinium ovalifolium*). [sm̩máy] hb.

1742. SM'OOGYIT, SM'OOGYID-, SMGYIGYET. *n.* chief. [sm̩ʔɔ́·gʸɩtʰ] pr. [sm̩gʸigʸɛ́tʰ] hb,pr.
 1742.1 sm'ooygyit, sm'ooygyid-. [sm̩ʔɔ́·ygʸɩtʰ] hb.
 1742.2 sm'oygyit, sm'oygyid-. [sm̩ʔɔ̀ygʸɩtʰ] k.

1743. SM'UKSDOX. *v.t.* take out. [sm̩ʔuksdɔ́x̣] m,pr.

1744. SMWÜS. *n.* blanket. [sm̩wɨs] pr.

1745. SMXSO. *n.* dugout canoe; pirogue; Indian canoe.

1746. SMYA'AWIN. *n.* right hand. [sm̩yáʔʌwɩn] k.
 1746.1 smya'awn. [sm̩yáʔʌwn̩] pr.

1747. S'NDZOKS. *v.i.* make camp. [sʔn̩ʒɔ́qs] pr.

1748. SNLAYDITSKS. *v.i.* signal; make a sign. [sn̩láydɩcʰks] m,pr.

1749. SNYÉEKWT, SNYÉEKWD-. *v.t.* hold. [sn̩yéʌkʷʰtʰ] k,m.

1750. SOO. *n.* food taken from a feast to be redistributed. [sɔ·] m.

1751. SO'AX. *n.* robin. [sɔ́ʔax̣] k,m.
 1751.1 sóo'k, sóo'g-. [soʌʔqʼ] k,m.
 1751.2 so'ek, so'eg-. *v.i.* early. [šɔ́ʔeqʰ] m.
 1751.3 soog. *n.* the early morning. [sɔ·g̣] m,pr.

1752. SP'AA. *v.i.* beat time. *n.* percussion stick (a percussion instrument used in dances). [spʔa·] pr.

1753. SPAGAYT-, SPAGAYD- among; between. [spáɣ̣aytʰ] hb.

1754. SPANAXNOX. *n.* supernatural being; place where a supernatural being dwells (Note: always in the sea). [spanax̣nɔ́x̣] pr.

1755. SPA'OL. *n.* bear den. [spʌʔɔ́l] pr.

1756. SPASAAMI. *n.* bear den. [spʌsá·mi] pr.

1757. SPAYGANGAN. *n.* forest. [spaygạngạ́n] k,m.

1758. SPEEXSK, SPEEXSG-. *v.i.* weave cedarbark. [spe·x̣skʰ] m,pr.

1759. SPINOOꞭ. *n.* shoulder blades. [spɩnɔ́·ɬ] hb.

1760. STAHYAA. *v.i.* continue; keep going. [stʌhyá·] m,pr.

1761. STAKALAAꞭ. *v.t.* follow; keep track of. [stʌkʰalá·ɬ] m,pr.

1762. STA'ONM HAXBÉEXSK. *n.* carpenter saw (*lit:* hand on one side saw). [st̄ʰa̅ʔɔ́nm̥hax̣bɛ́·ʌx̣skʰ] hb.

1763. STIMBÓODMGYILHAWLI. *n.* train; steam locomotive. Note: neologism. [stīmbóʌdm̥gʸɩlháwli] hb.

1764. STI'MOON, STI'MOON. *n.* humpback salmon; pink salmon. [stɩʔmɔ́·n] k.
1764.1 stm'oon. [stm̥ʔɔ́·n] pr.
1764.2 stmóon. [stm̥ɔ̓ʌn] hb.

1765. STOX, LAXSTOX. *v.i.* sleep. [stɔx̣] k. [lax̣stɔ́x̣] k.

1766. STS'OOL. *n.* beaver. [scʔɔ·l] hb.
1766.1 sts'óol [scʔɔʌl] k,pr.

1767. STS'OOLALOP, STS'OOLALOB-. *n.* marine isopods. [scʔɔ́·lalɔ́pʰ] hb.
1767.1 süts'oolalop, süts'oolalob-. [sɨcʔɔ́·lalɔ́pʰ] hb.

1768. STUKWLIIN. *n.* rabbit. [stukʷlí·n] hb.
1768.1 stükwlíin. [stɨkʷlíʌn] hb.
1768.2 stukliin. [stuklí·n] k.
1768.3 stükwɬiin. [stɨkʷʰɬí·n] m.
1768.4 stükwɬíin. [stɨkʷʰɬí·ʌn] pr.

1769. STÜTI. *n.* nettles. [stɨ́ti] m.

1770. STUUL, SÜKSTUUL. *v.t.* accompany. [stu·l] hb. [sɨkstú·l] hb.
1770.1 stúul. [stu·ʌl] pr.

1771. STÚUNꞭ, GASTÚUNꞭ. *v.i.* whisper. [stu·ʌnɬ] k. [g̣astu·ʌnɬ] k.

1772. STUU'PL. *n.* back of house; rear of house. [stu·ʔpʾl̥] pr.

1773. ST'U'UTSK, ST'U'UTSG-. *v.t.* blacken; make black. [stʔúʔucʰkʰ] k,m.

1774. SU- new. [su] m,pr.

1775. SÜGWALAK, SÜGWALAG-. *v.i.* start a fire. [sɨ̆gʷálʌkʰ], [s̄ɨgʷálʌkʰ] hb,m.

1776. SUGYET, SUGYED-, SUGYEDMGYET. *n.* a murderer (Note: plural form indicates a murderer of more than one victim). [sugʸɛ́tʰ] m,pr. [sugʸɛ̀dm̥gʸɛ́tʰ] m,pr.

1777. SUKYOOXT. *n.* fresh grass. [sukʸʰɔ́·x̣tʰ] pr.

1778. SÜLAKS. *v.i.* build a fire. [sɨlʌ́ks] pr.
1778.1 süleks. [sɨlɛ́ks] pr.

1779. SUWILIIN. *v.t.* bother; chase; go after. [suwɩlí·n] m,pr.
1779.1 süwiliin. [sɨwɩlí·n] k,m.
1779.2 suwalíinsk, suwalíinsg-. [suwalíʌnskʰ] pr.
1779.3 süwiliinsk, süwiliinsg-. *n.* hunter. [sɨwɩlí·nskʰ] k.
1779.4 suwiliinsk, suwiliinsg-. [suwɩlí·nskʰ] hb.
1779.5 suliinsk, suliinsg-. [sulí·nskʰ] k,pr.
1779.6 sulíinsk, sulíinsg-. [sulí·ʌnskʰ] pr.

1780. SÜLUUNA. *v.t.* dry. [sɨlú·nɑ] pr.

1781. SÜMAALSK, SÜMAALSG-. *v.i.* tell a lying story. *v.t.* betray. [sɨma·lskʰ] m,pr.

1782. SUMAXS. *plural of* sup'as.

1783. SÜMELA. *v.i.* hurry up. [sɨmɛ́lɑ] m,pr.

1784. SUMSIKSWANTK, SUMSIKSWANTG-. *plural of* swantk.

1785. SUNAAŁ. *v.i.* tired. [suná·ɬ] hb,k,pr.
1785.1 suunaał. [su·na·ɬ] pr.

1786. SUP'AS, SUMAXS. *v.i.* young. *n.* a young person. [supʔás] pr. [sumáx̣s] pr.

1787. SÜS'AAKS, LÜSA'AAXS. *v.t.* make laugh; *v.i.* laugh. [sɨsʔá·qs] pr. [lɨsaʔá·x̣s] pr.
1787.1 süs'aaxs. [sɨsʔá·x̣s] k,pr.

1788. SÜTYEEL. *v.t.* trade. [sɨtʰyɛ́·l] k,m.

1789. SUU. *v.i.* swing. [su·] pr.

1790. SUU. *v.i.* go ahead; have permission. [su·] pr.

1791. SÜÜ. *n.* mouth of a river. [sɨ̈·]pr.

1792. SUUGYE'AWIN. *adv.* just now. [su·gʸɛ́ʔʌwɩn] pr.

1793. SÜÜLGAS. *n.* forenoon. [sɨ̈·lgʌs] pr.

1794. SUULG. *v.i.* dreaded; dangerous. *n.* something fearful; center; middle; hip (*anat*); waist (*anat*). [su·lg] pr.
1794.1 süülg. [sɨ̈·lg] pr.
1794.2 süülk, süülg-. [sɨ̈·lkʰ] k.

1795. SÜÜLGA'AATK, SÜÜLGA'AATG-. *n.* midnight. [sɨ̈·lgɑʔá·tʰkʰ] pr.
1795.1 süülga'áatk, süülga'áatg-. [sɨ̈·lgaʔáʌtʰkʰ] hb.

1796. SÜÜLGASAH. *n.* noon. [sɨ̈·lgasáh] hb.

1797. SUUL'KNSK, SUUL'KNSG-. *v.i.* hesitate; despair (Note: because something is too difficult or dangerous). [sú·l?k̓n̩skʰ] m,pr.

1798. SUUNS, GASUUNS. *v.i.* blind. [su·ns] hb,k,pr. [g̣asú·ns] k.

1799. SUUNSM'YUUT, SUUNSM'YUUT-. *n.* blind man. [sù·nsm̩?yú·tʰ] pr.

1800. SUUNT, SUUND-, GYIKSUUNT. *n.* summer. [su·ntʰ] hb,k.
1800.1 súunt, súund-. [su·ʌntʰ] k,pr.

1801. SUUWANOO. *v.t.* bother; pester. [su·wanó·] k,m.
1801.1 suwanoyx. [suwanóyx̣] k,m.
1801.2 suwüno. *v.t.* tease; pester. *v.i.* complain. [suwɨnɔ́] m.

1802. SUU'WEENTK, SUU'WEENTG-. *v.i.* have teeth erupt. *n.* false teeth; dentures. [su·?wɛ́·ntʰkʰ] m,pr.
1802.1 su'weentk, su'weentg-. [su?wɛ́·ntʰkʰ] m.

1803. SÜWIIHÓON. *n.* twins. [sɨwi·hɔ́ʌn] m,pr. *lit:* makes big fish.

1804. SUWILAAY'MSK, SUWILAAY'MSG-. *v.i.* teach. *n.* teacher. [suwɩlá·y?m̩skʰ] m.

1805. SÜXSAASÜX. *n.* thorn bush. [sɨxsa·sɨx] pr.

1806. SÜ'YENS. *n.* springtime. [sɨ?yɛ́ns] m.

1807. SWAN. *v.t.* blow (Note: reference includes but it not restricted to the shamanistic curing practice). [swan] hb. [swʌn] pr.
1807.1 swantk, sumsikswantk. *v.i.* blow. [swʌntʰkʰ] k. [sùmsɩkswʌ́ntʰkʰ] k.

1808. SWEDA, SIKSWEDA. *n.* sweater (neologism). [swɛ́da] hb. [sɩkswɛ́da] hb.

1809. SWETMTS'AALXS. *n.* sweater coat. [swɛ̀tʰm̩c?á·lx̣s] hb.

1810. SXAT'UUSA. *n.* dam. [sx̣at?ú·sa] m,pr.

1811. SXAYTSK, SXAYTSG-, SAXSAYTSK. *v.t.* hurt; wound. [sx̣aycʰkʰ] k. [sʌx̣sáycʰkʰ] k.

1812. S'YAAN. *n.* ocean floor; lake bottom. [s?ya·n] pr.

1813. S'YOON. *n.* glacier. [s?yɔ·n] pr.
1813.1 s'yóon. *n.* snow slide; avalanche. [s?yɔ·ʌn] m.

T

1814. T'AA, WAN. *v.i.* sit. *n.* lake. [t?a·] k,pr. [wan] k,pr (Note: plural for verb only).
1814.1 t'áa. [t?a·ʌ] k,pr.

1815. -T'A'A. deceased (used as a suffix for kinship terms). [t?á?a] k.

1816. TAAGAN. *n.* planking (*naut*). [tʰa·gán] hb.
  1816.1 taagandmbóot. [tʰa·gándm̥boʌtʰ] hb.

1817. T'AAK, T'AAG-. *n.* whirlwind. [tʔa·qʰ] m.
  1817.1 t'ak, t'ag-. [tʔɑqʰ] hb.
  1817.2 t'a'k, t'a'g- *v.t.* wind; wring out. *n.* water spout. [tʔɑʔkʼ] hb.
  1817.3 t'aakyil. *v.t.* twist. [tʔá·kʸʰɩl] hb.
  1817.4 t'a'kyl. [tʔáʔkʸʼḷ] hb.

1818. TAALSGMTS'ÓOXS, TIKTAALSGMTS'ÓOXS. *n.* hose; socks; stockings. [tʰá·lsgm̥cʔɔ́·ʌx̣s] hb. [tʰɩktʰá·lsgm̥cʔɔ́·ʌx̣s] hb.

1819. T'ÁA'Pɬ, T'ÜPT'ÁA'Pɬ. *v.i.* hammer (Note: plural form denotes to hammer repeatedly it does not mark a plural subject). [tʔaʌʔpʼɬ] hb. [tʔɨptʔáʌʔpʼɬ] hb.

1820. T'ÁA'PNSK, T'ÁA'PNSG-. *n.* nail (building tool). [tʔáʌʔpʼn̥skʰ] m. *See also* txáa'pnsk.
  1820.1 t'aa'pnsxk, t'aa'pnsxg-. [tʔá·ʔpʼn̥sx̣kʰ] hb.
  1820.2 t'áa'pxnsk, t'áa'pxnsg-. [tʔaʌʔpʼx̣n̥skʰ] hb.

1821. T'AAS. *n.* arrow; bird arrow; toy arrow; spearhead. [tʔa·s] hb,m.
  1821.1 t'aax. [tʔa·x̣] hb.

1822. T'A'AWIL, T'A'AWIL. *n.* halibut hook (hb,k); trolling hook (k,m). [tʔáʔawɩl] hb,k,m.
  1822.1 t'a'wil. [tʔáʔwɩl] hb,k,m.
  1822.2 t'a'awül. [tʔáʔawɨl] hb.
  1822.3 t'a'awl. [tʔáʔawḷ] hb.

1823. T'AGAAɬ. *n.* olachen nets (Note: made of nettles fibre). [tʔagá·ɬ] hb.

1824. T'A'Iɬ. *v.i.* bend (causative intransitive). [tʔáʔiɬ] k,m.

1825. T'A'K, T'A'G-, T'IKT'A'K. *n.* terrace (*spec*: subterranean terraces over which a house is built). [tʔʌʔkʼ] hb. [tʔɩktʔʌʔkʼ] hb.

1826. T'AK, T'AG-. *n.* cedar bark (*spec*: when it is so sticky that you can't pull it off the tree). [tʔɑqʰ] m.

1827. T'ALWEYT, T'ALWEYD-. *v.t.* meet. [tʔalwέytʰ] k.

1828. T'APXAAT, T'APXAAD-. *num.* two (of flat objects). [tʔʌpx̣á·tʰ] hb,m,pr.

1829. T'APXADUUL. *num.* two (of humans). [tʔʌpx̣ɑdú·l] hb,m,pr.

1830. T'APXALDOOL. *num.* seven (of humans). [tʔʌpx̣ɑldɔ́·l] hb,m,pr.

1831. T'APXOOLDAAT, T'APXOOLDAAD-. *num.* seven (of persons aboard a conveyance). [tʔʌpx̣ɔ́·ldá·tʰ] hb,m,pr.

1832. T'APXOOLDA'ON. *num.* seven (of measures). *n.* seven fathoms.
[tʔʌpx̣ɔ́·ldaʔɔ́n] hb,m,pr.

1833. T'APXOOLSXN. *num.* seven (of long objects). [tʔʌpx̣ɔ́·lsx̣n̩] hb.

1834. T'APXOOLD. *num.* seven (of round or flat objects). [tʔʌpx̣ɔ́·ld] hb,m,pr.
1834.1 t'apxoolt, t'apxoold-. [tʔʌpx̣ɔ́·ltʰ] hb,m,pr.

1835. T'APXOOLTK, T'APXOOLTG-. *num.* seven (of canoes). [tʔʌpx̣ɔ́·ltʰkʰ] hb,m,pr.

1836. T'APXOOLTSXN. *num.* seven (of long objects). [tʔʌpx̣ɔ́·lcʰx̣n̩] hb,m,pr.

1837. T'AWGOGAT, T'AWGOGAD-. *plural of* xsolk.

1838. T'AXT'ÓOSK, T'AXT'ÓOSG-. *n.* golden shiner (*Notemigonus crysoleucas*); minnow. [tʔʌx̣tʔɔ́·ʌskʰ] m.
1838.1 t'axtẋóogn. [tʔax̣tx̣ɔ́·ʌg̣n̩] hb.

1839. T'AXT'OOX. *v.t. & v.i.* suck. [tʔax̣tʔɔ́·x̣] hb.

1840. T'AXWANS, T'AXWANS. *n.* adze. [tʔax̣wʌ́ns] hb. *See also* daxwans.

1841. T'AXYAAKW, T'AXYAAGW-. *v.t.* hold. [tʔax̣yá·kʷʰ] m.
1841.1 t'axyakw, t'axyagw-. [tʔax̣yákʷʰ] k.

1842. T'ÉES. *n.* bowstring. [tʔe·ʌs] m,pr.

1843. T'EEG-. *v.i.* eat ravenously. [tʔe·g̣] hb.
1843.1 t'ex. [tʔɛx̣] k,m.

1844. TGWAH. *n.* glass; any glass object. [tʰgʷah] hb.

1845. T'IIBN. *n.* sea lion; walrus. [tʔí·bn̩] hb,k,m,pr.
1845.1 t'íibn. [tʔíʌbn̩] hb,k,m,pr.

1846. T'I'IK, T'I'IG-. *n.* navel. [tʔíʔikʰ] pr.

1848. T'IIL. *v.i.* fast (in getting something accomplished). [tʔi·l] hb.
1848.1 t'iild. [tʔi·ld] m,pr.
1848.2 t'iilt, t'iild-, lilt'iild. [tʔi·ltʰ] k. [lɩltʔí·ld] k.
1848.3 t'iin. [tʔi·n] hb.

1849. T'IIMUU. *n.* leech. [tʔi·mú·] hb.

1850. T'ÍIN. *n.* fish trap. [tʔiʌn] m,pr.

1851. T'IISK, T'IISG-. *v.t. & v.i.* forget. [tʔi·skʰ] hb.

1852. TKADZEMSK, TKADZEMSG-, TKADZEMSK. *n.* boiled whole fish.
[tʰkaʒέmskʰ] k. [tʰkaʒέmskʰ] k.

1853. T'K'UULTK, T'K'UULTG-. *v.i.* crooked; twisted. [tʔkʔú·lt^hk^h] hb.

1854. TKWABÁANL. *v.i.* spin. [t^hk^wʌbá·ʌnɬ] m,pr.

1855. TKWIDZOOX. *n.* outside edge. [t^hk^wiʒɔ́·x̣] m,pr.

1856. TKYI- down; downward. [t^hk^yi] hb,m,pr.

1857. TKYIDAAWL. *v.i.* sink. [t^hk^yɩdá·wɬ] m,pr.

1858. TKYIDZÓOL. *v.i.* slide down. [t^hk^yiʒɔ́·ʌl] m,pr.

1859. TKYI'NIITSK, TKYI'NIITSG-. *v.i.* look down. [t^hk^yiʔní·c^hk^h] m,pr.

1860. TKYIT'UUS. *v.t.* knead; press down. [t^hk^yitʔú·s] m,pr.

1861. TKYIYAA. *v.i.* go down (to); walk down (to); descend (to). *n.* dusk. [t^hk^yiyá·] m,pr.

1862. T'MBA. *n.* hip and upper leg (above the knee). [tʔm̩bá] hb.
 1862.1 t'mbaa. [tʔm̩bá·] pr.

1863. T'MGAWS. *n.* head. [tʔm̩gáws] pr.

1864. T'MGAY. *n.* arm (pr); shoulder (k). [tʔm̩gáy] k,pr.

1865. T'MK'O. *n.* backbone; vertebrae. [tʔm̩qʔó] hb.

1866. T'MKYAA, T'MWAALXS. *v.i.* walk to the front; step out. [tʔm̩kyá·] hb. [tʔm̩wá·lx̣s] hb.

1867. T'MLAANI, T'IKT'MLAANI. *n.* neck. [tʔm̩lá·ni] k,pr. [tʔɩktʔm̩lá·ni] k,pr.

1868. T'MLAAM. *n.* leg (below the knee). [tʔm̩ɬá·m] pr.
 1868.1 t'mlam. *n.* shin bone; tibia. [tʔm̩ɬám] pr.

1869. T'MMIIS. *v.t.* & *v.i.* paint; write. *n.* a painting; written material. [tʔm̩mí·s] hb.

1870. T'MYAA. *v.i.* fast (in motion). *n.* a fast-moving thing. [tʔm̩yá·] hb,pr.

1871. T'OOK, T'OOG-. *v.t.* & *v.i.* suck. [tʔɔ·q^h] pr.
 1871.1 t'óok, t'óog-. [tʔɔ́·ʌq^h] m.
 1871.2 t'oox. [tʔɔ·x̣] pr.
 1871.3 da'óox. [dʌʔɔ́·ʌx̣] m.

1872. T'ÓOL. *n.* snout of a bull sea elephant; sack of a bull hooded seal. [tʔoʌl] hb.

1873. T'OO'TSIP, T'OO'TSIB-. *n.* fort; fortress (*spec*: the cone of an extinct volcano used as a place of refuge and owned by a particular lineage. In latter times they were used as gardens).

[t?ɔ́·?cʾɩp^{h}] k,m.
1873.1 t'o'otsip, t'o'otsib-. [t?ɔ́?ɔc^{h}ɩp^{h}] k,m.
1873.2 t'uu'tsip, t'uu'tsib-. [t?ú·?cʾɩp^{h}] k,m.
1873.3 t'u'utsip, t'u'utsib-. [t?ú?uc^{h}ɩp^{h}] k,m.

1874. T'OYAKS. *v.t.* say goodbye to; thank. [t?ɔ́yʌqs] m.
1874.1 t'oyust, t'oyusd-. [t?ɔ́yust^{h}] pr.

1875. T'UUS. *v.t.* push. [t?u·s] pr.
1875.1 t'uuskm t'uusg-. *v.t.* & *v.i.* sweep. [t?u·sk^{h}] k.
1875.2 t'usk, t'usg-, lilt'usk. [t?usk^{h}] k. [lɩlt?usk^{h}] k.

1876. T'U'U'TSGM'OL. *n.* black bear. [t?ú?u?cʾgṃ?ɔ́l] hb.

1877. T'U'UTSK, T'U'UTSG-. *v.i.* black (colour). *n.* iron; knife; butcher knife; black (colour). [t?u?uc^{h}k^{h}] hb,k,pr.
1877.1 t'u'usk, t'u'usg-. [t?ú?usk^{h}] k.
1877.2 t'ut'u'usk, t'ut'u'usg-. plural for *knife* only. [t?ut?ú?usk^{h}] k.
1877.3 nadist'u'utsk, nadist'u'utsg-. plural for *black* only. [nadɩst?ú?uc^{h}k^{h}] k.
1877.4 t'o'tsk, t'o'tsg-. *v.i.* & *n.* black (colour). Note: archaic in hb. [t?o?c^{h}k^{h}] hb.

1878. TXA'AAXT, TXA'AAXD-. *n.* place in front of door; place outside of house. [tx̣a?á·x̣t^{h}] k,m.

1879. TXAALPDAAT, TXAALPDAAD-. *num.* four (persons aboard a conveyance). [txa·lpda·t^{h}] hb.
1879.1 txalpdaat, txalpdaad-. [tx̣alpdá·t^{h}] hb,m,pr.

1880. TXAALPX. *num.* four (of round or flat objects). [tx̣a·lpx̣] hb,m,pr.

1881. TXAALPXL'ON. *num.* four (of measures). *n.* four fathoms. [tx̣á·lpx̣ḷ?ɔ́n] hb,m,pr.

1882. TXAALPXSK, TXAALPXSG-. *num.* four (of canoes). [tx̣a·lpx̣sk^{h}] hb,m,pr.

1883. TXAAMSM. *n.* Raven, the Culture Hero. [tx̣á·msṃ] m,pr.

1884. TXAAP, TXAAB-. *num.* four (of abstract, round, and flat objects). [txa·p^{h}] hb.
1884.1 txalp, txalb-. *num.* four (of flat objects). [tx̣alp^{h}] hb.

1885. TXAA'PNSK, TXAA'PNSG-. *n.* nail (building tool). [tx̣á·?pʾṇsk^{h}] pr.

1886. TXA'APSXN. *num.* four (of long objects). *n.* four half-fathoms. [tx̣ā́?apsx̣ṇ] hb,m,pr.

1887. TXAL- against. [tx̣al] hb.

1888. TXALAAM. *v.i.* be good for (requires a human in benefactive case). [tx̣alá·m] k,m.

1889. TXALAAN. *v.i.* be behind (in place); be after. [tx̣alá·n] pr.

1890. TXALPXDOOL. *num.* four (of persons). [tx̣alpdɔ́·l] hb,m,pr.

1891. TXALYAA. *v.i.* develop; enlarge; expand; grow; increase. [tx̣alya·] k,m.
1891.1 Txalyaa baask. *The wind is getting stronger.*
1891.2 Txalyaa sgeetk. *It's getting dark.*

1892. TXANAAẄ. *n.* mooring; landing place (*spec*: the one just down from the speaker's house). [tx̣aná·ÿ] m.

1893. TXA'NII. *v.i.* all. [tx̣aʔní·] hb,m.

1894. TXA'OOGASTETI. *n.* stinging nettle (*Urtica dioica*); hedge nettle (*Stachys cooleyae*). [tx̣aʔɔ́·gastʰɛ́tʰi] hb.

1895. TXAS- along the surface. [tx̣as] hb.

1896. TXAW, TXAW. *n.* halibut. [tx̣aw] hb,k,m,pr. [tx̣aw] k.

1897. TXOOXK, TXOOXG-, 'YAAK, 'YAAX. *v.t.* & *v.i.* eat. [tx̣ɔ·x̣kʰ] k,m. [ʔya·qʰ] k. [ʔya·x̣] k.
1897.1 t'xok, t'xog-. [tʔx̣okʰ] k.

1898. TS'A'A. *n.* clam. [cʔáʔa] m.
1898.1 ts'a'ag. [cʔáʔag] pr.
1898.2 ts'ak, ts'ag-, gȧdzak. [cʔaqʰ] k,m. [g̣aʒaqʰ] k.

1899. TS'A'ADZIKS, TS'A'AKSIKS. *v.i.* dirty; dusty; soiled. *n.* dirt; dust. [cʔáʔaʒɩks] hb,m. [cʔáʔaksɩks] hb,m.
1899.1 ts'a'adziks. [cʔáʔaʒɩks] pr.
1899.2 ts'a'aks. [cʔáʔaks] k.
1899.3 ts'a'iks. [cʔáʔɩks] k.

1900. TS'AAL. *v.i.* filet fish; cut salmon for smoking. *n.* half-smoked salmon. [cʔa·l] m,pr.
1900.1 ts'aal. [cʔʌ·l] m.

1901. TS'AALBIKSN. *v.t.* wring out. [cʔá·lbɩksn̩] pr.

1902. TS'AANS. *n.* armpit. [cʔa·ns] k.
1902.1 TS'MTS'AANS. [cʔm̩cʔá·ns] k.

1903. TS'AA'TS, TS'AA'DZ-. *v.i.* pull out (extract) an arrow. [cʔa·ʔcˀ] pr.

1904. TS'AAW. *n.* viscera; insides of body; inside part of anything. [cʔa·w] k,m.
1904.1 ts'aaẅ. [cʔa·ÿ] k,m,pr.

1905. TS'ÁAWIL. *v.t.* rob. [cʔáʌwɩl] m.
1905.1 ts'a'wił. [cʔaʔwɩł] pr.

1906. TS'AAY. *v.i.* be full; burp. [cʔá·y] pr.

1907. TS'AGM'AAX. *v.i.* be hungry. [c?ʌgṃ?á·x̣] pr.

1908. TS'AGMGAYT, TS'AGMGAYD-. *n.* cap (*lit*: nose on the hat). [c?ág̣ṃgáyt^h] m,pr.

1909. TS'AGYAGYEMK, TS'AGYAGYEMG-. *n.* old moon. [c?ágʸʌgʸέmk^h] hb.
   1909.1 ts'akyagyemk, ts'akyagyemg-. [c?ákʸ^hʌgʸέmk^h] m.

1910. TS'AK, TS'AG-. *n.* China slipper; giant chiton; gumboot. [c?ak^h] hb,k.

1911. TS'AK, TS'AG-. *n.* clam. [c?ɑq^h] hb.
   1911.1 ts'ak, ts'ag-. [c?ɑk^h] hb.
   1911.2 ts'ax, ts'ag-. [c?ɑx̣] hb.

1912. TS'AK, TS'AG-, GATS'AA'TSAX. *n.* nose. [c?ɑq^h] m. [g̣ɑc?á·?c'ʌx̣] pr.
   1912.1 ts'ax, ts'ag-. [c?ɑx̣] pr.

1913. TS'AKSNÁAS, TS'AKTS'AKSNÁAS. *n.* bracelet. [c?ʌksnáʌs] k. [c?ʌ̀ks?ʌksnáʌs] k.
   1913.1 ts'üksnaaxs. [c?ɨksná·x̣s] hb.

1914. TS'AKTS'IIK, TS'AKTS'IIG-. *n.* wagon; automobile; vehicle; anything with wheels. [c?ʌkc?í·k^h] pr.

1915. TS'AKY, TS'AGY-, TS'AKYTS'AK. *v.i.* be out (of a fire); be extinguished. [c?akʸ^h] k,m,pr. [c?ʌkʸ^hc?ák^h] pr.

1916. TS'AL, TS'IKTSALT. *n.* face; eyes. [c?al] k,m. [c?ɩkc^hált^h] k.
   1916.1 ts'al. *n.* eye [c?ʌl] m.
   1916.2 ts'e'l. *n.* face; eyes. [c?ε?l] pr.

1917. TS'ALAA, TS'ÜKTS'ALAA. *n.* (large) basket (hb,m); basket for fish (k); anything in a basket (pr). [c?ʌlá·] hb,pr. [c?ɨkc?ʌlá·] hb.
   1917.1 ts'elaa. [c?εlá·] k,m.
   1917.2 ts'ilaa. [c?ɩlá·] hb,pr.

1918. TS'ALAASÜ. *n.* canyon; gorge; rapids. [c?ʌlá·sɨ̆] k,pr.
   1918.1 ts'elaasik, ts'akts'alaasik. [c?εlá·sɩk^h] k. [c?ʌ̀ks?ʌlá·sɩk^h] k.

1919. TS'ALAAY. *v.t.* visit. [c?ʌlá·y] m.
   1919.1 ts'alaayüü. [c?ʌlá·yɨ̆·] pr.

1920. TS'ALAKS. *n.* whirlpool. [c?alʌks] pr.
   1920.1 ts'alaks. [c?ʌlʌks] m,pr.
   1920.2 ts'a'lks, ts'iktsa'lks. [c?a?lks] k. [c?ɩkc?á?lks] k.
   1920.3 ts'elaks. [c?εlʌks] pr.

1921. TS'AMTI. *n.* lightning. [c?ámt^hi] k.
   1921.1 ts'amti. [c?ʌmt^hi] pr.
   1921.2 ts'mti. [c?ḿt^hi] hb.
   1921.3 ts'its'amti. *n.* thunderbird. [c?ic?ámt^hi] k.

1922. TS'AP, TS'AB, TS'APTS'AP. *n.* town; tribe. [cʔapʰ] k. [cʔʌpcʔápʰ] k̄.
 1922.1 ts'apɨ. *v.i.* take cooked food out of the fire.
 1922.2 ts'apts'ap, ts'apts'ab-. *n.* wren; tomtit. [cʔʌpcʔápʰ] pr.

1923. TS'AS. *n.* golden eyed sea duck; whistler (*orn*); tree duck; wood duck. [cʔas] hb.

1924. TS'ATS'A. *n.* hail. [cʔacʔá] pr.
 1924.1 ts'a'tsa. [cʔáʔcʼʌ] k.
 1924.2 ts'ats'aa. [cʔacʔá·] hb.

1925. TS'ATS'AAWD. *n.* Athapascan Indian. [cʔʌcʔá·wd] m,pr.

1926. TS'AWAAL. *n.* finger. [cʔʌwá·l] pr.
 1926.1 ts'üüwald. [cʔɨ̈·wáld] pr.

1927. TS'AWES. *n.* smiling berries; salal (*Gaultheria shallon*). [cʔɑwɛ́s] hb.

1928. TS'AWX, GATS'AWGYIT. *v.i.* deaf. [cʔawx̣] k. [gɑcʔáwgʸɩtʰ] k.
 1928.1 ts'éeg. [cʔe·ʌg] pr.
 1928.2 ts'éex. [cʔe·ʌx̣] pr.

1929. TS'ASKW, TS'ASGW-, TS'AKTS'ASKW. *n.* louse; lice. [cʔaskʷʰ] k. [cʔʌkcʔáskʷʰ] k.
 1929.1 ts'eskw, ts'esgw-. [cʔɛskʷʰ] pr.

1930. TS'II, LAMDZAX. *v.i.* come in; go in; enter. [cʔ·] k,pr. [lámʒʌx̣] pr.

1931. TS'I'I. *n.* grandmother (address: MM, FM, MMZ, FMZ).

1932. TS'ÍIBASEE. *v.i.* be overcast (*lit*: The sky closes its eyes). [cʔí·ʌbʌsɛ́·]

1933. TS'ÍIGA. *n.* top shells. [cʔí·ʌgɑ] hb.
 1933.1 ts'íik, ts'íig-. *v.i.* be leaking. [cʔi·ʌkʰ] m,pr.

1934. TS'IIŁ. *n.* (common) snipe; sandpiper. [cʔi·ɬ] hb.

1935. TS'IINGYEMK, TS'IINGYEMG-. *n.* eclipse. [cʔí·ngʸɛ́mkʰ] hb.

1936. TS'IINGYIGM'AATK, TS'IINGYIGM'AATG-. *n.* eclipse of the moon. [cʔí·ngʸigm̥ʔá·tʰkʰ] hb.

1937. TS'IIP, TS'IIB-. *v.t.* tie; tie up. [cʔi·pʰ] m,pr.
 1937.1 ts'íip, ts'íib-. [cʔi·ʌpʰ] m,pr.

1938. TS'IIWKWSA. *v.i.* bail out a canoe. [cʔí·wkʷʰsɑ] m.

1939. TS'IŁINA'A, TS'ÜKTS'IŁINA'A. *n.* apron. [cʔiɬináʔɑ] hb.
 1939.1 ts'iɬina'ka. [cʔiɬináʔqʼɑ] hb.

1940. TS'IYOOLGY. *n.* kingfisher; bullroar. [c?iyɔ́·lgʸ] pr.
1940.1 ts'iyoolky, ts'iyoolgy-. [c?iyɔ́·lkʸʰ] pr.
1940.2 ts'iyoolk, ts'iyoolg-. [c?iyɔ́·lkʰ] hb.
1940.3 ts'ioolk, ts'ioolg-. [c?iɔ́·lkʰ] k.

1941. TSKAH, TSKAH. *n.* (Pacific) herring; alewife; American shad. [cʰkah] k. *See also* sgah.
1941.1 tskah. [cʰkʌh] k.

1942. TS'LMGAA, TS'LMT'AA. *v.t.* take in. [c?l̩m̩gá·] m,pr. [c?l̩m̩t?á·] pr.
1942.1 ts'lmgáa. [c?l̩m̩gá·ʌ] m.

1943. TS'LM'MA'A. *v.t.* roast; put in the oven. [c?l̩m̩?má?a] k,m.

1944. TS'LMT'AA. *plural of* ts'lmgaa.

1945. TS'LM'WIIHAAW. *v.i.* call out while coming into a house; give greeting; announce oneself. [c?l̩m̩?wí·há·w] pr.

1946. TS'M'AATK, TS'M'AATG-, TS'ÜTS'MAATK. *v.i.* sweet. [c?m̩?á·tʰkʰ] k,m,pr. [c?ɨc?m̩á·tʰkʰ] k.

1947. TS'M'AAX, TS'M'AAG-. *n.* mouth. [c?m̩?á·x̣] m,pr.

1948. TS'MAAY. *n.* barnacles; greatgrandparents; greatgrandchildren. [c?m̩á·y] hb.

1949. TS'M'AN'ON. *n.* palm of hand. [c?m̩?an?ɔ́n] k.

1950. TS'MGAL. *n.* anus. [c?m̩gál] m.
1950.1 ts'mgéelm. [c?m̩gé·ʌlm̩] m.

1951. TS'MGA'NA. *n.* door frame; window frame. [c?m̩gá?na] hb.

1952. TS'MHON. *n.* red cod; red snapper. [c?m̩hɔ́n] hb.
1952.1 ts'mhoon, ts'ikts'imhoon. *n.* grey cod. [c?m̩hɔ́·n] k. [c?ɩkc?ɩmhɔ́·n] k.
1952.2 ts'moon. [c?m̩ɔ́·n] k.

1953. TS'MHUUTSA. *v.i.* flow (k). *n.* a deep place in a stream under the roots of a large tree (m). [c?m̩hú·cʰa] k,m.
1953.1 ts'mhúutsa. [c?m̩hú·ʌcʰa] m.

1954. TS'MKSIYETS, TS'MKSIYEDZ-. *v.t.* chop out. [c?m̩ksiyécʰ] m.
1954.1 ts'mksüyets, ts'mksüyedz-. [c?m̩ksɨyécʰ] m.

1955. TS'MLÓOB. *n.* cave. [c?m̩lɔ́ʌb] pr.
1955.1 ts'mlúub. *n.* fish pond (trap). [c?m̩lú·b] hb.

1956. TS'MLUULP, TS'MLUULB-. *plural of* luulp.

1957. TS'MMUU. *n.* ear. [c?m̩mú·] k,pr.
1957.1 ts'muu, ts'ikts'mow. [c?m̩ú·] k. [c?ɩkc?m̩ɔ́w] k.

1958. TS'M'ÓOTSN. *n.* palm of hand. [cʔm̩ʔɔ́ʌcʰn̩] pr.

1959. TS'MSEE. *n.* knee joint. [cʔm̩sé·] k.

1960. TS'MSMHÓON. *n.* grey diving bird. [cʔm̩sm̩hɔ́ʌn] pr.

1961. TS'MT'II. *n.* nape of neck. [cʔm̩tʔí·] pr.

1962. TS'MT'ÓOŁ. *n.* (room) behind the fireplace. [cʔm̩tʔɔ́·ʌɬ] hb.

1963. TS'MTS'AX. *n.* nostril. [cʔm̩cʔáx̣] k.

1964. TS'MTSOXS. *n.* sole of foot. [cʔm̩cʰɔ́x̣s] k.

1965. TS'MUUHÓON. *n.* pectoral fin. [cʔm̩ú·hɔ́ʌn] hb.

1966. TS'MYUUP, TS'MYUUB- *n.* menstruation closet (Note: a place (hole) under the house where a girl stayed during her first menstruation. She was confined to this closet, fasting, for seven days). [cʔm̩yú·pʰ] pr.

1967. TS'OGAT'AXTXAYŁ. *n.* bat (*zool*). [cʔog̣atʔax̣tx̣áyɬ] hb.

1968. TS'OO, TS'OO'TSAXT. *v.t.* split open; pull out of a skin. *v.i.* split a skin. [cʔɔ·] pr. [cʔɔ́·ʔcʼʌx̣tʰ] pr.
1968.1 ts'ook. *v.i.* life (of fog); clear (of fog); disappear (of fog); subside (of a flood). [cʔɔ·kʰ] pr.

1969. TS'OOKS. *v.t.* to drain the water off; dry. [cʔɔ·ks] m,pr. *See also* dzooks.

1970. TS'ÓOŁIK, TS'ÓOŁIG-. *v.i.* go out (*spec*: of tide in the morning). *n.* kindling; zero tide; neap; neap tide. [cʔɔ́ʌɬɩkʰ] hb,m.

1971. TS'OOŁUU. *n.* fork of a river; a slow eddy. [cʔɔ́·ɬu·] m,pr.

1972. TS'OOX. *n.* salmon belly, dried or smoked. [cʔɔ·x̣] hb.
1972.1 ts'ooxs, gats'óoxs, ts'ikts'ooxs. *n.* shoes; soles (of shoes); a tougher material at the bottom of leggings to cover the soles of the feet. [cʔɔ·x̣s] k,m. [g̣acʔɔ́·-x̣s] hb. [cʔɩkcʔɔ́·x̣s] k.
1972.2 ts'óoxs, ts'ükts'óoxs. [cʔɔ·ʌx̣s] hb. [cʔɨkcʔɔ́·ʌx̣s] hb.

1973. TS'ÜGA'AAM. *n.* liquorice root; polypody fern (*Polypodium glycyrrhiza*). [cʔĭgaʔá·m] hb.

1974. TS'UULBAKSK, TS'UULBAKSG-. *v.i.* sink. [cʔú·lbʌkskʰ] m,pr.

1975. TS'USK, TS'USG-, SISUUS. *v.i.* small; little. [cʔuskʰ] k. [sɩsú·s] k.
1975.1 ts'uusk, ts'uusg-. [cʔu·skʰ] pr.
1975.2 ts'üüsk, ts'üüsg-. [cʔĭ·skʰ] pr.
1975.3 ts'úusk, ts'úusg-. [cʔuʌskʰ] k.

1976. TS'UUP, TS'UUB-, TS'IKTS'ÚUP. *n.* tail. [cʔu·p^h] k,m,pr.
[cʔɩkcʔúʌp^h] k.
1976.1 ts'úup, ts'úub-. [cʔuʌp^h] k.

1977. TS'UU'TS, TS'UU'DZ-. *n.* bird; penis. [cʔu·ʔc˃] k,pr.
1977.1 ts'úu'ts, ts'úu'dz-. [cʔu·ʌʔc˃] m.
1977.2 ts'u'u'ts, ts'u'u'dz-. [cʔúʔuʔc˃] hb.

1978. TS'U'U'TSM'AATK, TS'U'U'TSM'AATG-. *n.* night hawk; mosquito hawk; bull bat. [cʔúʔuʔc˃m̩ʔá·t^{h}k^h] hb.
1978.1 tsu'u'tsm'áatk, ts'u'u'tsm'áatg-. [cʔuʔuʔc˃m̩ʔaʌt^{h}k^h] hb.

1979. TS'UWAAN. *n.* end. [cʔuwá·n] pr.

1980. TS'ÜWAAS. *n.* pygmy salmon. [cʔɨwá·s] hb.

1981. TS'ÜWAASMMÜSOO. *n.* pygmy sockeye salmon. [cʔɨwá·sm̩mɨsɔ́·] hb.

1982. TS'U'U'TSMHÚUPL. *n.* night birds (Note: a general class which includes bats, owls, night hawks, and chicken hawks. [cʔúʔuʔc˃m̩húʌp!] hb.

1983. TS'UWAANGYIT, TS'UWAANGYID-. *n.* the youngest child in a family.
[cʔuwá·ng^{y}ɩt^h] pr.

1984. TS'UWAANƚ. *n.* a point; something pointed. [cʔuwá·nƚ] m,pr.

1985. TS'ÜBAA. *v.i.* run a short distance; lame. [cʔɨbá·] pr. *See also* dzabaa.

1986. TS'ÜLUU. *v.i.* take one's own lunch, provisions, etc.

1987. TS'ÜÜBAASK, TS'ÜÜBAASG-. *n.* gale; strong wind. [cʔɨ̆·bá·sk^h] pr.

1988. TS'UUNDEE. *n.* the limit; the best. *excl.* You're the best!
[cʔu·ndé·]
1988.1 ts'üünde. [cʔɨ̂·ndɛ] m.

U

1989. UKSBAASK, UKSBAASG-. *n.* offshore wind. [ʔuksbá·sk^h] hb.

1990. UKSDAAWƚ. *v.i.* drown; fall overboard; go out to sea. [ʔuksdá·wƚ] pr.
1990.1 uksdawƚ. [ʔuksdáwƚ] pr.

1991. UKSDOXƚ. *v.t.* take out. [ʔuksdɔ́x̣ƚ] m,pr.

1992. UKSHAAYTK, UKSHAAYTG-. *v.i.* stand out; stand near the water.
[ʔukshá·yt^{h}k^h] pr.

1993. UKSHALHOOLT, UKSHALHOOLD-. *v.i.* full. [ʔukshalhɔ́·lt^h] pr.

1994. UK'WEY. *plural of* wey. *plural of* 'wey.

1995. U'LIS. *n.* great grandparent; great grandchild (address and reference:

great grandparent, great grandchild, MZChChCh). [ʔúʔlɩs] k.

1996. ÜM'AM. *plural of* miik.

1997. UMGOOKS. *n.* sacrifice. [ʔumgɔ́·ks] pr.

1998. UMHON. *v.i.* go trolling. [ʔumhɔ́n] k.

1999. UMKSIWA̲, UMKSIWA̲. *n.* Caucasian. [ʔumksiwá] k.

2000. UNX. *n.* box. [ʔunx̣] k,m.
2000.1 ünx. [ʔɪ̈nx̣] k,m.

2001. UU. *v.i.* fish; go fishing. [ʔu·] hb,pr.

2002. ÜÜK, ÜÜG̲-. *n.* coho salmon. [ʔɪ̈·qʰ] hb.

2003. UULA̲. *n.* seal; hair seal; harbour seal. [ʔú·lɑ] k,m,pr.
2003.1 üüla̲. [ʔɪ̈́·lɑ] hb,k,m,pr.

2004. UUMƚ, U'UUMƚ. *n.* bucket. [ʔu·mɨ] k. [ʔuʔú·mɨ] k.
2004.1 üümƚ. [ʔɪ̈·mɨ] k.

2005. UUNIKSIK, UUNIKSIG-. *n.* ashes; coals. [ʔú·nɩksɩkʰ] hb,k.
2005.1 uunsik, uunsig-. [ʔú·nsɩkʰ] hb.

2006. UUSK, UUSG-. *v.i.* stink. [ʔu·skʰ] m,pr.
2006.1 üüsk, üüsg-. [ʔɪ̈·skʰ] m,pr.

2007. ÚUST, ÚUSD-. *plural of* waah.

2008. UUT, UUD-. *v.t.* bake (Note: in coals, ashes, or with hot stones). [ʔu·tʰ] hb,k.
2008.1 úut, úud-. [ʔu·ʌtʰ] k.

2009. UUTK, UUTG-. *v.t.* call by name. [ʔu·tʰkʰ] k.

2010. ÜÜ'ÜÜNK, ÜÜ'ÜÜNG-. *n.* a clumsy person. [ʔɪ̈·ʔɪ̈́·nkʰ] k,m.

2011. ÜÜX. *n.* coho salmon. [ʔɪ̈·x̣] m,pr. *See also* üük̲ *and* wüüx.

2012. UWEP, UWEB-. *plural of* weep.

W

2013. WAA, WÜTWAA. *v.t.* meet. [wa·] k. [wɨtʰwá·] k.
2013.1 wey, wük'wey,uk'wey. *v.t.* find. [wɛy] k. [wɨkʔwɛ́y] m. [ʔukʔwɛ́y] m.
2013.2 'wey. [ʔwɛy] m.
2013.3 waatk, waatg-. *v.i.* be found. [wa·tʰkʰ] k.
2013.4 'waatk, 'waatg-. [ʔwa·tʰkʰ] m.

2014. WAA. *n.* hips. [wa·] m.
2014.1 Nadu waan? *What's your name?* (*lit: From whose hips*

did you come?
2014.2 wáatk, wáatg-. *v.i.* come from; be from. [wa·ʌtʰkʰ] m.
2014.3 wáa, úust. *n.* name. [wa·ʌ] k. [ʔu·ʌstʰ] k.
2014.4 waah. [wa·h] k.
2014.5 wee. [wɛ·] pr.

2015. WA'A, WA'WAX. *v.t.* bury. *v.i.* dig. [wáʔɑ] pr. [wáʔwʌx̣] k.
2015.1 wa'ax. [wáʔʌx̣] pr.

2016. WAADMɨK, WAADMɨG-. *v.i.* pregnant. [wá·dm̩ɨkʰ] pr.

2017. WAADZDM'AN'ON. *n.* watch. [wá·ʒdm̩ʔanʔɔ́n] hb. *See* waats.

2018. ẄAAK, ẄAAG-. *n.* coho salmon. [ÿʌ·qʰ] k,m,pr.
2018.1 ẅaax, ẅaag-. [ÿʌ·x̣] k,m,pr.

2019. WAAKS, LUWAAKS. *v.t. & v.i.* paddle; row. [wa·ks] k. [luwá·ks] k.

2020. WAAKY, WAAGY-. *n.* Mountain goat kid. [wa·kʸʰ] k.
2020.1 'wáayg. [ʔwaʌyg] hb.

2021. WEEL, SAGAYT WEEL. *v.t.* do. *v.i.* be; do. [wɛ·l] k.
[saɣaytʰwɛ́·l] k.

2022. WELI, WILWELI. *v.t.* carry. [wɛ́li] k. [wɩlwɛ́li] k.

2023. WAAL'K. *n.* bufflehead (*orn*). [wa·lʔk˃] hb.

2024. WAALXS. *plural of* yaa.
2024.1 walaxs.

2025. 'WA'AMANÍITS, 'WA'AMANÍIDZ-. *v.i.* careless. [ʔwàʔamaní·ʌcʰ] k.
2025.1 wahmaníits, wahmaníidz-. [wɑhmaní·ʌcʰ] m.

2026. WAAN. *v.t. & v.i.* obey. [wa·n] k.
2026.1 wáan. [wá·ʌn] k.

2027. 'WAAN, WÜK'WAAN. *n.* tooth; teeth. [ʔwa·n] hb,k,m,pr.
[wɨkʔwá·n] k.
2027.1 'wen. [ʔwɛn] k.

2028. 'WAANM NAK'YIIK. *n.* lower teeth. [ʔwá·nm̩nɑkʸʔí·kʰ] pr.

2029. 'WA'ANM TS'UUSK. *n.* milk teeth. [ʔwáʔanm̩cʔú·skʰ] pr.

2030. WAAP, WAAB-. *n.* house. [wa·pʰ] m,pr.
2030.1 walp, walb-. [walpʰ] k.
2030.2 weep, weeb-, uwep. [wɛ·pʰ] k. [ʔuwɛ́pʰ] k.
2030.3 weelp, weelb-. [wɛ·lpʰ] pr.

2031. WAAPXSEN. *n.* gambling house. [wa·px̣sɛ́n] pr.

2032. WAAS. *n.* a monster (*spec*: a wooden effigy which comes to life).
[wa·s] k,m.

2033. WAAS, WAAS. *n.* rain. [wa·s] hb,k,pr. [wa·s] k.
2033.1 wáas. [waʌs] hb,k,pr.
2033.2 wees. [wɛ·s] k.

2034. WAASAAL. *v.t.* handle roughly; force (human object). [wa·sá·l] pr.

2035. 'WAASK, 'WAASG-. *v.t.* find. *v.i.* be found; come from. [ʔwa·skʰ] k.
2035.1 'waatk, 'waatg-. [ʔwá·tʰkʰ] pr.

2036. WAASMYEEN. *n.* foggy rain; mist. [wa·sm̩yɛ́·n] hb,m.

2037. 'WA'AT, 'WA'AD. *v.t.* sell; trade. [ʔwáʔʌtʰ] k.

2038. WAATS, WAADZ-. *n.* clock; any time piece. [wa·cʰ] hb.

2039. 'WA'AWÉE. *v.i.* be in doubt. [ʔwaʔawɛ́ʌ] k.
2039.1 wahwe. [wɑhwɛ́] m.

2040. WAAXS. *n.* (house) wren. [wa·x̣s] hb.
2040.1 weexs. [wɛ·x̣s] hb.

2041. WAAY, HUWAY, LUWAY, WUWAAY. *v.t. & v.i.* paddle; row. [wa·y] k,m,pr. [huwáy] pr. [luwáy] pr. [wuwá·y] k.
2041.1 way. [way] k.
2041.2 waay. *n.* propeller (*naut*). [wa·y] hb.
2041.3 waayt, waayd-. *n.* pectoral and ventral fins. [wa·ytʰ] hb.
2041.4 weeyt, weeyd-. [wɛ·ytʰ] hb.

2042. WAAYBN. *v.i.* pregnant (of dogs; note: insulting term when used for a human being). [wá·ybn̩] k,m.

2043. WAGAGYIK, WAGAGYIG-. *n.* low tide (k); high tide (m). [wɑgɑgʸíḳʰ] k,m.

2044. 'WAH- without. [ʔwɑh] hb,m.

2045. 'ẄAH. *n.* candlefish; olachen; (whitebait) smelt. [ʔÿʌh] hb,k,pr.

2046. WAHAAS. *n.* rope (Note: made of fireweed fibres). [wɑhá·s] hb.

2047. WAH'A'AYIN. *n.* an unforgivable offense; a commoner. [wahʔáʔʌyɩn] k,m.

2048. 'WAHGA'TMK'AAY. *n.* vest; brassiere. [ʔwɑhgɑ̣́ʔtʼm̩qʔá·y] hb.

2049. 'WAHK'ALIGYETK, 'WAHK'ALIGYETG- *v.i.* virgin; unmarried; untouched (Note: can refer to either sex). [ʔwahqʔàligʸɛ́tʰkʰ] pr.

2050. WAHLII. *v.i.* bald. [wɑhlí·] hb.

2051. WAHLIILGYIT, WAHLIILGYID-. *n.* the one who didn't wake up. [wɑhlí·lgʸɩtʰ] hb.

2052. WAHLIIMI. *n.* one having no song. [wahlí·mi] hb.

2053. 'WAH'NTS'II'TS, 'WAH'NTS'II'DZ-. *n.* one without a grandmother (Note: an insulting name). [ʔwahʔn̥cʔí·ʔcʼ] hb.

2054. 'WAHTI TXAS'NIITGA. *v.i.* take time out; do two things at the same time. *n.* time used to do something outside the ordinary routine. [ʔwáhtʰitx̣asʔní·tga] m.

2055. WAHWAA. *v.i.* be puzzled. [wʌhˆwá·] k. *See also* 'wa'awée.

2056. 'WAH'WAA'NSK, 'WAH'WAA'NSG-. *v.t.* & *v.i.* disobey. [ʔwahʔwá·ʔn̥skʰ] m.
2056.1 'wa'waa'nsk, 'wa'waa'nsg-. [ʔwaʔwá·ʔn̥skʰ] pr.
2056.2 'wax'wa'nsk, 'wax'wa'nsg-. *v.i.* stubborn. [ʔwax̣ʔwáʔn̥skʰ] hb.

2057. WAH'YOOKS. *v.t.* trust. *v.i.* hope. [wahʔyɔ́·ks] k.

2058. ẄAK, ẄAG-. *n.* coho salmon; silver salmon. [ÿʌqʰ] hb,m.
2058.1 ẅax. [ÿʌx̣] hb. *See also* üüx.

2059. WAKAWAA. *n.* jellyfish. [wʌɣawá·] hb.

2060. 'WALOOMSGYETK, 'WALOOMSGYETG-. *n.* a fool. [ʔwalɔ́·msgʸɛ́tʰkʰ] hb.

2061. WAȽ. *n.* yellow cedar. [wʌɬ] hb,k.
2061.1 waɬ. [waɬ] hb.

2062. WAȽAAS. *n.* huckleberry (colour). [waɬá·s] k,m.

2063. WAN. *n.* deer. [wʌn] hb,k,m,pr.

2064. WAN. *plural of* t'aa.

2065. WA'NAA. *v.t.* plant. [wʌʔná·] k.

2066. WAS, WISWAS. *n.* blanket. [was] hb,m. [wʌs] k,m,pr. [wɩswʌ́s] k.
2066.1 wask, wasg-. *v.i.* be dressed. [wʌskʰ] k,m.
2066.2 wasn. *v.t.* & *v.i.* dress. [wʌ́sn̥] k,m.

2067. WA'TAXK, WA'TAXG-. *v.i.* whistle. [wáʔtʼax̣kʰ] k.
2067.1 xs'wa'taxk, xs'wa'taxg-. [x̣sʔwʌ́ʔtʼʌx̣kʰ] m.

2068. 'WA'TOKW, 'WA'TOGW-. *n.* female slave. [ʔwaʔtʼokʷʰ] k,m.

2069. 'WATSA. *n.* land otter; river otter. [ʔwacʰa] hb,k,m. [ʔwʌcʰa] pr.

2070. 'WATS'AMU. *n.* someone who never listens; Otter-no-ears (an insult name). [ʔwácʰʔamú] hb.

2071. WA'TUK, WA'TUG-. *n.* ling cod. [wáʔtʼukʰ] hb.

2072. WAXȽ. *n.* beaver's tail. [wax̣ɬ] k.

2073. WAXWOX. *n.* moth. [wax̣wóx̣] hb,k.

2074. WAYTO. *adv.* far away. [waytʔó] k,m.

2075. WEGI. *n.* brother (address: ♂B, ♂MZS, ♂FBS). [wέgi] k.

2076. WEKY, WEGY-, WAGEE. *n.* brother. (reference: ♂B, ♂MZS, ♂FBS).
[wεkʸʰ] k. [wʌgé·] k.

2077. WIGYATK, WIGYATG-. *v.i.* homesick. [wɩgʸátʰkʰ] k.

2078. WIHAAWTK, WIHAAWTG-. *v.i.* cry; weep. [wihá·wtʰkʰ] k,m.
2078.1 wiihawtk, wiihawtg-. [wi·háwtʰkʰ] pr.

2079. 'WIIK'OOLI. *n.* one with long hair. [ʔwi·qʔɔ́·li] pr.

2080. WIILEE. *v.i.* wide. [wi·lé·] m,pr.

2081. 'WIILEEKS. *v.i.* big; large. [ʔwi·lé·ks], [ʔwi·lέ·ks] hb,k,pr.

2082. 'WIILEEKSM GASGAAWT. *v.i.* be of a large size.

2083. WII'NAK, WII'NAG-. *v.i.* long, tall. [wi·ʔnʌ́kʰ] m,pr.
2083.1 'wii'nak, 'wii'nag-. [ʔwi·ʔnʌ́kʰ] m.
2083.2 wi'nak, wi'nag-. [wiʔnákʰ] k,m.
2083.3 'wi'nak, 'wi'nag-. [ʔwiʔnákʰ] k.

2084. WIIT'IS. *v.i.* big; large. [wi·tʔís], [wɩ·tʔís] k,m.

2085. WILAA'KLS. *v.i.* clever. [wɩlá·ʔkḷs] k,m.

2086. WILAAN. *v.i.* fart (Note: woman's word; *see also* p'aasü).
[wɩlá·n] m,pr.

2087. WILAAY. *v.t. & v.i.* know. [wɩlá·y] pr.
2087.1 wilaask, wilaasg-. *n.* relative. [wɩlá·skʰ] k.
2087.2 wilaaysk, wilaaysg-. [wɩlá·yskʰ] k.
2087.3 wülaaysk, wülaaysg-. [wɨlá·yskʰ] k.

2088. WILADZAP, WILADZAB-. *v.i.* lucky; healthy; competent (especially in hunting). [wɩlaʒʌ́pʰ] pr.
2088.1 wiladzep, wiladzeb-. [wɩlaʒέpʰ] pr.
2088.2 wukdzap, wukdzab-. [wukʒʌ́pʰ] m.

2089. WILDUULGYIT, WILDUULGYID-. *n.* war. [wɩldú·lgʸɩtʰ] hb.

2090. WILGAK'OOSK, WILGAK'OOSG-. *n.* council. [wɩlgaqʔɔ́·skʰ] pr.

2091. WILGYET, WILGYED-, WILGIGYET. *n.* colour. [wɩlgʸέtʰ] hb.
[wɩlgigʸέtʰ] hb.

2092. WILIINGYIT, WILIINGYID-. *n.* grasshopper (hb); spider (m,pr: especially a large spider, which, if found in the house, is a omen of death). [wɩlí·ngʸɩtʰ] hb,m,pr.

2092.1 wuliingyit, wuliingyd-. [wulí·ngʸɩtʰ] hb.

2093. WILMAXLAGAAP, WILMAXLAGAAB-. *n.* a narrow channel. [wɩlmʌ̀x̣lagá·pʰ] pr.

2094. WIL'NAK, WIL'NAG-. *adv.* far away. [wɩlʔnákʰ] m.
2094.1 'wil'nak, 'wil'nag-. [ʔwɩlʔnákʰ] pr.

2095. WINIIŁK, WINIIŁG-. *n.* pregnant seal; pregnant sea mammal. [winí·ɬkʰ] hb.
2095.1 wiwiniiłk, wiwiniiłg-. *n.* a large pregnant seal. [wiwini·ɬkʰ] hb.

2096. WITS'IIN. *n.* mouse; deer mouse; harvest mouse. [wɩcʔí·n] m.
2096.1 wüdzíin. [wiʒíʌn] hb.
2096.2 wüts'íin. [wɨcʔí·ʌn] m,pr.

2097. W'NAK, W'NAG-. *n.* skunk cabbage. [wʔn̥áqʰ] hb.
2097.1 w'nax, w'nag-. [wʔn̥áx̣] hb.

2098. WO'AML. *n.* eyelashes. [wɔ́·aml̥] k.
2098.1 'wo'ml. [ʔwɔ́ʔml̥] pr.

2099. WOK, WOG-. *v.i.* sleep. [wɔqʰ] k.
2099.1 wox, wog-. [wɔx̣] k.

2100. WOO. *v.t. & v.i.* hunt on the water. [wɔ·] k.
2100.1 wóo. [wɔ·ʌ] k.

2101. WO'OGL. *v.t.* roll up. [wɔ́ʔɔgl̥] k,m.

2102. WOOMS. *n.* devil's club (*Oplopanax horridum*). [wɔ·ms] hb,k.

2103. WOOMXK, WOOMXG-, WAXWOOMASK. *v.i.* suffer. [wɔ·mx̣kʰ] k. [wʌx̣wɔ́·mʌskʰ] k.

2104. WOOPX. *n.* forehead. [wɔ·px̣] m,pr.

2105. WOOXT. *v.i.* stay overnight. [wɔ·x̣tʰ] k.

2106. WOYT, WOYD-, WÜKWO'YT. *v.t.* invite. [wɔytʰ] k. [wɨkwɔ́ʔytʰ] k.

2107. WUK'AK'AA'LK, WUK'AK'AA'LG-. *plural of* k'aa'lk.

2108. WUK'AW. *v.t. & v.i.* dig. [wukʔáw] hb.

2109. WUKTS'AN. *n.* clouds (esp. cirrus). [wukcʔán] k.

2110. WÜLIILMTGWAH. *n.* eyeglasses. [wɨlí·lm̥tʰgʷah] hb.

2111. WÜŁEEXS. *n.* copper bush, grouse berry (hb: *Cladothamnus pyrolaeflorus*); huckleberry (m). [wɨɬɛ́·x̣s] hb,m.

2112. WÜSIN- along the inside. [wɨsɩn] hb.

2113. WÜSINBAA. *v.i.* run along the inside. [wɨsɩnbá·] hb.

2114. WÜSINSGÜÜ. *n.* hip of roof. [wɨsɩnsgɨ́·] m.

2115. WÜDZII. *n.* reindeer; caribou; moose; elk. [wɨʒí·] hb,m,pr.

2116. WÜLIIL. *v.t.* anoint; rub. *n.* eye(s); eyeball(s). [wɨlí·l] k,pr.
2116.1 wülíil. [wɨlíʌl] k.

2117. WÜNAA'TSX. *v.t.* whip. [wɨná·ʔcʼx̣] k.

2118. WÜNDO. *n.* cheek; salivary gland; tobacco; anything you put in your mouth to dissolve. [wɨndɔ́] k.

2119. WÜNDO UMKSIWA. *n.* tobacco. [wɨndɔ́·ʔumkšɩwɑ́·] k.

2120. WÜNEEY. *n.* food. [wɨné·y] k.

2121. WÜNGAWS. *n.* brain. [wɨngáws] k.

2122. WÜNOO. *n.* something impossible; insurmountable trouble. [wɨnɔ́·] pr.

2123. ẄÜÜX. *n.* coho salmon. [ÿɨ̈·x̣] k,m,pr. *See also* üüx.

X

2124. XA. *n.* (male) slave. [x̣a] k.
2124.1 xaa, gaxhay. [x̣a·] k. [gɑx̣háy] k.
2124.2 xáa. [x̣a·ʌ] k.

2125. XAAYG. *v.i.* upset a canoe. [x̣a·yg] pr.

2126. XABAALDA. *n.* southwest direction. [x̣abá·ldɑ] pr.

2127. XADIYAAẄ. *v.i.* receive a burial payment. [x̣adiyá·ÿ] pr.

2128. XADZIKS. *n.* minnows. [x̣áʒɩks] hb.

2129. XA'IŁETK, XA'IŁETG-. *v.i.* be full of blood; bloody. [x̣ɑʔiɬétʰkʰ] hb.
2129.1 x'iłetk, x'iłetg-. *v.i.* & *n.* bruise. [x̣ʔiɬetʰkʰ] hb.

2130. XALDAWK, XALDAWG-. *n.* medicine. [x̣ɑldáwkʰ] pr.
2130.1 xaldawxk, xaldawxg-. [x̣aldawx̣kʰ] m.

2131. XASANIIS. *v.i.* climb a mountain. [x̣asaní·s] k,m.

2132. XBA'ALA. *n.* squall; storm from the south. [x̣báʔalɑ] pr.
2132.1 xba'la. *n.* southwest wind. [x̣báʔla] hb.
2132.2 xbaalax. *n.* south wind. [x̣bá·lɑx̣] hb.

2133. XBAALMGÜÜLKA. *n.* southwest wind. [x̣bá·lm̩gɨ́·lkʰɑ] hb.

2134. XBAK, XBAG-. *v.t.* & *v.i.* fold. *n.* crest of a wave; a wave breaking.

[x̣baqʰ] hb.
2134.1 xbax. [x̣bax̣] hb.
2134.2 xpagmgoop, xpagmgoob-. *v.i.* die. *n.* death. Note: a euphemism, "the wave breaks," i.e., he is dead. [x̣pagṃgɔ́·pʰ] hb.

2135. XBEEXSK. *v.t. & v.i.* saw. [x̣be·x̣skʰ] pr.
2135.1 xpeesxɨ. [x̣pɛ́·sx̣ɨ] k,m.

2136. XBIDAXS. *n.* starry flounder. [x̣bídax̣s] m.

2137. XBIHATS'AL. *n.* devilfish; giant squid; giant octopus. [x̣bihac?ál], [x̣bīhʌc?ʌ́l] hb.

2138. XBIIL. *n.* end. [x̣bí·l] pr.
2138.1 exbilataab. *the end of the table.*

2139. XBIMOOKSK, XBIMOOKSG-. *n.* half-breed; métis. [x̣bimɔ́·kskʰ] pr.

2140. XBIYEE. *n.* half. [x̣biyé·] pr.

2141. XBÓOLGN. *n.* night birds (includes bats, owls, chicken hawks, and night hawks). [x̣bóʌlgṇ] hb.

2142. XDII. *v.t.* eat with. [x̣dí·] pr.
2142. Dm xdiiyu Dzoon. *I will eat with John.*

2143. XÉEX. *n.* foam. [x̣ɛʌx̣] k.

2144. XÉEXS. *v.i.* cry; weep. [x̣ɛ·ʌx̣s] pr.

2145. XGUULA. *v.t.* scold; tell off. [x̣gú·la] pr.

2146. XGÜÜS, GAXGÜÜS. *v.i.* catch salmon (*spec*: in the Autumn when they are red and in the fresh water. [x̣gï·s] pr. [gax̣gḯ·s] pr.

2147. XGWATKS. *v.i.* feel cold. [x̣gʷʌtʰks] pr.

2148. XGYET, HUXGYET, GAXGYET. *v.i.* kill with witchcraft. *n.* cannibal. [x̣gʸɛtʰ] k. [hux̣gʸɛtʰ] k, plural for *v.i.* only. [gax̣gʸɛ́tʰ] k, plural for *n.* only.

2149. XLU'AN'ON. *v.i.* receive burial payment at the feast after the funeral. [x̣lu?an?ɔ́n] pr.

2150. XɫAAɫ. *n.* snowberry. [x̣ɨa·ɨ] pr.

2151. XɫIIẄ. *v.i.* burst. [x̣ɨi·ÿ] pr.

2152. XɫIM- around. [x̣ɨɩm] pr.

2153. XɫIMGAAWSK, XɫIMGAAWSG-. *v.i.* thin. [x̣ɨɩmgá·wskʰ] pr.

2154. XɫIP, XɫIB-. *n.* end. [x̣ɨɩpʰ] pr.

2155. XƗKOOY. *v.t.* pay back. [x̣ɨkɔ·y] pr.
    2155.1 xɨkooytk, xɨkooytg-. *v.i.* be paid for. [x̣ɨkɔ·ytʰkʰ] pr.

2156. XƗU. *n.* female genital organs; pudendum; vulva. [x̣ɨu] m.

2157. XƗÜP'IINS. *n.* cow parsnip leaves (base of the compound leaf which supports the three leaflets; used in imitative magic, it is rubbed on fishing gear to insure success in fishing). [xɨʉp?i·ns] hb.

2158. XMAALGASK, XMAALGASG-. *n.* payments for cremation. [x̣má·lgʌskʰ] pr.

2159. XPAAK, XPAAPÜK. *v.t. & v.i.* fold. [x̣pa·kʰ] k. [x̣pa·pʉkʰ] k.
    See also xbak.
    2159.1 xpax. [x̣pɑx̣] m.

2160. XPISMSGÜÜ. *v.i.* bend; lean over. [x̣pɩsm̩sgɨ́·] k,m.

2161. XP'IYEEN. *v.i.* smoke. [x̣p?iyɛ́·n] k,m.

2162. XPOOLGYIMƗK, XPOOLGYIMƗG-. *v.t.* smother to death.

2163. XSAAN. *n.* mosquito larvae; mosquito pupae. [x̣sa·n] m.

2164. XSAANG. *v.t.* doubt; disbelieve. [x̣sa·nġ] pr.

2165. XSAN, GAXSAN. *v.i.* gamble. [x̣san] k. [ġɑx̣sán] k.
    2165.1 xsen. [x̣sɛn] pr.
    2165.2 Dm xse'enu. *I'm going gambling.*

2166. XSATS'ÍI'PA. *n.* necktie. [x̣sɑc?íʌ?pʼɑ] hb.

2167. XSDAA. *v.i.* win a war. [x̣sda·] pr.

2168. XSGYAALST, XSGYAALSD-. *v.i.* make a purchase. [x̣sgʸa·lstʰ] m,pr.

2169. XSGYEN. *n* gum. [x̣sgʸɛn] k,m.

2170. XSGYIIK, XSGYIIG-. *n.* eagle. [x̣sgʸi·kʰ] hb.
    2170.1 xsgyíik, xsgyíig-. [x̣sgʸiʌkʰ] pr.

2171. XSIIT, XSIID-. *v.t., v.i., & n.* vomit. [x̣si·tʰ] k,pr.
    2171.1 xsíit, xsíid-, laxsíit. [x̣siʌtʰ] k. [lɑx̣síʌtʰ] k.

2172. XS'IƗEETK, XS'IƗEETG-. *n.* red (colour: high chroma). [x̣s?iɨé·tʰkʰ] hb.

2172. XSIWOOX. *n.* dream. [x̣siwɔ́·x̣] k,m.

2173. XSK'AANAXS. *n.* toes. [x̣sk?á·nʌx̣s] pr.

2174. XSOOGMLAXA'YENS. *n.* killing frost; strong north wind at the beginning of winter. [x̣sɔ́·gml̩ɑ́x̣ɑ?yɛ́ns] hb.
    2174.1 xsoomlax'yens. [x̣sɔ́·mlɑx̣?yɛ́ns] hb.

2175. XSLAX'OSMT'AYS. *n.* quilt. [xslax?ósmt?áys] m,pr.

2176. XSMAŁIITK, XSMAŁIITG-. *n.* green, blue-green, yellow-green (colour). [xsmaɨí·tʰkʰ] hb.

2177. XSMŁÍISK, XSMŁÍISG-. *n.* yellow-green(colour). [xasmɨíʌskʰ] k,m.

2178. XASOO. *n.* boat; canoe. [xasó·] hb.
2178.1 xso, gaxso. [xso] pr. [gaxsó] pr.
2178.2 xsoo. [xso·] k,m.

2179. XSOL. *n.* one who is ahead. [xsol] k,m.
2179.1 xsolk, t'awgogat. [xsolkʰ] k. [t?awgógatʰ] k.
2179.2 xsolgat, xsolgad-. *v.i.* ahead; first. [xsólgatʰ] k,m.

2180. XSOOX. *n.* scab; serum coming from a sore or scab. [xso·x] k,m.

2181. XSP'IYAAN. *n.* smoke-blue (colour). [xsp?iyá·n] hb.

2182. XSP'O. *v.i.* crackle. [xsp?o] hb.
2182.1 xspo'nsk, xspo'nsg-. *v.t.* break. *n.* crackle (of twigs breaking). [xspó?nskʰ] hb.

2183. XSTAAMG. *n.* noise. [xsta·mg] pr.
2183.1 xstaamx, xstaamg-. [xsta·mx] k,m.

2184. XST'AXT'OOX. *n.* orange (colour). [xst?axt?ɔ́·x] hb.

2185. XSTELTK, XSTELTG-. *v.i.* talk. [xstɛltʰkʰ] pr.

2186. XST'OOK, XST'OOG-. *v.i.* sleep. [xst?ɔ·qʰ] pr.
2186.1 xst'oox, xst'oog-. [xst?ɔ·x] k.

2187. XSU'USK, XSU'USG-. *n.* hawk. [xsú?uskʰ] k,m. *See also* xts'u'u'ts.

2188. XSUWOXAN. *v.i.* dream. [xsuwɔ́xan] k,m.

2189. XSWAXŁAAS. *n.* pink, huckleberry (colour). [xswaxɨa·s] hb.
2189.1 xswałaask, xswałaasg-. [xswaɨá·skʰ] hb.
2189.2 xswałaask, xswałaasg-. [xswaɨá·skʰ] k,m.

2190. XS'WAANX, XS'WAANG-. *n.* herring eggs. [xs?wa·nx] k,pr.
2190.1 xswang. [xswang] pr.

2191. XSWATAXK, XSWATAXG-. *v.i.* whistle. [xswʌ́tʌxkʰ] pr.
2191.1 xs'wa'taxk, xs'wa'taxg-. [xs?wʌ́?t˃ʌxkʰ] m.

2192. XSWN. *v.i.* sit in a row. [xswn̩] hb.

2193. XSWOOXSK, XSWOOXSG-. *v.i.* dive. [xswɔ·xskʰ] m,pr.

2194. XSYAANAK'ALMOS. *n.* yellow, yellow-orange (colour). [xsyá·naq?almós] hb.
2194.1 xs'yaanak'almoos. [xs?yá·naq?almó·s] hb.

2195. XT'O'TS. *v.i.* be in black; be in mourning. [x̣tʔoʔc̓] hb.

2196. XTS'A'ASI. *n.* ankle; leg below the knee. [x̣cʔàʔɑsí] hb.
2196.1 xts'a'asii. [x̣cʔàʔɑsí·] pr.

2197. XTS'I, GAXTS'II. *n.* fog. [x̣cʔi] k. [gɑx̣cʔí·] k.
2197.1 xts'ii, gagts'ii. *v.i.* thick. [x̣cʔi·] m,pr.
[gɑɣ̣cʔí·] pr.
2197.2 xts'íik, xts'íig-. *n.* ribbon worm. [x̣cʔi·ʌq^{h}] hb.

2198. XTS'U'U'TS. *n.* hawk. [x̣cʔúʔuʔc̓] hb.

Y

2199. YAA. *v.t.* give away. [ya·] k,m.
2199.1 ya'an. *v.t.* pass around. [yáʔan] m.
2199.2 ya'ansk, ya'ansg-. *n.* distribution; the act of passing around something. [yáʔansk^{h}] m.
2199.3 yaask, yaasg-. *v.i.* give a gift (*spec*: by a woman to her husband's relatives at the ear piercing of her children. [ya·sk^{h}] k,m.
2199.4 yaaws. *v.t.* remember with a gift. [ya·ws] m.
2199.5 yaws. [yaws] k.

2200. YAA, ŁOGA, WAALXS. *v.i.* go; step; walk. [ya·] k,pr. [ɬóg̣ɑ] pr.
[wa·lxs] pr.
2200.1 yee. [yɛ·] pr.

2201. 'YAAGITS'M'AKS. *n.* tidal wave. [ʔyá·gɩcʔṃʔáks] hb.

2202. YAAK, YAAG-. *n.* earthquake. [ya·k^{h}] k.
2202.1 yáak, yáag-. [ya·ʌk^{h}] k.
2202.2 'yaak, 'yaag-. [ʔya·k^{h}] hb.

2203. YAAKW, YAAGW, GAYAAKW, NIGYITYAAKWS. *v.i.* give a potlatch. *n.* potlatch; distribution of gifts in a feast (lúulgyit). [ya·k^{wh}] hb,k. [g̣ɑyá·k^{wh}] k, more than one person giving potlatches. [nig^{y}ityá·k^{wh}s] k, one person giving many potlatches.
2203.1 yeekw, yeegw, gayeekw, nigyityeekws. [yɛ·k^{wh}] k.
[g̣ɑyɛ́·k^{wh}] k. [nig^{y}ityɛ́·k^{wh}s] k.

2204. 'YAAK, 'YAAG-. *plural of* t'xok.
2204.1 'yaax, 'yaag-.

2205. YAAMX. *v.t.* bait; lure; trick. *v.i.* tricky. *n.* bait. [ya·mx̣] k.
2205.1 yaamgask, yaamgasg-, yaxyaamgask, yakyáamgasg-. *v.i.* imitate a deer or seal as a lure. *n.* fraud. [yá·mg̣ɑsk^{h}] k,m.
[yʌx̣yá·mg̣ɑsk^{h}] k. [yʌqyá·ʌmg̣ʌsk^{h}] m.

2206. YAAMOOKS. *v.i.* snow. [ya·mɔ́·ks] m,pr.

2207. YAANABIYAALS. *n.* falling star; meteorite; shooting star.
[yá·nabiyá·ls] hb.

2208. 'YAANAK'ALMOOS. *n.* yellow, yellow-orange (colour).
[?yá·naq?almó·s] hb.
2208.1 yinak'almóos. [yínaq?almó-s] k,m,hb.

2209. YAANAT'IIBN. *n.* dark grey (colour). [yá·nat?í·bn] hb.

2210. YAANAT'O'TSK, YAANAT'O'ISG-. *n.* rust colour (*spec*: orange to orange-yellow with increased value and decreased chroma).
[yá·nat?ó?chkh] hb.
2210.1 yinat'o'atsk, yinat'o'atsg-. *n.* purple, violet (colour).
[yɩnat?ó?ʌchkh] k,m.

2211. YAANST, YAANSD-. *n.* sea prune; Black Katy chiton. [ya·nsth] k.
2211.1 'yens. [?yɛns] hb.

2212. 'YAA'NTSK, 'YAA'NTSG-. *v.i.* be afraid, hesitate (*spec*: when going into water or rain because it is cold). [?yá·?nchkh] m.

2213. YAAWHMX. *v.i.* give a message for someone. [yá·wɨmx] hb.
2213.1 yawhmx, yikyawhmx. *v.i.* give advice; give the facts.
[yáwɨmx] k,m. [yɩkyáwɨmx] k.

2214. YAAWXK, YAAWXG-. *v.i.* eat. [ya·wxkh] pr.
2214.1 yáaxk, yáaxg-. [yaʌxkh] k.
2214.2 yawxk, yawxg-. [yawxkh] k.

2215. YAAXH. *v.i.* spit. [ya·xɨ] k,m.
2215.1 yexh, yikyáak. [yɛxɨ] k. [yɩkyáʌkh] k.

2216. 'YAGADOX. *v.t.* take down. [?yàɣadóx] pr.

2217. YAGAGAKSÜÜLMXS. *n.* half-tide (going out). [yàɣagaksí·lmxs] hb.
2217.1 'yagaksüülgyimxs. [?yàɣaksí·lgyɩmxs] m.

2218. 'YAGAGOO. *v.i.* go down. [?yàɣagó·] pr.

2219. 'YAGAGWINUUSK, 'YAGAGWINUUSG-. *n.* waterfall. [?yàɣagwɩnú·skh] pr.

2220. 'YAGAGYEMK, 'YAGAGYEMG-. *n.* new moon. [?yàɣagyέmkh] hb.

2221. 'YAGASE'IK, 'YAGASE'IG-. *v.t.* pull down. [?yàɣasé?ikh] pr.

2222. 'YAGAY. *adv.* already. [?yágay] hb.

2223. YANG. *n.* mould. [yang] m.
2223.1 yeenk, yeeng-. [yɛ·nkh] hb.
2223.2 yenk, yeng-. *v.i.* mouldy. [yɛnkh] hb.

2224. YANS. *n.* leaf; leaves. [yans] k.
2224.1 'yens. [?yɛns] hb,k,m,pr.

2225. 'YAK, 'YAG-. *v.t.* hang. [?yaqh] k.
2225.1 'yax. [?yax] k.
2225.2 'yaxk, 'yaxg-. *v.t.* follow [?yaxkh] k,m.

2226. YEE. *n.* spring salmon; Chinook salmon; king salmon. [yɛ·] k,pr.
2226.1 yeeh. [yɛ·h] m.
2226.2 yéeh. [yɛʌh] hb.

2227. 'YE'E. *n.* grandfather (address: FF, FFB, MF, MFB). [ʔyɛ́ʔɛ] k.
2227.1 'ye'es. *n.* grandfather (reference: FF, FFB, MF, MFB. [ʔyɛ́ʔɛs] k.

2228. YEEN. *n.* fog. [yɛ·n] hb,pr.
2228.1 yéen. [yɛʌn] k.

2229. YEE. *n.* fat. [yɛ·] m,pr.
2229.1 yeey, yikyeey. [yɛ·y] hb,pr. [yɩkyɛ́·y] pr.
2229.2 yey. [yɛy] k,pr.

2230. YEL. *v.t.* drill. [yɛl] k.
2230.1 yaltk, yaltg-. [yʌlt^{h}k^h] k.
2230.2 yeltk, yeltg-, yïlyeltk. [yɛlt^{h}k^h] k. [yɨlyɛ́lt^{h}k^h] k.

2231. YELGAN. *n.* drilling stick; firedrill. [yɛ́lgạn] k.

2232. YEƚ. *n.* fish slime. [yɛƚ] k.
2232.1 yiƚ. [yɩƚ] m.
2232.2 yeƚiksk, yeƚiksg-. *v.i.* slide. [yɛ́ƚɩksk^h] pr.
2232.3 yeƚsk, yeƚisg-. *v.i.* slippery. [yɛ́ƚɩsk^h] m,pr.
2232.4 yeƚk, yeƚg-, yiƚyeƚk. *v.i.* smooth. [yɛƚk^h] k,pr. [yɩlyɛ́ƚk^h] k.
2232.5 yiƚk, yiƚg-. [yɩƚk^h] pr.

2233. YENI. *n.* marten. [yɛ́ni] hb,k,m.

2234. 'YENSAGAWGAW. *n.* crow chiton; hairy mopalia (*Mopalia hindsii*). [ʔyɛ́nsạgawgạ́w] hb.

2235. 'YETS, 'YETS-. *v.t.* club. [ʔyɛc^h] k.
2235.1 yetsisk, yetsisg-. *n.* land animal. [yɛ́c^{h}ɩsk^h] hb.
2235.2 ye'tsisk, ye'tsisg-. [yɛ́ʔcʼɩsk^h] hb,pr.
2235.3 ya'tsisk, ya'tsisg-. [yáʔcʼɩsk^h] hb.
2235.4 yetsk, yetsg-, yïkyetsk. [yɛc^{h}k^h] k. [yɨkyɛ́c^{h}k^h] k.

2236. YIWKWDELT, YIWKWDELD-. *num.* eight (of abstract, flat, or round objects). [yiwk^{wh}dɛ́lt^h] hb.
2236.1 yukwdeelt, yukwdeeld-. [yuk^{wh}dɛ́·lt^h] hb,pr.

2237. YIWKWDELTSXN. *num.* eight (of long objects). [yɩwk^{wh}dɛ́lc^{h}x̣n̩] hb.
2237.1 yukwƚeetsxn. [yuk^{w}ƚɛ́·c^{h}x̣n̩] hb,pr.

2238. YOO. *v.i.* roast fish. [yɔ·] k.
2238.1 yóo. [yɔʌ] pr.

2239. YOOKS, YOOYAKS. *v.i.* wash; wash one's face. [yɔ·ks] k,pr. [yɔ́·yʌks] k.

2240. YÜGAH, YÜGÜÜ. *n.* halibut hook. [yɨgáh] k,m. [yɨgɨ́·] k.

2241. YUITSK, YUITSG-, YU'ITSK. *n.* necklace; necktie; anything around the neck. [yuɩc^{h}k^h] k. [yú?ɩc^{h}k^h] k.
2241.1 'yutisk, 'yutisg-. [?yútɩsk^h] m.
2241.2 'yuu'tisk, 'yuu'tisg-. [?yú·?t˃ɩsk^h] hb.
2241.3 yúutsk, yúutsg-. [yuʌc^{h}k^h] k,m.
2241.4 yúutk, yúutg-. [yu·ʌt^{h}k^h] m.
2241.5 'yuutk, 'yuutg-, 'yik'yuutk. *v.t.* carry around the neck. [?yu·t^{h}k^h] k. [?yɩk?yú·t^{h}k^h] k.

2242. YÜKSMOOTS, YÜKSMOOTS-. *n.* an east-southeast wind in the autumn. [yɨksmɔ́·c^h] hb.

2243. YUKWŁA'ADOOL. *num.* eight (of humans). [yuk^{w}ɬá?adɔ́·l] hb,pr.

2244. YUKWŁA'ALDAAT. *num.* eight (of persons aboard a conveyance). [yuk^{w}ɬá?aldá·t^h] hb,pr.

2245. YUKWŁA'AL'ON. *n.* eight fathoms. *num.* eight (of measures). [yuk^{w}ɬá?ʌl?ɔ́n] hb,pr.

2246. YUKWŁA'ATK. *num.* eight (of canoes). [yuk^{w}ɬá?at^{h}k^h] hb,pr.

2247. YÜÜ. *v.i.* hide. [yɨ̈·] k,m.
2247.1 yúu. [yuʌ] k.

2248. YUUP, YUUB-. *n.* land; earth; soil; ground; dust; dirt. [yu·p^h] k,pr.
2248.1 yúup, yúub-. [yu·ʌp^h] k,pr.

2249. YUUSL, YÜKYUUSL. *n.* (small) cedar basket. [yú·sḷ] hb. [yɨkyú·sḷ] hb.

2250. 'YUUTA, YIK'YUUTA, GYET. *n.* man. [?yú·t^{h}ɑ] k,pr. [yɩk?yú·t^{h}ɑ] k. [g^{y}ɛt^h] pr.
2250.1 'yúuta. [?yúʌt^{h}ɑ] k,pr. [?yú·ʌt^{h}ɑ] k,pr.

G

H

R

U

V

W

REFERENCES CITED

Boas, Franz
1912 Tsimshian texts, new series. Publications of the American Ethnological Society volume 3.

Hindle, Lonnie and Bruce Rigsby
1973 A short practical dictionary of the Gitksan language. Northwest Anthropological Research Notes volume 7 number 1.

Susman, Amelia
1940 Tsimshian materials. Manuscript. Philadelphia: American Philosophical Society Library.

PART II

A Reference Grammar for the Coast Tsimshian Language

PREFACE TO THE 1979 EDITION

The purpose of this reference grammar is to provide bilingual teachers, teachers' aides, and other interested persons with a nontechnical introduction to the Coast Tsimshian language. This grammar is designed to be used in conjunction with the Practical Dictionary of the Coast Tsimshian Language. It is also designed for persons who speak and write English and who understand the basic grammatical structure of English. It is not intended as a set of lesson plans. However, the teacher of Tsimshian might use it as a guide for developing instructional materials. The grammar should also prove useful to advanced students of Tsimshian.

The idea for a reference grammar for Tsimshian was conceived in Metlakatla, Alaska, in the summer of 1976, during a community workshop in Tsimshian grammatical analysis. This project was given further impetus by the language workshop sponsored by the Hartley Bay Band in Hartley Bay, British Columbia, during the summer of 1978. The participants of both these workshops have contributed enormously to the completion of the reference grammar. Finally, the Museum of Man has supported the preparation of this manuscript as well as much of the field research upon which it is based.

While an enormous amount of time and effort has gone into the preparation of the grammar, even after more than ten years of fieldwork and analysis, it is still only a beginning. Many of the more sophisticated and complex intricacies of Tsimshian syntax and semantics still remain to be studied. The interrogative, negative, and complex sentence structures have not been so thoroughly studied as to provide a complete understanding. This manuscript undoubtedly contains errors, omissions, and other shortcomings, for all of which the author alone is responsible.

John Dunn
Norman, Oklahoma
1979

TABLE OF CONTENTS

THE ALPHABET AND PRONUNCIATION

1. The Tsimshian alphabet has twenty-two simplex letters.

letter form	letter name	near English equivalents	phonetic symbols
a	a	at, pot, but	æ, ɑ, ʌ,
b	bee	bat	b
d	dee	dog	d
dz	dee-zed	adze	d^z
e	e	let, late	ɛ, e
g	gee	get	g
h	aitch	hat	h
i	i	hit, heat	ɩ, i
k	kay	keep	k
l	ell	let	l
ɬ	barred-ell		ɬ
m	em	map	m
n	en	nap	n
o	o	ought	ɔ
p	pee	pat	p
s	ess	sat, shade	s, s
t	tee	tap	t
ts	tee-ess	let's	t^s
u	u	suit	u
w	double-u	wash, now	w
x	ach	loch (Scot)	x̣
y	yod	yes, boy	y

The Tsimshian orthography also includes a large number of complex letters. These will be described in the following sections.

2. There are six classes of Tsimshian speech sounds: stop consonants, affricates, continuant obstruents, laryngeal glides, sonorants (including nasals, glides, and the liquid ell), and vowels.

3. The stop consonants are b, d, g, k, p, and t. There are two kinds of gee and kay: ordinary and backed. Backed gee and kay, pronounced by pulling the back of the tongue back against the uvula, are indicated by underlining (g̲, k̲). There are two series of voiceless stops: plain (k, k̲, p, t) and checked or glottalized (k', 'k, k̲', 'k̲, p', 'p, t', 't). In some checked stops the glottalic closure coincides with the consonant closure and the vocal cords are released after the consonant is released. This type of glottalization is indicated by an apostrophe after the consonant letter (k', k̲', p', t'). In some checked stops the glottalic closure occurs before the consonant closure. This latter type of glottalization is indicated by an apostrophe before the consonant letter ('k, 'k̲, 'p, 't).

b	bee	ban	b
d	dee	dash	d
g	gee	gift	g
g̲	back-gee		g̣

letter form	letter name	near English equivalent	phonetic symbol
k	kay	kiss	k
k̲	back-kay		q
k'	kay-apostrophe		kˀ
'k	apostrophe-kay		ˀk
k̲'	back-kay-apostrophe		qˀ
'k̲	apostrophe-back-kay		ˀq
p	pee	pan	p
p'	pee-apostrophe		pˀ
'p	apostrophe-pee		ˀp
t	tee	tin	t
t'	tee-apostrophe		tˀ
't	apostrophe-tee		ˀt

4. The affricates are dz, ts, ts', and 'ts.

dz	dee-zed	adze	d^{z}
ts	tee-ess	let's	t^{s}
ts'	tee-ess-apostrophe		t^{s}ˀ
'ts	apostrophe-tee-ess		ˀt^{s}

5. The continuant obstruents (fricatives) include ess (s), barred-ell (ɫ), and ach (x). The ess can be pronounced either as the ess in sip or as the esh in ship. The barred-ell is produced much like an ess, except that the tip of the tongue touches the alveopalatal ridge behind the upper incisors and the air flow is around one or both sides of the tongue. Barred-ell is a lateral like ell and a fricative like ess. The ach (x) is a uvular fricative. During its production the back of the tongue is pulled back close to the uvula.

s	ess	lease	s
		leash	s
ɫ	barred-ell		ɫ
x	ach	loch (Scot)	x̣

6. The laryngeal glides.

h	aitch	help	h
'	glottal stop		ʔ

7. The sonorants include the semivowels yod (y), double-u (w), and dotted-double-u (ẇ), the liquid ell (l), and the nasals em (m) and en (n). The dotted-double-u is an unrounded double-u and is pronounced without any pursing of the lips. There are two series of sonorants, plain and checked. In the checked series the vocal cords are closed then released before the sonorant itself is released.

y	yod	yes, boy	y
'y	checked-yod, apostrophe-yod		ˀy
w	double-u	wet, how	w
'w	apostrophe-double-u		ˀw

letter form	letter name	near English equivalents	phonetic symbols
ẅ	dotted-double-u		ÿ
'ẅ	apostrophe-dotted-double-u		ʔÿ
l	ell	late	l
'l	apostrophe-ell		ʔl
m	em	man	m
'm	apostrophe-em		ʔm
n	en	no	n
'n	apostrophe-en		ʔn

The sonorants em, en, and ell can carry syllable peaks (indicated by underlining).

m̲	syllable-em, em-underline	fascism	m̩
'm̲	apostrophe-em-underline		ʔm̩
n̲	en-underline	fasten	n̩
'n̲	apostrophe-en-underline		ʔn̩
l̲	ell-underline	able	l̩
'l̲	apostrophe-ell-underline		ʔl̩

The underlining of the syllabic sonorants is an optional orthographic convention and is often omitted by proficient user of Tsimshian. Some, following the Gitksan system, prefer to write the syllabic sonorants as im, in, and il.

8. Vowels may be short or long. The long vowel is indicated by a double letter (aa, ee, ii, oo, uu). The long vowel is pronounced in one of three ways: (1) sustained, i.e., with an even pitch, (2) with a falling pitch and offglide to the vowel sound in the English word "what," (3) with a glottal interruption or constriction.

a	short a	hat	æ
a̲	back a	hot, hut	ɑ, ʌ
aa	long a	had	æ·
áa	falling a		æʌ
a'a	interrupted a		æʔæ
e	short e	wet	ɛ
ee	long e	wed, wade	ɛ·, e·
ée	falling e		ɛʌ, eʌ
e'e	interrupted e		ɛʔɛ, eʔe
i	short i	hit, heat	ɩ, i
ii	long i	hid, heed	ɩ·, i·
íi	falling i		ɩʌ, iʌ
i'i	interrupted i		ɩʔɩ, iʔi
o	short o	fought	ɔ
oo	long o	fraud	ɔ·
óo	falling o		ɔʌ

letter form	letter name	near English equivalents	phonetic symbols
o'o	interrupted o		ʔ
u	short u	boot	u
uu	long u	food	u·
úu	falling u		uʌ
u'u	interrupted u		uʔu

There are two types of the letter u, the ordinary or rounded u as shown above and the unrounded u (indicated by the dieretic mark) which is pronounced without pursing the lips.

ü	unrounded-short-u, dotted-short-u		ɨ, ɪ̵
üü	dotted-long-u		ɪ̵·

The underlining of the back a (a̲) and the acute accent over the falling vowels (áa) are optional orthographic conventions and are often omitted by proficient users of Tsimshian. Some prefer to write the falling vowels as ah, eh, ih, oh, uh.

THE DISTRIBUTION OF SOUNDS

1. The letters b, d, dz, g, and g̲ generally occur between vowels and before vowels when they (b, d, etc.) are not part of a consonant cluster. The letters k, k̲, p, and t generally occur at the ends of words and in clusters. There are a few exceptions to this pattern, e.g., kyooxk (grass), puksk (to spit, spitoon), taag̲an (planking for a boat), taalsgmts'ooxs (stocking).

2. If a glottalized segment occurs before a vowel, the glottalic closure coincides with the consonant closure and the vocal cords are released after the consonant is released (k', k̲', p', t'). If the glottalized segment occurs after a vowel, the glottalic closure occurs before the consonant closure ('k, 'k̲, 'p, 't); if such a glottalized segment is word final, the vocal cords are unreleased thruout the production of the consonant sound. When a glottalized segment occurs between vowels, it is of the former type (k', p', t') if the second of the two vowels has the greater stress; it is of the latter type ('k, 'p, 't) when the first of the two vowels has the greater stress.

3. The g, k, k', and 'k can be unrounded or rounded. If they are unrounded but come before a round vowel (u, o), a yod offglide (y) is inserted between the unround consonant and the round vowel. If they are round but come before an unrounded vowel (a, e, i, ü), a double-u offglide is inserted between the round consonant and the unround vowel. Sometimes a double-u offglide is added to round k at the end of a word. Sometimes a yod offglide is added to unround k at the end of a word. A yod offglide is often inserted after an unround g, k, etc., even if the following vowel is unround.

4. The back a (a̲) generally occurs in syllables with a k̲, k̲',

'k, g, x, or glottal stop, and in unstressed syllables. The ü generally occurs in unstressed syllables.

STRESS

1. In most Tsimshian words, the primary stress is on the last syllable. However, if the last syllable is a suffix or a connective (see appropriate sections), the penultimate (next to last) syllable receives the primary stress. In a few other words the penultimate syllable is stressed.

2. Words with penultimate stress.

awta	porcupine
amgyeeka, gyiika,	beach
badzi	lift
bana	bag net
didiiya	hills
duula	tongue
dziiwkwsa	bail water out of a canoe or boat
gadnaada	who
ga'nah	mast
ganawelii	carrying strap
ganhada	Raven People
ganiliimi	keep singing
gawagani	the act of making peace
gawdi	all
gayna	road, trail
ginadziiga	be grounded at low tide
goyim, gooym	spring (season)
goy'pa	bright, moon, daylight
güülka	westerly, West, west wind
gwe'a	poor
gwesga	that
gwis'naba'ala	button blanket
gwüsmati	mountain goat skin coat
gyenti	sea cucumber
gyigyaani	up above
gyilhawli	woods, forest
gyits'iipta	yesterday
haak'otssemii	table knife
ha'awiini	not yet be, not yet do, Not yet!
hanhani	temple(s) (body part)
hani	thin
hat'aapa	(stone) pestle
hats'anaasüü	good luck (plural agreement form)
hats'iiwkwsa	bailer
haymaadm	mortheast wind
hum'tsa	kiss
k'asgi, kawsk	unripe
k'awtsi	oil, grease
k'aym	almost

klusms	Nass River
k̲'ool̅i	scalp
k̄sa̲ts'iiba	tie one's hair in a coil on top of the head (Note: signifies a warrior and a brave man)
k'üüti	a box for picking berries
k'wiinti	salmon stomach
k'yabeelda	cliff
laguula, laguulaẅ	burn
laxst'ooga	sleep
laxsüülda	ocean
legi	chordaria algae
ligyimti	cotton, flannel, wool
liimeti	wool
liimi	sing, song
liiwaa'pah	cabin (of a boat)
loog̲awdi	be empty
lukłihooya	underclothes
luuna, süluuna	dry
luwi	alder tree
łakłgwt'iina	steep valleys
łog̲a	go, step, walk (plural agreement form)
łuunti	angry
maadm	falling snow, snowflakes
maanwineeya	left over food
maaxay	rainbow
magwa'lah, magwa'lü	deep winter
mati	mountain goat
maxłye'tsü	give a great potlatch
mela	be in a hurry
mi'yuuta	mannish, a mannish woman
moksa	sour
mü'wa̲tsa	act crazy, a crazy person
naasu̅	raspberry
nak'eeda	muskrat
nip'a'la	button
nla'ida	light house, signal
noosü	wolverine
nüwa̲'na	seed(s)
p'aatsah	fucus algae
saali	invite
sag̲awdi	be nothing there
sag̲ayna	fall down (inanimate absolutive)
sami	meat
smk̲'awtsi	olachen grease
stü̅ti	nettles
sümela	hurry up
sweda	sweater
sxat'uusa	dam
t'mlaani	neck
t'oo'tsip	fortress
ts'alaasü	canyon
ts'alaayüü	visit

ts'iig̲a	top shells
ts'mg̲a'na	door frame, window frame
ts'mhuutsa	flow
üüla	seal
weli	carry
'wa̲tsa	land otter
wa̲'tuk	ling cod
wegi, weky	brother
'wiik̲'ooli	one with long hair
xba'ala, xba'alax	squall
xbaalmgüülka	southwest wind
xguula	scold
xsats'ii'pa	necktie
'yuuta	man

3. When a word ends in a complex consonant cluster, a vowel is sometimes used to break up the cluster. Such a vowel is called an epenthetic vowel. In Tsimshian the epenthetic vowels in final consonant clusters are a (as in "what"), i, or ü. They are always unstressed.

aadit	fisherman
aadzak̲	long enough
aadza̲ks	arrogant
a'adzik	straight
aalks, aaliks	servant
aalx, aalax	quick tempered
aa'pax	remember
algyax	speak
asgaabax	chatter-box
aya'ag̲as	a good hunter
ayaawx, ayaawüx	custom
ayawül	competent
ayn, ayin	no
ba'wis	monkey, bigfoot
baxg̲aksüülgyimxs	half-tide (coming in)
biiltsük	red sunset
daamsax	faint
dalbaksk	shorten
dooyaxs	strong
dzak'wüsk	animal
g̲aakłik	rat
g̲a'awis	newborn baby girl
g̲ałdik	to one side
g̲anooksinsk	gunnel
g̲ansigiidask	yeast
g̲asg̲adzax	ants
gugweelaks	polished, shiny
gułxbaa'laxs	nightmare
güüdax	ask
güünaks, güünks	dry
gwaanaks, gwaanks	cooked, faded
gwanüks	spring (of water)
gyelk̲, gyelag̲	outside

ha'ayin	put down (a baby or child)
haa'ytisk	house posts
haayuk	soul, spirit
hastaaleks	third finger (ring finger)
ha'yn, ha'yin	place upright
hoyax	correct
k'łik'agun	crush
kł'üüngyaxs	stomp on, trample
k'oodzax	break, die
k'oolax	warm one's back by the fire, dull
k'o'oldzax	carry on one's shoulder
ksłüüdat	down below, the bottom one
k'waadamłk	pregnant
k'wa'adis	miss, be lost
kwłna'anax	broken
la'abal	hurry
la'agwil	wrap up, cover
laamdzax	come in (plural absolutive)
laxts'a'adzaks	field, garden
ligyi'alax	leave in anger
logask	wet
lu'apüs	sew
luudisk	learn, store up provisions for the winter
luulgyit	feast
ła'ayask	climb
ła'gyin	bend
łałuungyit	slave
łgwüłuugyit	plug
łi'awin	brant
łukwt'a'yin	grandchild
małiłk	tell
manbulask	erupt (of a geyser)
naksmya'win	right hand
na'tsiks	fish tail, caudal fin, tail fin
nuungat	take hold of
p'algyüxsk	heavy
p'asaxk	split
saaldzik	groan
sa'awan	put into a box
saho'yagnsk	inner bark (used for stencils) (Note: the stress is on the o)
si'ndoonik, sndooyntk	garden
smhu'adzax	brook
smii'kask	song sparrow
snlayditsks	signal
t'a'awil	halibut hook
t'oo'tsip	fortress
t'oyaks	say goodbye to, thank
ts'a'adziks	dirty
ts'aawil	rob
ts'oołik	neap tide
ts'uulbaksk	sink
u'lis	great grandparent, great granchild

SOUND CHANGES - VOWELS

1. Short vowels are often lengthened when they are stressed.

łaats, łakłats	scraper
g̲aax, g̲akg̲ak	black bass
aalx, alx	short tempered
baa'lx, ba'lx	corpse, ghost
daaw, daw	ice, frozen
dziiw̓, dziw̓	dolphin
dzoox, dzox	ashamed
eesk, esk	promise
haaps, ha'ps	lid
holtk, hooltk	full
hon, hoon	fish
hupl, huupl	dark
k̲'aawts, k̲'awts	labret
k̲'ah, k̲'ak̲'aah	cut, wound
laakws, lakws	light
mooksk, moksk	white
pts'aan, pts'an	totem pole
t'aak̲, t'ak̲	whirlwind
ts'uusk, ts'usk	small
xaa, xa	(male)slave
małiłk, ma̲kmaałiłk	tell

2. The vowel a often alternates with the vowel e.

anaay, aney	biscuit
baał, beł	cut open
batsk, betsk	arrive
dalpk, delpk	short
dzap, dzep	build
g̲anaaxs, g̲aneexs	ladder, steps
haaywaas, haywees	south wind, southeaster
hadaay, hadeey	rudder
hayatsk, hayetsk	a copper (potlatch plaque)
k'yap, k'yep	ten (of animals)
'naaxł, 'neexl	killerwhale
sah, seh	day
saksk, seksk	clean
sayp, seyp, seeyp	bone
waa, wee	name
'waan, 'wen	tooth
waap, weep	house
waas, wees	rain
waayt, weeyt	pectoral and ventral fin
yaa, yee	walk, go, step

3. The vowel a sometimes alternates with the vowels e and a̲ (as in "what').

dal, del, da̲l	fight
dap, dep, da̲p	liver
lak, lek, la̲k	fire, firewood

mask, mesk, ma̲sk red
ts'al, ts'e'l̄, ts'a̲l face

4. The vowel a sometimes alternates with the vowel a̲ (as in "father").

k'waas, k'was, k'wa̲s, k'wa̲a̲s broken
kwdaaxs, kwdaxs, kw̄da̲xs leave
naks, 'na̲ks marry, spouse
p'as, p'a̲s grow
xbax, xba̲k crest of a wave

5. The vowel e sometimes alternates with the vowel i.

dzem, dzim boil
gyeps, gyips high
gyet, gyit person
gyeeka, gyiika beach

6. The vowel e sometimes alternates with the vowels a and i.

ban, ben, bin belly

7. The vowel u sometimes alternates with the vowel o.

lu'uts, lo'ots elderberry
ɬiyuun, ɬioon elk
moo'mx, muu'mk̄ smile
t'o'tsip, t'u'̄utsip fortress
t'o'tsk, t'u'utsk black

8. The vowel u alternates with the vowel ü, and the glide ẅ alternates with the glide w. In general younger people use the plain u and w where older people use ü and ẅ.

üüla, uula seal
üümɬ, uumɬ bucket
dziiẅ, dziiw porpoise
üüsk, uusk stink
laaẅ, laaw trout

9. Long vowels may become diphthongs.

hayaaxk, hayawxk fork
k'ayeet, k̲'ayeyt sculpin
l̄üksg̲oot, ̄luksg̲oyt crazy, stubborn, foolish
ts'mmuu, ts'ikts'mmow ear
sm'oogyit, sm'ooygyit chief
hats'iiwkwsa bailer (from ha-ts'ii-aks)
ɬool, ɬoowl̲ push thru the water

10. A short vowel followed by ell may become a long vowel with the ell deleted.

walp, waap house

SOUND CHANGES INVOLVING BOTH VOWELS AND CONSONANTS

1. When a long vowel is followed by a glottalized segment, the glottalization often "bleeds" into the vowel, changing it into an interrupted vowel. Sometimes the following consonant is also deleted.

bii'k, bi'ik	tell a lie
ha'k̲, ha'ak̲, ha'a	goose
haɫe̅'pa, ha̅ɫa'apa	scraper
hanaa'k̲, hana'a	woman
haw'ts̅, ha'u'ts	cormorant
k'waa'tis, k'wa'a'tis	be lost
naak̲, na'ax, na'g̲a, na̲'a̲	woman's dress, skirt
nee'k̲, ne'ix	anal fin, dorsal fin
nts'i̅i̅'ts, nts'i'i'ts	grandmother
soo'k̲, so'ax	robin
ts'uu̅'ts, ts'u'u'ts	bird, penis

2. When glottalized k and glottalized back-k occur between vowels, they often simplify to a glottal stop.

q̲ak'ay, q̲a'ay	wing
lu'kwil, lu'wil	many, really, very
sa̲'kaɫ, sa̲'a̲ɫ	divide, settle an estate

3. An interrupted long vowel often becomes a falling vowel.

be'a̲x, béex	tear, tear up
bu'i̅l, búul	warn
gwe'a, gwée	poor
gyi'a̲ɫ, gyíiɫ, gyii'tɫ	male sockeye salmon in red phase
la'a̲gwil, láawil	wrap up, cover
lo'op, lóop	rock, stone, cement
lükso'a̲k̲, lüksóox	door, doorway

SOUND CHANGES - CONSONANTS

1. Back-k often becomes x when it occurs at the end of a word.

naak̲, na'ax	woman's dress, skirt
nee'k̲, ne'ix	anal fin, dorsal fin
soo'k̲, so'ax	robin
lükso'a̲k̲, süksoox	door, doorway
aak̲, aax	mouth
iimk̲, iimx	beard

2. Gy often simplifies to y when it occurs after an ell.

algyax, alyax	speak
p'algyüxsk, p'alyüxsk	heavy

3. Glottalized segments often simplify by losing the glottalization and then becoming voiced.

k'wili, gwülii	three (general number)
gasgoos, k'ask'oos	crane, stork
k'ask'adzn, gasgadzn	ants
ts'awes, dza'west	salal
galdzap, galts'ap	town
'naaxɬ, naaxɬ	killer whale
'naa, naa	bait

4. The glottal stop in initial position sometimes alternates with aitch.

aɬo, haɬo	cloth

5. Ell sometimes alternates with en.

manbu'nsk, manbulask	erupt (of a geyser)
k'yilaam, k'yi'nam	give

THE FORMATION OF THE PLURAL - REDUPLICATION

1. The ordinary way to show the plural number is by reduplication. Reduplication is a morphological device in which part of a word is copied or repeated. Verbs agree in number with their absolutive (transitive object or intransitive subject). Adjectives agree in number with the nouns they modify. Verbs and adjectives show number agreement in the same way that nouns show number. There are several types of reduplication.

2. The most common type of plural reduplication consists of copying the first consonant of the word and prefixing it to the word along with a vowel and a kay (k). This type of reduplication is referred to as Class I, or CVk-, reduplication. The vowel that occurs in the prefix is determined by the first consonant of the prefix.

3. The most common vowel is a Class I plural prefix is i.

singular	plural	
dasx	dikdasx	squirrel
duuɬk	dikduuɬk	basket
duus	dikduus	cat
dziis	dzikdziis	weir
dziiẅ	dzikdziiẅ	dolphin
gyiik	gyikgyiik	fly (noun)
k'ya̲k	k'yikk'ya̲k	choke
seyp	sikseyp	bone
sgwaytk	siksgwaytk	stop
sgyet	siksgyet	spider
sk'uunsk	siksk'u'unsk	teach
swa̲ntk	sumsikswa̲ntk	blow
sweda	siksweda	sweater
sxan	siksxan	mat
taalsgmts'ooxs	tiktaalsgmts'ooxs	stocking
t'a̲'k	t'ikt'a̲'k	terrace (noun)
ts'al	ts'ikts'alt	face
ts'a'lks	ts'ikts'a'lks	whirlpool
ts'mhoon	ts'ikts'mhoon	grey cod
ts'mmuu	ts'ikts'mmow	ear
ts'ooxs	ts'ikts'ooxs	shoe
ts'uup	ts'ikts'uup	tail
yawɬmx	yikyawɬmx	advise
yeey	yikyeey	fat
yexɬ	yikyexɬ	spit
'yuuta	yik'yuuta	man
'yuutk	'yik'yuutk	carry around the neck

4. If the word begins with a glottal stop (') or an aitch (h), the vowel in the Class I plural prefix is a as in 'hat.' Note: words that begin with a glottal stop followed by a vowel are generally written without the initial glottal stop.

singular	plural	
alaays	ak'alaays	lazy
alaaskw	ak'alaaskw	weak
alx	ak'alx	angry
amalk	ak'amalk	scab
anaas	ak'anaas	skin (noun)
anool	ak'anool	allow
ap	hakhaps	bee
a'tsik	ak'a'atsik	straight
axbesx	hakhaxbesx	saw (noun)
aytk	ak'aytk	call by name
haa'ps	hakhaa'ps	cover
haks	hakhaks	scold
hałabiisk	hakhałabiisk	knife
hałe'pa	hakhałe'pa	knife
hałgyiik	hakhałgyiik	shore
hało	hakhało	cloth
oks	ak'oks	fall (verb)

5. If the word begins with a lateral (l, ł) or a nasal (m, n), the vowel in the Class I plural prefix is a as in 'what.'

laakws	laklaakws	light
laẅ	laklaẅ	trout
la'abl	lakla'abl	twinkle
libets'aẅ	laklobits'aẅ	kidney
luut	lakluut	wedge
lu'wl	laklu'wl	drip
łaats	łakłats	scraper
łgwt'iin	łakłgwt'iina	steep valley
łpun	łakłpun	whale
małiłk	makmaałiłk	tell
miilk	makmiilk	dance
naluułk	naknaluułk	nest

6. If the first consonant of the Class I plural prefix is uvular (g̠), the vowel is a as in 'father.'

g̠aax	g̠akg̠ak	black bass
g̠oom	g̠akg̠oom	ash(es)

7. If the first consonant of the Class I plural prefix is a bilabial stop (b, p'), the vowel is ü.

beed	bükbeed	bed
p'i'iłosk	p'ükp'i'iłosk	a square of dried seaweed

CLASS I IRREGULAR PLURALS

1. A number of Class I words are irregular in that they do not follow the vowel epenthesis rules stated in the previous section.

2. Class I irregular words in i.

singular	plural	
łaxs	łikłaxs	claw
łuunti	łikłuunti	angry
'nłomsk	nika'nłomsk	sacred

3. Class I irregular words in ü.

nłanagn	nłükłanagn	barrel
mihooks	mükmihooks	fragrant
sesoo	süksesoo	rattle (noun)
stuul	sükstuul	accompany
ts'iłina'a	tsükts'iłina'a	apron
yetsk	yükyetsk	animal
yuusl	yükyuusl	basket
'waan	wük'waan	tooth
'wey	wük'wey	find
woyt	wükwo'yt	invite

4. Class I irregular words in u.

gwüdaats	gukgwüdaats	jacket
gwis'naba'ala	gukgwis'naba'ala	button blanket
huutk	hukhuutk	call
moolksx	mukmoolksk	sour

5. Class I irregular words in a as in 'what.'

daxł	dakdaxł	hammer
saksk	saksaksk	clean
se'mx	sakse'mx	butter clam
ts'askw	ts'akts'askw	louse
ts'alaasik	ts'akts'alaasik	canyon
ts'alaa	ts'akts'alaa	basket
ts'aky	ts'akyts'ak	extinguished

6. Class I irregular words in oo.

mooksk	mookmooksk	white

CLASS II REDUPLICATION

1. In a few words the plural reduplication consists of copying the first consonant of the word and prefixing it to the word with a vowel and an ach (x). This type of reduplication is referred to as Class II, or CVx-, reduplication. All the words in this class contain a uvular consonant (g, k, k', x).

2. If the Class II word begins with a consonant (b, d, k'), the vowel in the prefix is a as in 'father.'

be'ax	baxbe'ax	tear up
da'axłk	daxda'axłk	able

singular	plural	
diilmx	daxdiilmx	answer
k'oomtk	gaxgoomtk	hope

3. If the word begins with a glide (w, y, '), the vowel in the prefix is a as in 'what.'

woomxk	waxwoomask	suffer
yaamgask	yaxyaamgask	lure
aadzak	ax'aadzak	reach across

CLASS III REDUPLICATION

1. In Class III, or CVC-, plural reduplication the first consonant of the principal syllable (the one with primary stress) + a vowel + the first consonant after the vowel are all prefixed directly to the principal syllable. In this morphological process diphthongs are considered as single vowel units unless there is no other consonant after the diphthong glide. The rules for determining the vowel of the prefix are generally the same as for the CVk- Class.

2. The most common vowel in a Class II plural prefix is i.

dal	dildal	fight
diduuls	dilduuls	alive
duup	dipduup	base of a mountain
gyelüks	gyilgyalks	feel
gyełk	gyiłgyełk	stab
gyiisk	gyisgyiisk	miss
lugyïis	lugyisgyiis	be wrong
naygyełxs	naygyiłgyełxs	tattoo
k'yi'nam	k'yilk'yi'nam	give
gwelk	gwilagweelk	burn
sagwaatk	gwitgwaatk	disappear
k'was	gwisgwas	break
was	wiswas	blanket
weli	wilweli	carry
yełk	yilyełk	smooth

3. If the principal syllable begins with a glottal stop (') or and aitch (h), the vowel in the prefix is a as in 'hat.'

adziks	adz'adziks	arrogant
algyax	al'algyax	speak
alx	al'alx	angry
axłk	ax'axłk	reach
haas	hashaas	dog
haats	hashaats	stump
haaxk	haxhaaxk	overburdened
ooy	ay'ooy	throw

4. If the principal syllable begins with a lateral or a nasal, the prefix vowel is a as in 'what.'

singular	plural	
lułap	lułapłap	deep hole
maatk	matmatg̱	dirty

5. If the principal syllable begins with a uvular, the prefix vowel is a as in 'father.'

g̱an	g̱ang̱an	tree
g̱awlg	g̱alg̱awlg	wind around
g̱awsk	g̱asg̱awsk	narrow
g̱ol	g̱alg̱ol	empty
ḵ'awsk	ḵ'asḵ'awsk	unripe
ḵ'os	g̱asg̱os	jump
ḵ'oylḵ	g̱alg̱oliḵ	dull

6. If the principal syllable begins with a bilabial stop, the prefix vowel is ü.

baa'lx	bülbaa'lx	ghost
basagn	büsbasag̱n	divide
p'axs	p'üxp'ax̱s	leggings

CLASS III IRREGULAR PLURALS

1. Class III irregular words in i.

baal	bilbaal	feel
baał	biłbaał	butcher

2. Class III irregular words in ü.

güüdax	gütgüüdax	ask
loop	lüploop	rock

3. Class III irregular words in a as in 'what.'

aam	am'aam	good
a'pax	ap'a'pax	remember
dzep	dzapdzep	make
g̱aldzap	g̱aldzapdzap	town
gwatk	gwatgwatk	lost
p'iiłn	p'ałp'iiłn	crush
ts'ap	ts'apts'ap	town
waa	watwaa	meet
yeltk	yalyeltk	drill

4. Class III irregular words in o.

luk'ol	luk'olk'ol	alone

5. Other Class III irregular words.

singular	plural	
daamsax	dmdaamsax	faint
daxda̲m	daxdmda̲m	hold fast
agwiiłems	agwiiłmłems	grandchild's spouse
p'algyüxsk	p'lp'algyüxsk	heavy

CLASS IV REDUPLICATION

1. In Class IV, or CV-, plural reduplication the first consonant of the principal syllable is copied and prefixed along with a vowel directly to the principal syllable. The rules for determining the vowel of the prefix are the same as for the CVk- and CVC- classes.

2. The vowel of the prefix is i after d, gy, or s.

laxdii	didii	hill
siipk	sipsiipk	sick
sm'ooygyit	smgyigyet	chief

3. After aitch (h) the vowel of the prefix is a as in 'hat.'

holtk	haholtk	full

4. After ł the vowel of the prefix is a as in 'what.'

ła'ayask	łałła'ayask	climb

5. After k̲' the vowel of the prefix is a as in 'father.'

k̲'o	k̲'ak̲'o	back (noun)
k̲'aa'lk	wuk̲'ak̲'aa'lk	thief
gyik̲'aak	k̲'aygyik̲'aak	waist, hip

6. After p the vowel of the prefix is u.

ptal	buptal	rib
pteeltk	bupteeltk	climb
pts'aan	bupts'aan	totem pole
pts'ih	bupts'ih	comb

CLASS IV IRREGULAR PLURALS

1. Most Class IV words are irregular.

2. Class IV irregular words in i.

beł	bibeł	butcher
'lax	lilak̲	needle

3. Class IV irregular words in ü.

singular	plural	
daalg	düdaalg	rebuke
dzał	dzüdzał	consume
güüdax	gügüüdax	ask
ksüühuutk	ksüühühuutk	call out
ts'm'aatk	ts'üts'm'aatk	sweet

4. Class IV irregular words in u.

daaw	dudaaw	ice
guuk	guhguuk	kill
ksiiw	ksuksiiw	scraper
t'u'usk	t'ut'u'usk	butcher knife

5. Class IV irregular words in a as in 'what.'

płoon	bapłoon	sea otter

6. Class IV irregular words in a as in 'father.'

ha'yin	haha'yin	place upright

7. Class IV irregular words in a as in 'hat.'

k'ah	k'ak'aah	wound

8. Class IV irregular words in e.

naa	ne'naa	snowshoe

CLASS V REDUPLICATION

1. In Class V, or -CV, plural reduplication the first consonant of the principal syllable and a vowel are suffixed directly to the vowel of the principal syllable, i.e., they are infixed between the vowel and any following consonant. The rules for determining the vowel of the infix are the same as for Classes I, III, and IV.

2. The vowel of the infix is i after d or y.

kwdii	lakwdiidi	hungry
yuutsk	yu'itsk	necklace

3. After n the vowel of the infix is a as in 'what.'

hana'a	hana'nax	woman
na'a	na'nax	dress

CLASS V IRREGULAR PLURALS

1. Class V irregular words in ü.

singular	plural	
łek	łiłük	bent

2. Class V irregular words in a as in 'what.'

sax	seesax	sharp
ts'oo	ts'oo'tsaxt	split
'wa'a	'wa'wax	dig
yooks	yooyaks	wash

3. Class V irregular words in a as in 'father.'

pla̲ksk	pliipla̲ksk	exhausted

4. Class V irregular words in o.

log̲ask	loolg̲ask	wet
lox̄	loolt̄	rotten

THE FORMATION OF THE PLURAL - DISTRIBUTIVES

1. Some words refer to things or states of being that by their very nature have special relationships to individual persons. These include body parts, clothing, special tools, states of mind, and kin relatives. Such words show the plural number by prefixing the distributive element ga-. This distributive element is to be translated as "each one his/her own ____."

2. Body parts.

singular	plural	
aak	ga'aak	mouth, mask
an'on	ga'an'on	hand
asii	gasasii	foot, leg
sii	gasüsii	foot
ban	gaban	belly
gayk	gagaykt	chest
goot	gogoot	heart
k'atsiweelt	gak'atsiwelt	finger
k'a'wts	gukk'a'w'ts	chin
kpal	gakpal	chin, jaw
ksiil	gaksiilt	teardrop
mmo	gamo	mother's milk, a suckling baby
muk	gamuukt	ear
ts'ak	gats'aa'tsax	nose
ts'al	gats'alts'al	face, eye
yexɬ	gayexɬ	saliva

3. Body parts may show the plural in other ways as well.

anaas	ak'anaas	skin
libets'aẅ	laklobits'aẅ	kidney
ɬaxs	ɬiklaxs	finger/toe nail
seyp	sikseyp	bone
t'mlaani	t'ikt'mlaani	neck
ts'al	ts'ikts'alt	face, eye
ts'mmuu	ts'ikts'mmow	ear
'waan	wük'waan	tooth
k'o	k'ak'o	back
ptal	buptal	rib
dap	dap	liver
iimx	iimx	facial hair
lii	lii	body hair
gaws	nak'awst	head hair

4. Clothing, tools, etc.

aat	ga'aat	net, seine
alah	ga'alah	chimney, smoke hole, vent, vent cover
gaayt	gagaayt	billed hat

singular	plural	
ksłüüsk	guksłüüsk	shirt
kwdus, kwduus	gukwdus	woman's knife
na'a	ganaa'nax	woman's dress
sgyen	gaxsgyen	lead, pitch, gum

5. States of body and mind.

alx	ga'alx	angry, brave
amadaalk	ga'amadaalk	praise, worship, speak well of
amawaal	amagawaalt	wealthy
buu	gabuu	blow, sound, have an orgasm
dzook	gadzook	ashamed

6. Kin relatives.

agwinübiip	agwiganübiip	great uncle (FMB, MMB, ref.)
agwinügwat	agwiganügwat	uncle (FB, MZH)
agwi'nts'i'i'ts	agwiga'nts'ii'ts	great aunt
nts'ii'ts	nagandzi'isk, naganüts'ii'tsk	grandmother
'naks	ganiwnaks, ganiwnskt	spouse

7. Kin terms may show the plural in other ways as well.

agwiiłems	agwiiłmłems	grandchild's spouse
agwii'o'os	agwiitxal'o'os	second cousin (FZCC, MBCC)
'naks	lax'naks	spouse (Note: this plural form refers to the spouses of one person)
weky	wagee	brother (B, MZS, FBS, male speaking)

8. Other distributives.

aamndep	aamngadep	a good amount
aamsganak	aamsgaganak	just long enough
k'oł	gak'oł	year
k'yabeelda	k'yigaxbeelda	cliff
łgum'yee	gakłgum'yee	old dog salmon
ts'ak	gadzak	clam

THE FORMATION OF THE PLURAL - ITERATIVES

1. Words that refer to some aspect of time or succession may indicate the plural number by prefixing the adverbial element gyik-. This element normally means "again," but in the vocabulary list in this section, it functions as a true plural.

singular	plural	
gyemk	gyikgyemk	month, moon, sun (Note: the plural also means "more than a month past" or "more than a month from now")
gyet	gyikgyet	man, person, human being
k'ooł	gyikk'ooł	year
suunt	gyiksuunt	summer
ksuut	gyiksuut	autumn
sxaytk	gyiksxaytk	dark (noun)

THE FORMATION OF THE PLURAL - INTENSIVES

1. Some words show the plural number by prefixing the intensive element lu-. This element is related to lu'kwil or lu'wil which means "very."

ayawa	ayaluwa	shout
baałk	labaalxk	abdominal surgery
baas	lübaas	afraid
duway	luway	paddle (a canoe)
güünks	luunks	be dry
güünaks	luuna̲ks	be dry
gwa̲tk	laxgwa̲tks, laxgwīida̲ks	be cold
gyeb	lapł	draw water, dip water
gyigyooks	llooks	float
gyipaayk	la̲paayk	fly (verb)
gyipayk	līpayk	fly (verb)
hadiks	la̲heediks	swim
ksinaałk	lūsanaałk	breathe
kwdii	lakwdiidi	hungry
kwtii	lukwtidi	hungry
kwłaask	nukwłaask	kick
'niidz	lu'niitsk	see (Note: plural also means "to stare at")
sgwaytk	lisgwaytk	stop, rest (Note: this form is used if the absolutive is human)
	siksgwaytk	stop, rest (non-human absolutive)
siin	lusiin	dizzy (plural also means "drunk")

singular	plural	
sgüü	lisgüü	put down, lay down, lie down, be lying down
süs'aaks	lüsa'aaks	laugh, make laugh
t'iilt	lilt'iild	fast, quick
waaks	luwaaks	paddle, row
waay	luwaay, huwaay, wuwaay	paddle, row
xsiit	laxsiit	vomit

THE FORMATION OF THE PLURAL - ISOMORPHICS

1. Some words, especially those referring to natural species, have the same form for both singular and plural.

aalks	servant
aatk	night
adawx	legend, story
aks	water, drink
aɬdigaws	humming bird
aws	sand
biẅaatk	phosphorescent algae
dap	liver, count, measure, try
gaax	raven, black
gagoom	seagull
gaxaax	berry bushes in bloom
gool	loon
goom	ashes
ha'a	goose
hagwn	oyster, mussel
iimx	beard
k'askoos	sandhill crane
lak	fire, firewood, fuel
lii	body hair, fur, feather
lo'ots	elderberry
lo'ox	eel
la'ask	seaweed
maas	bark (of a tree)
maay	berry
moon	salt water, sea
moos	thumb
'naaxɬ	killer whale
nuu	halibut hook
ol	bear
onxɬ	water lily
t'a'awil	halibut hook
t'axwans	adze
daxwans	adze
tkadzemsk	boiled whole fish
tskah	herring

umksiwa	European person
k'amksiwa	European person
waas	rain

THE FORMATION OF THE PLURAL - SUPPLETIVES

1. In a number of verbs and adjectives the plural agreement form ismorphologically unrelated to the singular form, i.e., they are not related by any transparent morphological mechanism. In such words the number of the absolutive has evidently become a part of the semantic characterization of the verbs and adjectives themselves.

singular	plural	
adigult'aa	adigulwan	continue, endure
aksyaa	akswaalxs	accumulate, increase, brighten, get fat, spread across
alobaa	alok'ooɬ	run quickly
amap'as	amamaxs	attractive
awül'mak	awült'aɬ	put away, put aside
baa	k'ol	run
batsk	maxsk	arrive, stand up, come in
batsgn	maxsn	place upright
baxyaa	baxwaalxs	walk up
daxsmt'aa	daxsmwan	mind, obey, sit still
dzabaa	dzak'ol	lame ("runs a short distance")
dzagayaa	dzagawaalxs	go across
dzak	düü	kill, die, be dead
gaksk	liwdsk	wake up
gatgyet	gatleet	strong
gyimɬ	siguunaks	wipe
ha'linook	ha'lilaaɬk	bed
haytksn	maxsn	place upright
k'aas	mukmoolsk	sour
ksüü	ksoox	go out, exit
kwdaxs	kwdaaɬaxs	leave
kwɬiyaa	kwɬiwaalxs	walk across
k'yeexk	huut	escape, flee, run away
miik	üm'am	ripe, rain cloud, storm
münyaa	münwaalxs	ascend, go up, walk up
nook	laaɬk, leɬk	lie down (animate absolutive)
p'axs	maxs	grow, develop
p'eegl	p'eegn	tear out and turn over

singular	plural	
sagyooks	saalooksk, salilooks	drift away
xswooxsk	saxswooxsk	dive (Note: this word might also be considered an irregular Class II reduplicative)
sgüü	doo, laɬk	put down, lay down, lie down, be lying down
sgyeetk	skatktanik	easy
sit'aatk	sigyootk	start off (e.g., in a canoe or on skis)
sup'as	sumaxs	young (person)
t'aa	wan	sit
t'mkyaa	t'mwaalxs	walk to the front
t'u'utsk	nadist'u'utsk	black (Note: this word might also be considered a complex plural with an intensive element (na') and a Class III plural prefix (dis-))
txooxk	'yaak, 'yaax	eat
ts'a'adziks	ts'a'aksiks	dirt, dirty
ts'lmgaa	ts'lmt'aa	take in
waa	uust	name
yaa	ɬoga, waalxs	go, step, walk

DERIVATIONAL REDUPLICATION

1. Reduplication is also used to form new words, i.e., it is a derivational mechanism. Unlike the plural reduplication (an inflexional mechanism) the reduplicated derivations often copy the vowel as well as one or more consonants of the model syllable. Reduplicated derivations function to express repeated activity or state of being (iterative), intensification, natural species, body parts, and perhaps even a "derivational plural."

2. Class I (CVk-) derivations.

source	form	meaning and (function)
?		
	wakawaa	jelly fish (natural species)

3. Class II (CVx-) derivations.

source	form	meaning and (function)
?		
	maxmeex	grouse (natural species)
?		
	naxnox	supernatural (intensive?)
	halaxsa'nax'nox	beach knotwood (natural species)
t'ook		suck
	t'axt'oox	suck (intensive, iterative)
	t'axt'oosk	golden shiner (natural species)
?		
	ts'ogat'axtxayɫ	bat (natural species)
wok		sleep
	waxwox	moth (iterative, intensive, natural species)

4. Class III (CVC-) derivations with the vowel copied.

source	form	meaning and (function)
aamadzap		complete
	aamadzapdzap	perfect (intensive)
?		
	aw'aawsk	curly hair (intensive, iterative)
baa		run
	babaa	tremble (iterative)
?		
	ba'nba'n	break bread (iterative)
buu, aks		blow, water
	buhbuu'aks	splash (intensive)
?		
	galipliip	thunder (intensive, iterative, natural species)
?		
	gasgadzax	ants (natural species)
	k'ask'adzn	ants (natural species)
güütks		search
	güsgüüts	wren, sparrow (iterative, natural species)

source	form	meaning and (function)
güül		pick, harvest
	gülgüül	search for (intensive) (Note: inanimate absolutive)
gwün, 'niidz		causal, look
	gwitgwiniiks	owl (intensive, natural species)
?		
	gyigyi'oosk	stubborn (intensive?)
gyiitk		flood
	gyitgyiitk	flood repeatedly (iterative)
hani		thin
	hanhani	temple (iterative, body part)
hayts		send
	hashayts	send (intensive?)
?		
	halhal	spinning top (iterative)
	laxhalhal	upstairs (?)
haw		say
	hawhaw	African lion (intensive, natural species)
huumsk		sniff
	huumhuumsk	sniff repeatedly (iterative)
k'odz		slice
	k'odzd'odz	butcher (iterative)
ksa, lax		out, on
	ksalaklak	fall down, fall out a window, be born (intensive)
lapł		dip water
	lapla'pgn	mix up, turn over, turn everything over (iterative, intensive)
lax, aks		on, water
	laxlagmks	calm, esp, just before the tide turns (intensive)
?		
	łakłakws	shake oneself (iterative, intensive)
?		
	łuluu	shake out (iterative, intensive) (Note: absolutive must be a flat object)
?		
	manhakhakwła	shoestring (iterative?)
?		
	maxlagalgaliis	Audobon's warbler (natural species)
naa		snowshoes
	'na'na	mallard (iterative, natural species)
gyet, sugyet		man, a person who has killed one victim
	sugyedmgyet	a murderer, a person who has killed more than one victim

source	form	meaning and (function)
?		
	ts'ats'a	hail (natural species)

5. Class III (CVC-) derivations with vowel epenthesis.

source	form	meaning and (function)
?		
	an'on	hand, arm (iterative, body part)
ban		belly
	binbentk	swim belly up, i.e., with a back stroke (iterative)
?		
	g̲atsg̲aats	dogfish shark (natural species)
	g̲asg̲aatsk	rough (intensive?)
gwaalk		burn
	gisagwlgwaalk	northern lights (iterative, intensive, natural species)
?		
	gwüsgwaas	blue jay (natural species)
	gwisgwaask	blue (intensive?)
g̲oos		jump
	g̲asg̲oos	stork (iterative, natural species)
?		
	g̲anyüsyetsa	suspenders (iterative)
?		
	hamhom	ankle (iterative, body part)
?		
	hashoosk	trouble (intensive?)
?		
	hathotxk	to boil (iterative, intensive?)
k'aa		cut, wound (noun)
	k̲'ag̲aa	harlequin duck (natural species)
kwɨaxs		kick
	kwligukwlaxs, kwlikwlaxs	utterly destroy by kicking (intensive, iterative)
k'waas		break
	k'wüsk'waasl	break up (iterative)
?		
	k̲'apk̲'oop	dwarf dogwood (natural species)
g̲oos		jump
	k̲'ask̲'oos	sandhill crane
dam̲		hold
	ludmdam̲	crush, squueze, hug (intensive)
looyk		move camp
	manliklooyg	be frightened, get excited (intensive)
?		
	mmo	milk, a suckling baby (iterative, body part)

source	form	meaning and (function)
moose (English)		
	mismuus	cow (natural species)
soo		food left over from a potlatch
	sasoo	rattle (iterative noun)
t'aa'pł		to hammer
	t'üpt'aa'pł	hammer repeatedly (iterative)
hoolt		full
	halhoolt	full (intensive)

6. Class IV (CV-) derivations.

source	form	meaning and (function)
?		
	dzigyidziip	tomorrow (iterative)
dziiws		daylight
	dzidziiws	still daylight (durative?)
gayk		chest (body part)
	k'ayk'ay	wing (iterative, body part)
gwaalk		burn
	gugweelaks	polished, shiny (intensive)
gyet		person
alu-		in front
	alugyigyet	talking chief, spokesman, the upper class (intensive)
k'al		empty
	k'algyigyet, gagyigyet	commoners (intensive)
ła-		past
	łagyigyet, łałagyigyet	the old people , i.e., from a former time (intensive)
sm-		real
	smgyigyet	chief (intensive address form)
gyi-		up
	gyigyaani	the interior, upriver (spatial iterative?)
	gyigyanngyał	to pray (iterative)
	gyigyooks	to float (iterative)
	gyigyootk	axe (iterative)
haw		say
	hahahaw	treasure (intensive)
?		
	hahangoot	destroy with malice (intensive)
lo'ox		eel
	hala'lox	sea monster
łuunti		angry
	łałuungyit, łiłuungit	slave
?		
	nalüksgyigyet	quilt (iterative)
?		
	nnaaw̓	lullaby (iterative)

source	form	meaning and (function)
t'iilt		fast
	didit'iil	go quickly (intensive)
ts'aaw		the inside
	ts'ats'aawd	Athapascan Indian (spatial iterative?)
ts'amti		lightning
	ts'its'amti	Thunderbird (intensive, iterative)
?		
	üü'üünsk	a clumsy person

7. Class V (-CV) derivations.

source	form	meaning and (function)
?		
	hmmoomax, mo'mx	smile
?		
	kwłna'anax	broken
łek		bend, twist
	łiłük	undo, untie (iterative)
?		
	łełap	smooth, plane (iterative)
sak̲		sharp
	saxsaasax	thornbush (iterative, natural species) (Note: this form is complex, being both Class II and Class V)

SOUND CHANGES ACCOMPANYING REDUPLICATION

1. Vowel changes.

łaats, łakłats	scraper
g̲aax, g̲akg̲ak̲	black bass
małiłk, makmaałiłk	tell
łek, łiłük	bent, crooked, twisted
sak̲, seesax	sharp
pla̅ksk, pliiplaksk	exhausted, overworked, beaten up
libets'aẅ, lakl̅obits'aẅ	kidney
sk'uunsk, sik̅sk'u'unsk	teach

2. The sound y is sometimes inserted after a long vowel and before a gy.

gyik̲'aak, k̲'aygyik̲'ak — hip, waist

3. The sound l is sometimes inserted after a long vowel and before a lateral sound (l, ł).

ła'ayask, la̲lła'ayask — climb

4. Long vowels may become diphthongs.

ts'mmuu, ts'ikts'mmou — ear

5. In some words prefixes are deleted in the reduplicated form.

sagwaatk, gwitgwaatk	disappear
laxdii, didii	hill
sm'ooygyit, smgyigyet	chief

6. Vowels are sometimes inserted into consonant clusters in order to make them easier to pronounce.

'nłomsk, nika'nłomsk	sacred
woomxk, waxwoomask	suffer
gyelüks, gyilgyalks	feel

7. The order of sounds is sometimes reversed.

k'oylk, galgolik	dull
logask, loolgask	wet
lox, loolt	rotten
ts'aky, ts'akyts'ak	extinguished

8. In some words suffixes are deleted or altered.

ts'al, ts'ikts'alt	face
waa, watwaa	meet
ap, hakhaps	bee
łgwt'iin, łakłgwt'iina	steep valley
lox, loolt	rotten

9. A glottalized k may become a g.

k'was, gwisgwas	break
k'oylk, galgolik	dull
k'os, gasgos	jump
k'oomtk, gaxgoomtk	hope

10. Glottalized y may simplify to plain y.

woyt, wükwo'yt	invite
naa, ne'naa	snowshoe
yuutsk, yu'itsk	necklace

11. Both k and k may become x at the end of a word.

gaax, gakgak	black bass
moolksx, mukmoolsk	sour
'lax, lilak	needle

12. Aitch and glottal stop alternate.

ap, hakhaps	bee

13. Ell and en alternate.

k'yi'nam, k'yilk'yi'nam	give

14. Some reduplication forms are compound.

swantk, sumsikswantk	blow

GRAMMATICAL SUFFIXES

1. There are ten suffixes which, when attached to words, change their grammatical relationships (actor, recipient of action, etc.) and sometimes their grammatical function (noun, verb, etc.).

2. The suffix -x (sometimes -k̲) derives a word that refers to a thing, place, or activity that is touched by or affected by the original word, or that is in some way a consequence of the original word. The relationship between the original word and the derived word is often metaphorical.

original word	derived word	meaning
naał		breath
	naałx	windpipe
xaa		air
	xeex	foam, bubles
k̲'aawts		labret
	k̲'aawtsx	gill
iim		quill
	iimk̲, iimx	beard, moustache
łaats		scraper
	łaatsx	salmon tails, split and smoked
moos		thumb
	'moosx	chewed fat
k̲'odz		cut
	k̲'oodzax	break (of a string), die (of a person)
k̲'o'a̲l		forget
	k̲'oolax	dull; warm one's back by the fire
moolks		crabapple
	moolksx	sour
güünks		dry
	lugüünksax	thirsty
xts'ii		thick
	xts'iik̲	ribbon worm

3. Three suffixes are used to express activity that affects some other thing or person. These suffixes are -t, -l, and -n.

4. The suffix -t changes a word to mean someone or something that uses (as an instrument) the original word.

gyemk		sun, moon
	gyemga̲t	astronomer
gyiims		cedar bark
	gyimst	match (originally shredded cedar bark used to start a fire)
g̲aks		awaken
	g̲akst	rattle (noun)

original word	derived word	meaning
waay		paddle, oar
	waayt	pectoral fin, ventral fin

5. The suffixes -l and -n change a word to mean a person, thing, or action that has as it goal, intention, or purpose, the original word or something similar to the original word.

buu		blow, sound (of a whale)
	buul, buu'l	warn
hasaax		lack
	hasaakl	desire
łoo		drift, swim (of a fish)
	łool, łoowl	push thru the water
p'uu		scatter (intransitive)
	p'uul	scatter (transitive)
t'a'k		water spout
	t'a'kyl	twist
saksk		clean (adjective)
	saksgn	clean (transitive)
sayp		bone
	saypn	harden (transitive), make hard
łeky		bent, crooked, twisted
	ła'gyin	bend (transitive)
hooks		come
hooksk		be with
	hooksn	put with, be put with
daxs		flounder
	daxsn	throw flat on the water, make skip along the water

6. Five suffixes are used to express various types of similarity to the original word. These suffixes are -k, -s, -sk, -tk, and -ts.

7. The suffix -k changes a word to mean some particular quality of the original word.

g̲atsg̲ats		dogfish
	g̲atsg̲atsk	rough
g̲aws		hair
	g̲awsk	thin
gwisgwaas		blue jay
	gwisgwaask	blue
k̲'apk̲'oop		bunch berry
	k̲'apk̲'oopk	red hot, lava
laalt		worm
	laaltk	slow
mooks		snow (on the ground)
	mooksk	white
sayp		bone
	saypk	hard

original word	derived word	meaning
was		blanket
	wask	dressed
yeł		fish slime
	yełk	smooth
p'iił		peel
	p'iiłk	mashed
ts'ii		come in
	ts'iik	be leaking

8. The suffixes -s, -sk, -ts, and sometimes -k, change a word to mean a particular thing or action that shares one or more qualities with the original word.

yaa		give away
	yaakw	potlatch
ts'oo		split open
	ts'ook	lift, clear (of fog), subside (of a flood)
beex		tear
	beexk	tear bark from a cedar tree
baał		cut open
	baałk	abdominal surgery
gatgyet		strong
	gatgyetk	jerk, push, throw down
noo		mother
	nook	lie down
ganaak		deer tracks
	ganaaxs	ladder, steps
gaapk		rake, scratch
	gaapxs	border, sill
loop		rock
	loo'pis	testes
moolk		nervous, irritated, on edge
	moolks	crabapple
süülk		middle
	süülgas	forenoon
ts'oox		salmon belly
	ts'ooxs	shoes
haaytk		stand up (intransitive)
	haa'ytisk	house posts
yaakw		potlatch
	yaask	give a gift at an ear piercing ceremony
yełk		smooth
	yełisk	slippery
yuutk		carry around the neck
	yuutsk	necklace
gab		eat
	ga'psk	eat berries off the "tree"
huum		smell
	huumsk	sniff around

original word	derived word	meaning
suwiliin		chase
	suwiliinsk	hunter
yaamx		tricky
	yaamgask	imitate a deer or seal as a lure
ya'an		pass around
	ya'ansk	distribution
gaamgn		pry
	gaamgants	oars
noo		mother
	noots	homosexual

9. The suffix -tk expresses a metaphorical similarity to the original word.

ban		belly
	binbentk	swim (float) belly up
galtsgan		three (of canoes)
	galtsgantk	three (of long things)
gan		wood, tree
	gantk	be erect, have an erection
ɨoo		drift, swim (of a fish)
	ɨo'otk	clouds

LEXICAL SUFFIXES

1. There are five sets of suffixes that can be related phonetically and semantically to independent lexical items. These suffixes are always unstressed.

2. The suffixes -sk, -ks, -kwsa, -aks, -üks, and -iks are related to the word for water, aks.

bu'nsk	splash
analysis: buu-n-aks (sound-make-water)	
manbu'nsk	erupt (of a geyser)
analysis: man-buu-n-aks (up-sound-make-water)	
gadziks	declare bankruptcy, sell out
(literally: throw water on everything)	
gwanüks	spring (of water)
gwaanaks	cooked, faded
laxlagmks	the calm before the tide shifts
analysis: lak-lak-m-aks (on-on-connective-water)	
ɨa'agynsk	glue (noun)
analysis: ɨa'agy-n-sk (be glued on-make-water)	
ts'alaks	whirlpool
analysis: ts'al-aks (eye-water)	
ts'iiwkwsa	bail water out of a canoe
hadziiwkwsa	dipper
analysis: ha-dziiwkwsa (instrument-bail water out of a canoe)	

3. The suffixes -gn, -gan, -xn, are related to the word for tree, wood, stick: gan.

batsgn	arrive in a boat
analysis: batsk-gan	(arrive-tree)
gaamgn	pry
gaamgnts	oars
k'awtsgn, k'awtsxn	one (long objects)
k'oopsxn	two (long objects)
Note: this suffix is used for all numbers referring to long objects. See the section on numerals.	
k'yiidzxan	point out
k'yiwaɫgn	ship worms
analysis: k'yi-waɫ-gan	(down-yellow cedar-wood)
lapl'pgn	mix up, turn over
yelgan	drill-stick, fire-drill
analysis: yel-gan	(drill-stick)

4. The suffixes -gyit and -git are related to the word for man: gyet.

gyitwaalgyit	raiders
analysis:gyitwaal-gyit	(attack-man)
laguulgit	burn the possessions of a dead person, the burnt possessions of a dead person
luulgyit	feast
ɫaɫuungyit	slave
sm'oogyit	chief
ts'uwaangyit	the youngest child in a family

5. The suffixes -bn and -n may be related to the word for belly: ban.

goopn	fish heart, soft palate
analysis: goop-ban	(wave-belly)
waaybn	pregnant (used to refer to dogs and, as an insult,to humans
analysis: waay-ban	(paddle-belly)

6. The suffixes -mx, -mk, and -x are possibly related to the word for respond: diilmx. They are used to refer to languages of dialects.

gaalmx, geelmx	Nass-Gitksan language
gyaanmx	Nass-gitksan language
gyitksanmx	Nass-Gitksan language
haydmx	Haida language
ɫingiitx	Tlingit language
sgüümx	Southern Tsimshian dialect

CARDINAL NUMBERS

1. The numbers in this section are used for counting things in general. In the following sections there are different sets of numbers which must be used to count specific kinds of things: living beings, human beings, long things, canoes (vehicles in general), humans aboard or in vehicles, volume measurements, linear measurements. Anything other than these specific classes of objects is counted using the numbers in this section.

k'üül	one
gu'pl	two
k'wili	three
txaalpx	four
kwstuuns	five
k̲'oolt	six
t̄'a̲pxoolt	seven
yuk̄wdeelt	eight
kstimoos	nine
kpiil	ten
kpiil di k'üül	eleven
kpiil di gu'pl	twelve
gu'pl wil kpiil	twenty
gu'pl wil kpiil di k'üül	twenty-one
k'wili wil kpiil	thirty

2. The numbers used for animals (non-human) are also used to count flat objects, e.g., skins, mats, clothing.

k'yaak	one
t'a̲pxaat	two
gwün	three
4 thru 7 same as the general numbers above	
k̲'andoolt	eight
9 same as the general number above	
k'yap	ten
k'yap di k'yaak	eleven
t'a̲pxaat wil k'yap	twenty

3. The numbers used for human beings are for the most part the same stems as those used for animals, but with an -ool suffix.

k'ool	one
t'apxaduul	two
gwüloon	three
txalpxdool	four
kstnsool	five
k̲'ooldool	six
t̄'apxaldool	seven
yukwɨa'adool	eight
ksta̲masool	nine
kpoo̅l	ten
kpool di k'ool	eleven
t'apxaduul wil kpool	twenty

4. The numbers used for long objects are for the most part the same stems as the general numbers, but with a -gn or -xn suffix (related to the word for tree: gan). This suffix is always unstressed.

k'awtsgn	one
k'oopsxn	two
galtsgan	three (The last syllable is stressed)
txa'apsxn	four
kwstu'ansxn	five
k'ooltsxn	six
t'apxooltsxn	seven
yukwdeeltsxn	eight
kstimootsxn	nine
kpiitsxn	ten
kpiil di k'awtsgn	eleven
k'oopsxn wil kpiil	twenty

5. The numbers used to count canoes and other vehicles consist for the most part of the general number stems with a -tk or -gantk suffix.

k'ameet	one
galbeeltk	two
galsgantk	three
txaalpxsk	four
kwstu'ansxn	five (same as the number for long objects)
k'ooltk	six
t'apxooltk	seven
yukwɨa'atk	eight
kstamoosk	nine
k'yepsk	ten

6. A special set of numerals is used to count human beings aboard canoes or in any conveyance or vehicle. This set consists of the general number stems and a -daat suffix. This suffix carries the primary stress.

k'widaat	one
gulapdaat	two
gwindaat	three
txaalpdaat	four
kwstunsdaat	five
k'oldaat	six
t'apxooldaat	seven
yukwɨa'adaat	eight
kstimoosdaat	nine
kbaldaat	ten

7. There are two sets of numbers used to count unit measures. The first set, with the stressed suffix -on (related to an'on: hand or arm) is used by most speakers of Tsimshian to count both linear and volume units of measure. Some, however, use it to count only volume units and use the second set for linear

units. The second set has a stressed suffix -gaay (related to the word for arm, chest, wing). When used as a noun, the first set (-on) refers to the specific number of fathoms.

volume or general	linear	
k'üülda'on	k'üüldmgaay	one
gupl'on		two
k'ul'on		three
txaalpxl'on		four
kwstunsal'on		five
k'oolda'on		six
t'apxoolda'on		seven
yukwɨa'al'on		eight
kstamoolsal'on		nine
kpal'on		ten

PROCLITICS

1. Morphemes that occur before nouns and verbs are called proclitics because they sometimes are prefixed directly to the word and at other times act as separate word prepositions. Proclitics express locative, aspectual, modal, case relational, and lexical meanings.

LOCATIVE PROCLITICS - STATIVE

1. Stative locative proclitics indicate the place or position of actions and things. The semantic dimensions of these proclitics include internal vs. external, tangent vs. nontangent, above, below, parallel, perpendicular, proximate, remote.

2. Ts'm- (locative, stative, internal)

ts'm'aatk	sweet
ts'm'aax	mouth
ts'm'an'on	palm of hand
ts'mg̲al	anus
ts'mg̲a'na	door frame, window frame
ts'mh̄uutsa	flow; a deep place in a stream under the roots of a tree
ts'mksiyets	chop out (see ksi-)
ts'mloob	cave
ts'mmuu	ear
ts'm'ootsn	palm of hand
ts'msee	knee joint
ts'mt'ii	nape of neck
ts'mt'ooł	a room behind the fireplace
ts'mts'ax	nostril
ts'mtsoxs	sole of foot
ts'muu hoon	pectoral fin (fish ear)
ts'myuup	menstruation closet

3. Lax- (locative, stative, tangent, above, parallel)

laxa, laxha	heaven, sky, storm, in the air
laxdii	hill
laxg̲ayna	street
laxgwiikw	spring time
laxhalhal	upstairs
laxhuu	sandbar
laxlag̲mks	calm (before the tide shifts)
laxmid̄iik	spring time
lax'naks	a woman who has two husbands
laxnap'aa	a high meadow
laxnap'aal	a cottonwood grove
lax'oh	the top, a patch of moss
lax'ool	eyelids
lax'oo waap	roof
laxs'neexs	top of foot
laxsniil	back of hand
laxst'uup'l	platform, stage

laxsüülda	ocean
laxsuumaay	summer time (new berry month, June)
laxsü'yens	spring time
laxt'aa	lake
laxts'a'adzaks	field, garden
laxwiihoon	summer time (salmon run month, July)
laxyuup	earth, ground

4. T'm- (locative, stative, tangent, above, perpendicular)

t'mbaa	hip and upper leg
t'mg̱aws	head
t'mg̱ay	arm
t'mḵ'o	backbone
t'mk̄yaa	walk at the front
t'mlaani	neck
t'nłaam	leg, shin bone
t'myaa	fast

5. Tkwi-, tkwa- (locative, stative, tangent, not above, parallel)

tkwabaanł	spin
tkwidzoox	outside edge

6. G̱ana- (locative, stative, tangent, not above, perpendicular)

g̱anahaaytk	lean against, stand against
g̱anawelii	carrying strap

7. Lag̱ax- (locative, stative, tangent, not above, bilateral)

lag̱ax'ag̱m	double headed axe
lag̱ax'alg̱yax	linguist
lag̱axniitsk	one who has "eyes in the back of his head"
lag̱axts'aap	a dying person, one who has begun talking to the dead, "talking in both houses"

8. Łüü, lukłi, lukwłi (locative, stative, proximate, below)

łüüwaap	under the house
lukłihooya	underclothes
lukłiwaap	under the house
lukwłiksłüüsk	undershirt
lukwłip'axs	underpants

9. Naḵ- (locative, stative, proximate, not below)

naḵ'axba'ala	on the south side
naḵhaaywaask	northeast
naḵsmya'win	right hand
naḵsuniisk	mirror, window

10. Alo-, alu- (locative, stative, remote, below)

alubaa, alobaa, aluḵ'oł	run quickly, i.e., out in front

alugigyet	talking chief, spokesman, people who live down in the open

11. sga, sxa, sa (locative, stative, remote, not below)

sxa'niist, sa'niist	mountain
sgadawɬ	go across
sganakt	length, duration
sga'ya'a	curtains
sxat'uusa	dam

LOCATIVE PROCLITICS - MOTION

1. Motion locative proclitics indicate motion in relation to the place or position of actions and things. The semantic dimensions of these proclitics include internal vs. external, afferent (motion toward), efferent (motion away from), ascending, descending, proximate, remote, geographic.

2. Ts'lm-, logm- (locative, motion, afferent, internal)

ts'lmgaa	take in
ts'lm'ma'a, ts'lmt'aa	roast, put in the oven
ts'lm'wiihaaw	call out while coming into a house, give a greeting, announce oneself
logmbaa	step into
logmt'aa	sit near

3. Ksi, ksa, ksü, xsa (locative, motion, internal source, efferent)

ksa'aamks	clear water
ksabuu	blow
kask'o'oɬ	forget
ksakwɬeel	be born (of animals)
ksalaklak	be born (of humans)
ksaɬoo	swim out
ksa'mesk	mother's milk
ksap'e'al	tear out
ksats'iiba	tie hair up in a coil
xsats'iipa	necktie
ksibuhbuu'aks	splash
ksigwaantk	rise (of the sun)
ksinaaɬ	breathe
ksits'al	tear drops
ksüɬootk	crawl out
ksawoox, xsuwoxan	dream

4. Agwil- (locative, motion, internal source, efferent, proximate)

agwilwan	set aside (plural object)

5. G̲ałdik- (locative, motion, internal source, efferent, ascending)

g̲ałdiksgüü	lie up at the side
g̲ałdikyaa	go aside, go up into the woods

6. Txa- (locative, motion, internal source, efferent, descending)

txa'aaxt	place down in front of the door
txanaaẅ	mooring (specifically the one just down from the speaker's house)

7. G̲alksi (locative, motion, internal, afferent and efferent)

g̲alksiłoosk	nose ring
g̲alksiyaan	go through

8. Wüsin- (locative, motion, internal)

wüsinbaa	run along the inside
wüsinsgüü	hip of the roof

9. Gwin- (locative, motion, not internal, afferent)

gwinse'ik	pull (non-human object)
gwinspiil	pull (human object)

10. Gwił- (locative, motion, not internal, efferent, proximate)

gwiłt'uus	push (human object)
gwił'aax	lip
gwiłwoh	get out

11. Gyis- (locative, motion, not internal, efferent, remote)

gyis	miss
gyisdawł	go away, leave
gyisg̲o	go to another place
gyisłaał	move (inanimate object)
gyistxalt'mtk	design, pattern, picture

12. Kwłi- (locative, motion, not internal, perpendicular)

kwłiwaalxs, kwłiyaa	walk across
kwłiyeetsk	pound
kwłna'anax	broken
kwłwoo	hunter

13. Hał- (locative, motion, not internal, parallel)

hałgyiik	beach
hałwn̲	sit in a row

14. Bax- (locative, motion, tangent source, tangent goal, ascending, parageographic)

baxbeega'aks	waterspout, gale
baxg̲aksüülgyimxs	half tide (coming in)

baxse'ik	pull up or stretch up along the ground
baxyaa, baxwaalxs	walk up along the ground

15.'Yag̲a- (locative, motion, tangent source, tangent goal, descending, parageographic)

'yag̲adox	take down
'yag̲aksüülgyimxs	half tide (going out)
'yag̲ag̲oo	go down
'yag̲agwinuusk	waterfall
'yag̲agyemk	new moon
'yag̲ase'ik	pull down

16. Man- (locative, motion, tangent source, non-tangent goal, ascending, parageographic)

ma̲'naxk	high, reach the top
manbu'nsk	erupt (of a geyser)
mangya'aglt	roll up (transitive)
manhakhakwła	shoestring
manliklooyg	be frightened, become excited
münyaa, münwaalxs	ascend (e.g., stairs, steps), go up, walk up
münlii	chest hair

17. Tkyi- (locative, motion, non-tangent source, tangent goal, descending, parageographic)

tkyidaawł	sink
tkyidzool	slide down
tkyi'niitsk	look down
tkyit'uus	knead, press down
tkyiyaa	go down (to), walk down (to), descend (to), dusk

18. Dzag̲am- (locative, motion, geographic, ashore)

dzag̲mdaawł	go ashore

19. Gyil- (locative, motion, geographic, upstream)

gyilhawli	forest, woods

20. Gyisi- (locative, motion, geographic, downstream)

gyisidaawł	downstream
gyisihaywaask	Northeast wind
gyisiyaask	North, North wind

21. Uks- (locative, motion, geographic, out to sea)

uksbaask	offshore wind
uksdaawł	drown, fall overboard, go out to sea
uksdoxł	take out
ukshaaytk	stand out, stand near the water

ASPECT PROCLITICS

1. Aspect elements indicate action or state as beginning, continuing, or terminated, etc.

2. The proclitics si-, sü, su- refer to a beginning or inceptive aspect.

sigootk	start thinking about, get an idea
sit'aa	begin
sit'aatk	start of, e.g., in a canoe or on skis
sügwalak	start a fire
sülaks	build a fire
sugyet	a murderer who has killed only one victim
sukyooxt	fresh (green) grass
sup'as, sumaxs	young, a young person
sugye'awin	just now
su'weentk	have teeth erupt, false teeth
suwilaay'msk	teacher, a teacher

3. Adigul- (continuing, enduring aspect)

adigult'aa, adigulwan	continue, endure

4. Gani- (continuing aspect)

ganiweel	continue
ganiliimi	keep singing

5. Sta-, sti- (continuing aspect)

stahyaa	continue, keep going
stakalaaɬ	follow, keep track of
sta'onm haxbeexsk	carpenter saw (literally: hand-stays-on-one-side-saw)
sti'moon	humpback, pink salmon

6. Gaxba-, gaxpa- (occasional aspect)

gaxba'alaskw	sometimes weak
gaxpaweel	do (something) sometimes

7. Huk- (habitual aspect)

hukalaays	always lazy, a lazy person
huk'al'algyax	speaker
huk'alaskw	always weak, a sickly person
hukaluk'aɬ	a fast runner
hukamadaal'kask	a worshiper
huk'at	a fisherman
hukbii'k	a liar
hukdzap	a jack of all trades
hukkwdek	a good hunter
hukwoomsk	always sick, sickly

8. Ła- (terminated or perfect aspect)

łagyigyet	the old people
łamaxsk	arrive (plural absolutive)
ła'nnak	a long time

9. Gwüldm- (beforehand)

gwüldmmaalsk	foretell, prophesy
gwüldm'niidz	foresee

10. Wil- (subsequential)

wiladzap	lucky, healthy, competent (especially in hunting)
wilduulgyit	war
wilgak'oosk	council
wilgyet	colour
wiliingyit	grasshopper, spider (especially a large spider, which, if seen in the house, is a omen of death), cave cricket
wilmaxlagaap	a narrow channel
wil'nak	far away

MODAL PROCLITICS

1. Modal elements indicate a particular attitude on the part of the speaker about the reality or fulfillment of the action or state being expressed.

2. Ap-, ap- (certainly, really)

ap'adziksmgyet	a snob
aplogawdi	empty, make empty
apsxawgan	wooden spoon

3. Am-, gam- (only, i.e., unimportant or unsubstantial)

amksiwah	European
amp'aal	cottonwood
amsahoon	fish weir
gamgaantk	door
gamgoot	pity
gamiilk	play
gamłabiisk	shavings
gamt'uu'tsk	charcoal, coal, volcanic rock

4. Kbi-, xbi- (half, i.e., not really)

kbidaxs, xbidaxs	starry founder
xbihats'al	devilfish, giant squid, giant octopus
xbilataab	the end of the table
xbimooksk	half-breed, metis

5. Liks-, lüks- (different, strange)

liksgoot, lüksgoot	crazy
liksoox, lükso'ak	door
likswaas	wind change at the end of a heavy rain
lükstaa	island
lüksts'ap	stranger
lükswaas	a sudden rain when the sun is shining
lüks'yens	weeds

6. Lu- (really)

lu'an'on	a person who pays for the burial of a dead person
lubaask	a southeaster
ludaaltk	meet
ludawłdagyemk	afternoon
ludep	try on for size
ludmdam, ludmis	crush, hug, squeeze
lugawsga'aaks	zero tide
lugyiis	be wrong, make a mistake
luho'nł	fill
luksüülk	right in the middle
lułguul	narrow
lu'niitsk	stare at
lu'ooks	wide
lusanaałk	miracle, wonder

7. Sis-, süs- (play, pretend, not serious or sincere)

sisdzooxs	cohabit ("play house")
sisgwangaatks	implore
süs'aaxs	laugh, make laugh

8. Sm- (real, genuine)

sm'algyax	language of the Coast Tsimshian
sm'alwilu, smhagwilhuu	burlap, gunny sack
sm'eesk	home brew, homemade berry wine
smgan	cedar
smgyigyet	chief (address form), the nobility, councillors, talking chiefs
smgyiik	woodpecker
smhaw	be sure
smhawksn	believe
smhaywas	a southeaster
smhu'adzax	a brook
smii'kask	song sparrow
smk'awtsi	olachen grease
smksiiyats	chop out
smlak	open fire
smmay	(oval leaf) blueberry
sm'ooygyit	chief
sm'uksdox	take out
smwüs	blanket

smxso	dugout canoe
smya'awin	right hand

9. 'Wah- (without)

wah'a'ayin	an unforgiveable offense, a commoner
'wahg̲a'tmk'aay	vest, brassiere
'wahk̲'aligyetk	virgin, unmarried, untouched
wahlīi	bald, prepubescent
wahliiilgyit	one who didn't wake up
wahliimi	one having no song
'wah'nts'ii'ts	one without a grandmother (an insult name)
'wahti txas'niitga	take time out, do two things at the same time, time used to do some- outside the ordinary routine
wahwaa	be puzzled
'wah'waa'nsk	disobey, stubborn
wah'yooks	trust, hope

CASE PROCLITICS

1. Case proclitics indicate particular relationships such as cause to be, resemble, instrument for, experience of, etc.

2. Am- (serving for)

amaalk	crust, scab
mag̲an	red cedar
amg̲o'insk	entertainment
amḡyeek	shore animals and plants
amgyiik	scoter
amhalaayt	shaman, a shaman's costume
amhaw	voice
amiilk	mask, disguise, effigy
amsg̲abuu	abundant, a lot
amuk̲s	listen, obey
amuus	corner

3. Ha- (instrument for)

ha'aks	dipper
hadaay	steer (a canoe), rudder
hadiiltk	dorsal fin of a cod
hadziiwkwsa	dipper for bailing out a canoe
hag̲agaytk	scissors
hag̲ayaan, ha'k̲ayaan	war club
hagyiłaam	carving knife
hagyooks	keel
hahahaw	treasure
hak'eentk	drill bit
hana'a	woman
hasiipk	disease

hat'aapa	pestle (made of stone)
hat'aaxs	a pole used for pushing a canoe in shallow water
hat'al	cedar bark strips used for making baskets
hayaaxk	fork

4. Ha'li- (place or time for)

ha'lidel	battlefield
ha'lidzook	world
ha'liksalaxlaka miyaanm	Christmas
ha'lik'üül	Monday
ha'ligu'pl	Tuesday
ha'lik'wili	Wednesday
ha'litxaalpx	Thursday
ha'likwstuuns	Friday
ha'liyaayx	Saturday
ha'lisgwayt	Sunday
ha'li'x'ẅah	March
ha'lilaxdzmdzm	March, April
ha'li'xxswaanxs	April
Ha'li'xła'ask	May
ha'li'xmaay	June
ha'lilaxłgumedmgaguum	May, June
ha'li'xstmoon	July
ha'li'xhoon	July
ha'lilaxstmhon	July, August
ha'lilaxts'awas	September, October
ha'linook	bed
ha'lit'ah	chair
ha'litoo	chest of drawers, cupboard, dresser
ha'liwaalxs	floor
ha'liwilduulgyit	battle ground

5. Ma-, mi-, mü- (act like)

mahana'a	effeminate, an effeminate man
magaayt, magayk	nightmare, sleep
mahaag	moss
małiitk	green, blue-green, yellow-green
ma'ol	an epileptic
mat'iibn	a person with webbed fingers
matxaw	a person with a nervous tic
mi'yuuta	mannish, a mannish woman
mü'watsa	act crazy, like an otter, a crazy person

6. Sa-, si-, sü-, s- (cause to be)

sa'kał	divide, settle an estate
sagayna	fall down (inanimate absolutive)
sagyaa	take off
sahakwdak	yew
sanaałk	be surprised, be astonished
sat'uus	push

sigwaan, sügwaanał	bake, cook
sigyemk	to heat
sihoon, gasihon	to smoke salmon
si'naa	to bait
s'ndzoks	make camp
si'nawōox	admonish, warn
st'u'utsk	blacken
süluuna	to dry (transitive)
sümaalsk	tell a lying story, betray
süwiihoon	twins

7. Sn- (cause to be)

snlayditsks	signal, make a sign
snyeekwt	to hold

8. Gwün- (order, cause)

gwünniidzn	show
gwünnuu	ask for, demand

9. Xs- (resemble)

xs'ileetk	red
xslax'osmt'ays	quilt
xsmałiitk	green, blue-gree, yellow-green
xsmłiisk	yellow-green
xsp'iyaan	smoke-blue
xsp'o	crackle
xspo'nsk	break, crackle (of twigs breaking)
xswaxłaas	pink, huckleberry colour
xsyaanak'almos	yellow

10. X- , xa- (experience, sense, eat)

xabaalda	Southwest
xadiyaaẅ	receive a burial payment
xa'iłeetk	bloody, bruise
xasaniis	climb a mountain
xba'ala	squall, storm from the South
xbak	fold, crest of a wave, a wave breaking
xpagmgoop	die, death, lit: the wave breaks
xdiī	eat with
xgwatks	feel cold
xgyēt	kill with witchcraft, cannibal
xp'iyeen	to smoke
xasoo, xso	canoe
xt'o'ts	be in black, be in mourning
sts'u'u'ts	hawk

LEXICAL PROCLITICS

1. Lexical proclitics are related both phonetically and semantically to independent lexical items.

2. Agwi- (collateral kin; from agwil (locative proclitic meaning "aside"))

agwibiip	great uncle (address)
agwinübiip	great uncle (reference)
agwidzi'is	great aunt (address)
agwin̲ts'i'its	great aunt (reference)
agwiłems	spouse of grandchild
agwinügwat	uncle (father's brother or mother's sister's husband)
agwi'o'os	second cousin

3. Aks- (opening up; from aks (water))

akslsgmmaadm	sleet
aksyaa, akswaalxs	accumulate, increase

4. Ama- (good; from aam (good))

amadaalk̲	praise, worship
amaniits	careful, watchful
amap'aas	attractive
amawaal	wealthy

5. Dax- (tightly, firmly; from dakł (tie around, encircling) and from daxs (flounder))

daxda̲m, daxdmda̲m	hold fast, restrain
daxwa̲ns	adze
daxya̲akw	hold fast, hold in hand

6. G̲an- (hard, wooden, long; from g̲an (tree))

g̲andaawłmgoot	shift position, take a rest
g̲andzooł	prepuce
g̲anhaayk	sparks
g̲anhadaay	wheel (of a boat)
g̲anlutgubaa	block (of a boat), double block
g̲anłaak	morning
g̲anłaan	armour
g̲anłaabiisk	drawknife, drawshave, spokeshave
g̲an'ooksnsk	gunnel
g̲anp'iyaan	chimney, stove pipe
g̲ansalg̲os	swing (recreation apparatus)
g̲ansigiidask	yeast
g̲ants'aa'ts	sticks used to spread out a skin for drying
g̲ants'iit	clam siphon
g̲an'uksgiłee	boom (of a boat)
g̲anyüsyetsa	suspenders

7. Gwis-, gwüs- (blanket, clothing; from gwa̲s (blanket))

gwisg̲an, gwüsg̲an	cedar bark mat coat, raincoat
gwis'naba'ala	button blanket
gwists'iik, gwüsdziik	fawn
gwüshalaayt	cape, robe
gwüsligyiyaa	traveling clothes

gwüsmati	mountain goat skin coat
gwüsnaygmgyaamk	Chilkat blanket
gwüs'ol	bearskin coat

8. Gyiɫ- (piercing; from gyeɫk (to stab))

gyiɫgyeɫ	to spear
gyiɫ'on	tattoo
gyiɫts'ax	nose ring
gyiɫweentk	woodpecker

9. Gyit- (man; from gyet (person))

gyitwaalgit	raiders, to get revenge
gyitwaaltk	war

10. Ƚgu-, ɫu (little; from ɫguɫk (little))

ɫgu'a̱ɫaan	brother-in-law (wife's brother)
ɫgüdelpk	very short
ɫguk'ooɫks	brother-in-law (husband's brother)
ɫguts'uusk	little
ɫguwaalks	prince
ɫguwoomɫk	child, infant
ɫgwiduuls	sister-in-law (woman speaking)
ɫgwüdzuus	sister-in-law (woman speaking)
ɫgwüɫuugyit	plug (for a boat)
ɫgwüsgaay	little finger
ɫgwüsgüü	happy
ɫgwüslis	nephew, niece

11. Ma̱s-, müs- (red; from mask (red))

ma̱s'aws	rouge, bridal shower (formerly the dressing of a bride for her wedding done by her future mother-in-law)
ma̱sxayloop	metridium anemone
müsiin	copper
müs'ol	cinnamon bear

12. Sg̱an- (woven mat; from sg̱an (woven mat))

sg̱ank'yiin	harpoon shaft, spear handle, spear shaft
sg̱anmoolksgm ts'm'aks	precious coral,sponges, esp. dead man's fingers
sg̱ansüxsaasüx	thorn bush

13. Ts'u-, dza-, dzi- (little; from ts'usk (little))

ts'uwaan	end
ts'üwaas	pygmy salmon
ts'uwaangyit	the youngest child in a family
ts'uwaanɫ	a point, something pointed
ts'übaa	lame (run a short distance)
dza̱baa, dza̱ḵ'oɫ	lame

dza̲buuksk	spitoon
dzā'west	salal
dzīg̲aws	salmon, split open and dried
dzin̄deh	when
dzügwiits	large sea urchin

14. 'Wii- (large; from 'wiileeks (big))

'wiik̲'ooli	one with long hair
wiilēe	wide
wii'nak	long, tall
wiit'is	big

15. Wün- (nourishment; from wüneey (food))

wündo	cheek, salivary gland, tobacco, anything you put in your mouth to dissolve
wüng̲aws	brain

COMPOUND WORDS

1. Compound words are formed with the connective -m-.

aadmmüsoo	a net for sockeye salmon (aat-m-müsoo: net-m-sockeye)
ałoomboot	sailboat (ałoo-m-boot: cloth-m-boat)
ałoomgyemk	flag
ap'adziksmgyet	a snob
biyaalsm'aatk	evening star
biyaalsmg̱anłaak	morning star
blag̱mloop	moss-green colour (bilax-m-loop: moss-m-rock)
daxłmluut	sledge hammer with wedge
duusmgyilhawli	bobcat, mountain lion
g̱aaydmboosn	rimmed hat (g̱aayt-m-boosn: hat-m-Boston; hat-m-boss)
g̱aaydmts'aalxs	hooded coat
g̱abog̱mp'axs	corduroy pants
g̱adiiłgmwas	fringed blanket
g̱aldmalgyax	talking chief, chief's assistant
g̱awsgmg̱an	pole (g̱awsk-m-g̱an: thin-m-tree)
g̱aydmsgyen	rubber hat (g̱aayt-m-sgyen: hat-m-pitch, gum)
gyemgmdziws	sun (gyemk-m-dziiws: light-m-day)
güünksmhoon	dried fish (güünks-m-hoon: dry-m-fish)

IDIOMS

1. Words are sometimes put together to form a new word with a new meaning. Sometimes a connective -a- is used to put the words together.

aamadzap	to fix (aam-a-dzap: good-a-build)
badzit'ool	sea elephant (badzi-t'ool: lift-snout)
baxbeega'aks	waterspout
buhbuu'aks	splash
deexłgagyemk	halo around the moon
gatgyetgabaask	gale, strong wind
dzaxag̱ayt	flying squirrel (dzag̱a-g̱ayt: across-chest)
g̱aaydibaa'lx	mushroom (g̱aayd-i-baa'lx: hat-ghost)
g̱aaydits'u'uts	mushroom, glans penis (hat-bird, hat-penis)
g̱anhadaay	wheel of a boat (g̱an-hadaay: wood-to steer)
g̱anlutgubaa	block, double block (g̱an-lu-tgu-baa: wood-really-outside-run)
g̱anp'iyaan	chimney (g̱an-p'iyaan: long-smoke)
g̱an'uksgiłee	boom (g̱an-'uks'-g̱awiłee: long-down out-blood vein)

THE NOUN PHRASE - NUMERALS

1. A numeral precedes the noun it numbers. It takes an -a or null enclitic connective: -a if it ends in a stop, affricate or fricative and null if it ends in a vowel or sonorant. Numerals for humans, long objects, canoes, humans aboard a conveyance, and unit measures can stand alone as nouns. General numerals are used for houses, dreams, masks, flowers, ghosts, spheres, abstract things, and anything else not specifically designated by the other classes. Animal numerals are used garments, skins, anything flat, e.g., mats, also for bak'wis (Bigfoot), hawhaw (a supernatural animal), and naxnox (supernatural beings). The numerals for canoes are used for any vehicle.

k'üül walp	one house
gu'pl uwalp	two houses
k'wili uwalp	three houses
k'üül xsiwoox	one dream
txaalpxa g̲a'aax	four masks
kwstuunsa g̲a'aax	five masks
k'üül baa'lx	one ghost
gu'pl bubaa'lx	two ghosts
k'yaaga ksɨüüsk	one shirt
t'apxaada guksɨüüsk	two shirts
gwün guksɨüüsk	three shirts
k'yaaga anaas	one pelt
kwstuunsa ak'anaas	five pelts
k̲'andooltga dikduus	eight cats
t'apxaduul wil kpool g̲axhay	twenty male slaves
t'apxaduul hana'nax	two women
txalpxdool smgyigyet	four chiefs
k̲'oopsxn bupts'aan	two totem poles
g̲abeeltk g̲axsoo	two canoes

DETERMINERS

1. Definite articles and demonstratives occur after the nouns they determine. The noun takes an -a or null enclitic suffix when it is followed by such a determiner. Determiners do not occur in the same noun phrase with numerals. The determiners are:

gwa'a	here, close to the speaker
gwasga	over there
doni	over there
awaan	over there, close to the hearer
gwi	definite
ta'a	deceased (used with kin terms only).

Example noun phrases:

waaba gwa'a	this house (by me)
waaba gwi	the house

waaba gwasga	that house
waaba awaan	that house (by you)
bübaa'ḷx gwa'a	these ghosts
gukstüüsga awaan	those shirts by you
agwiganübiiba gwa'a	these great uncles
agwiganübiiba ta'a	the deceased great uncles

ADJECTIVES

1. Adjectives, like numbers, come before the noun they modify. They take an -m enclitic suffix and must agree in number with the noun they modify. A noun phrase may have both a numeral and an adjective. Numerals come before adjectives. A noun phrase may have both an adjective and a determiner. A noun phrase may have more than one adjective.

t'apxaada sipsiipgm hashaas	four sick dogs
siipgm haasa gwa'a	this sick dog
sipsiipgm hashaasa gwi	the sick dogs
lu'am'aamagadgoodm hanaa'naga doni	those happy women
txalpxdool al'algm smgyigyet	four angry chiefs
mismasgm huwaap	the red houses
mismasgm huwaaba gwa'a	these red houses
gu'pl am'aamn łikłgułgm huwaap	two good little houses
t'apxaduul am'aamn gatgyetm yik'yuuta	two good strong men

Notes: 1) When an x comes before a vowel or m, it becomes g.
2) When the enclitic suffix -m comes after an m, it becomes -n.

POSSESSIVES

1. Possession is shown by placing the possessor noun after the noun that is owned. The two nouns (or noun phrases) are connected by the -a/null enclitic if the possessor is a common noun and by the -as/-s enclitic if the owner is a proper noun. Unless it is something that is considered to be a part of the owner, the possessed noun has a na- prefix. This prefix comes before the plural prefix. Some kinship terms do not have the na- prefix when they are possessed. This fact implies that some kinsmen are considered, in some way, part of one another.

gyigyeda huwaap	the colour of the houses
nahoon 'yuuta	the man's fish
nała'ta łikłgułgm yik'yuuta gwa'a	these little boys' ball
nahuwaaba am'aamn hanaa'naga gwa'a	these good women's houses

k'wili 'wileeksm nahuwaaba gatgyetgm yik'yuuta	the strong men's three big houses
nana'as Meli	Mary's dress
nawaabas Dzon	John's house
ts'e'ls Paul	Paul's face
noos Sala gwa'a	Sarah's mother here by me

Note: gwa'a determines noos, not Sala.

nagwadas Üünal	Arnold's father

POSSESSIVE PRONOMINALS

1. Possessive pronouns are expressed as enclitics or suffixes attaching to the words they possess. The na- prefix is used with pronominals in the same manner as with genitive nouns. The possessive pronominals are:

	singular	plural
1st person	-u	-m
2nd person	-n	-sm
3rd person	-t	-t

Example noun phrases:

nawaapt	his house, her house, their house
noot	his mother, her mother, their mother
nawaabn	your house (singular)
nawaabism	your house (plural)
nahuwaabism	your houses
ts'a'ln	your face
naga'aadism	your nets (plural)
nawaabm	our house
noom	our mother
ha'tsa'an'onm	our hands
'an'onu	my hand
asiiyu	my foot

Note: When -u comes after another vowel, a -y- is inserted between the two vowels.

naboodu	my boat
nagaxsooyu	my canoes
nagaaydn	your hat
nap'axsu	my pants
nagwidaadzit	his jacket, her jacket
ts'uwaangyidm łmktiin	your youngest sister (speaking to a boy)
ts'uwaangyidm łgaawgat	her youngest sister
ts'uwaangyidm łmktiit	his youngest sister
gwisgwaasgm naguksłüüsgu awaan	my blue shirts there by you
gwün gwisgwaasgm nagukłüüsgn	your three blue shirts

THE VERB PHRASE

1. The verb phrase consists of a temporal designator followed by a verb (TEMP VB).

2. The temporal designators are:

nah — completed or perfect
  e.g., nah dzap "already made"
dm — future and progressive
  e.g., dm dzap "will make," "is going to make," "is making"
ɨa — close to the present
  e.g., ɨa dzap "just beginning to make"
  nahɨa dzap "just finished making"
  ɨadm dzap "just about to start making"
wil — subsequent to another action or event
  e.g., wil dzap "and then made"
  nah wil dzap "and then already made"
  na'al dzap (variant of nah wil dzap)
  dm wil dzap "and now will be making"
  wil dm dzap (variant of dm wil dzap)
  nah ɨawil dzap "and then just finished making"
  nah ɨa'al dzap (variant of nah ɨawil dzap)
  na'al ɨa dzap (variant of nah ɨawil dzap)
  dm ɨawil "and now just about to start making"
  dm ɨa'al (variant of dm ɨawil)
  ɨawil dm (variant of dm ɨawil)
  ɨa'al dm (variant of dm ɨawil)
yagwa — present (used only with action verbs)
  e.g., yagwa dzap "be making right now," "is now making"

BASIC SENTENCE WORD ORDER

1. The basic word order of a Tsimshian sentence is (a) temporal designator, transitive verb, ergative noun phrase, absolutive noun phrase (TEMP VB_T ERG ABS), or (b) temporal designator, intransitive verb, absolutive noun phrase (TEMP VB_I ABS). Tsimshian is very unlike English in that Tsimshian does not have subjects and objects. The subjects of intransitive sentences and the direct objects of transitive sentences are in Tsimshian considered to be the same kind of noun phrase, i.e., they are considered to have the same grammatical function; they are both called absolutives. Subjects of transitive sentences in Tsimshian are called ergatives. Subjects of intransitive sentences are not considered to be like subjects of transitive sentences, as is the case in English.

English:	SUBJ TEMP VB_T OBJ	SUBJ TEMP VB_I
Tsimshian:	TEMP VB_T ERG ABS	TEMP VB_I ABS

Tsimshian		English
ERGATIVE	=	SUBJECT (with transitive verb)
ABSOLUTIVE	=	SUBJECT (with intransitive verb)
ABSOLUTIVE	=	DIRECT OBJECT

2. The -a/null enclitic connective attaches to the verb when it is followed immediately by the absolutive. The same enclitic attaches to an ergative when it is followed by an absolutive.

TEMP VB_I+a ABS

TEMP VB_T ERG+a ABS

If the absolutive is a proper noun, then the enclitic connective is -as/-s (intransitive verb) or -at/-t (transitive verb).

Some intransitive sentences:

a) Yagwa baa wan (Yagwa TEMP; baa VB_I; wan ABS; the deer is is running)
b) Nah siipga hana'a (Nah TEMP; siipk VB_I; -a; hana'a ABS; the woman was sick)
c) Yagwa baas Meli (Yagwa TEMP; baa VB_I; -s; Meli ABS; Mary is running)
d) Ƚadm siipgas Dzon (Ƚadm TEMP; siipk VB_I; -as; Dzon ABS; John is about to be sick or John is soon going to be in pain)

Independent pronouns (see appropriate section) and kinship terms have all the syntactic properties of proper nouns in Tsimshian.

e) Yagwa baas nagwadu (Yagwa TEMP; baa VB_I; -s; nagwadu ABS; my father is running)
f) Ƚadm siipgas nooyu (Ƚadm TEMP; siipk VB_I; -as; nooyu ABS; my mother is going to be sick)

3. The enclitic connective -da is attached to the verb when it precedes an ergative. At the same time a -t enclitic attaches to the temporal designation.

TEMP+t VB_T+da ERG+a ABS

Proper noun ergatives and absolutives in transitive sentences take the -t form of the connective: -dit (before an ergative) or -at/-t (before an absolutive).

Some transitive sentences:

a) Yagwat niisda ts'uu'tsa laalt (Yagwa TEMP; -t; niits VB_T; -da; ts'uu'ts ERG; -a; laalt ABS; the bird sees the worm; Note: the ts in niits simplifies to s when the -da enclitic is attached)
b) Ƚat niisda ts'uu'tsat Jack (Ƚa TEMP; -t; niits VB_T; -da; ts'uu'ts ERG; -at; Jack ABS; the bird just now saw Jack)

c) Ƚat niisdit Meli ts'uu'ts (Ƚa TEMP; -t; niits VB_T; -dit; Meli ERG; ts'uu'ts ABS; Mary just now saw the bird)
d) Ƚat niisdit Melit Jack (Ƚa TEMP; -t; niits VB_T; -dit; Meli ERG; -t; Jack ABS; Mary just now saw Jack)

4. In transitive sentences in which there is an especially close semantic relationship between the transitive verb and the absolutive such that the transitive verb greatly limits what the absolutive could be, then the absolutive can be incorporated into the verb. Then the sentence pattern

TEMP+t VB_T+da ERG+a ABS

becomes

TEMP VB_T+m+ABS+a ERG,

i.e., the absolutive becomes a part of the verb as a compound word and the ergative functions syntactically as an absolutive.

Some examples of absolutive incorporation:

a) Ƚawil aadmhoonu (Ƚawil TEMP; aat VB_T; -m-; hoon ABS; -u ERG; and then I was just seining for fish or I was just now fish-seining)
b) Yagwa suwiliinsgmwudziis Dzon (Yagwa TEMP; suwiliinsk VB_T; -m-; wudzii ABS; -s; Dzon ERG; John is hunting caribou or John is caribou-hunting)
c) Yagwa łeemlaks nagwat (Yagwa TEMP; łee VB_T; -m-; lak ABS; -s; nagwat ERG; his father is hauling firewood)

5. An indirect object follows the absolutive in the sentence word order. A -da enclitic attaches to the absolutive. The connective between the transitive verb and the ergative is -a/null and there is no -t enclitic on the temporal designation.

TEMP VB_T+a ERG+a ABS+da INDOBJ

a) Nah k'yi'nam 'yuuta hoonda haas (Nah TEMP; k'yi'nam VB_T; 'yuuta ERG; hoon ABS; -da; haas INDOBJ; the man used to give the dog fish)
b) Ƚa k'yi'nam hana'a ła'tida k'abatgüüłk (Ƚa TEMP; k'yi'nam VB_T; hana'a ERG; ła't ABS; -(i)da; k'abatgüüłk INDOBJ; the woman just gave the child a ball)

The proper noun variant of da is -das when it comes before an indirect object.

c) Ƚa k'yi'nams Üünal hoondas nagwadit (Ƚa TEMP; k'yi'nam VB_T; -s; Üünal ERG; hoon ABS; -das; nagwadit INDOBJ; Arnold just gave his father a fish)

6. Instrumental, benefactives and locatives have the same pattern as indirect objects:

TEMP VB_T+a ERG+a ABS+da INST

TEMP VB_T+a ERG+a ABS+da BENF

TEMP VB_T+a ERG+a ABS+da LOC

a) ƀa gwin'oy 'yuuta ła'tida hana'k (ƀa TEMP; gwin'oy VB_T; 'yuuta ERG; ła't ABS; -(i)da; hana'k LOC; the man just now threw the ball to the woman).
b) ƀa k'al'oy 'yuuta hana'kada ła't (ƀa TEMP; k'al'oy VB_T; 'yuuta ERG; hana'ka ABS; -da; ła't INST; A man just now hit a woman with a ball)
c) ƀadm k'aga 'yuuta liksoogada hak'aga (ƀadm TEMP; k'aga VB_T; 'yuuta ERG; liksook ABS; -(a)da; hak'aga INST; A man is about to open a door with a key)
d) Nah wasn yeen galts'apda ła ganłaak (Nah TEMP; wasn VB_T; yeen ERG; galts'ap ABS; -da; ła ganłaak LOC; fog used to blanket the village in the morning)
e) Nah wasn yeen galts'apda lax likst'aa (Nah TEMP; wasn VB_T; yeen ERG; galts'ap ABS; -da; lax likst'aa LOC; fog used to blanket the village on the island)
f) Nahła dzabas Dzon waapdas Meli (Nahła TEMP; dzap VB_T; -as; Dzon ERG; waap ABS; -das; Meli BENF; John just finished building a house for Mary)

PRONOMINALS

1. Ergatives and instrumentals can be expressed by pronominals. Pronominals are proclitics and enclitics which attach to the verb phrase. The ordinary pronominals for absolutives are the same as the possessive pronominals. They are attached to the end of the verb.

	singular	plural
first person	-u	-m
second person	-n	-sm
third person	-t	-t

TEMP VB_I+absPRO

a) ƀadm baayu.	I'm about to run.
b) ƀadm k'olm.	We're about to run.
c) ƀadm baan, 'nii?	And now you're about to run, aren't you?
d) ƀa'aldm k'olsm, 'nii?	And now you're about to run,
e) ƀa baat.	He's just now running.
f) ƀa k'olt.	They're just now running.

When an absolutive pronominal occurs in a sentence with a noun ergative, a -t enclitic must be attached to the temporal designation.

TEMP+t VB_T+absPRO ERG

a) ƀawilt niidzu ol.	And just now the bear has seen me.
b) ƀawilt niidzn ol.	And just now the bear has seen you.
c) ƀawilt niidza ol.	And just now the bear has seen him, her, it.

d) Ławilt lu'niisda ol. — And just now the bear has seen them.

e) Ławilt lu'niidzm gyibaaw. — And just now the wolf has seen us.

f) Ławilt lu'niidzism gyibaaw. — And just now the wolf has seen you (pl).

If an absolutive pronominal occurs in a sentence with a proper noun ergative, the -it/-t enclitic must attach to the end of the word immediately preceding the proper noun ergative.

g) Ławilt niidzut Dzon. — Then John just now sees me.
h) Ławilt niidznt Dzon. — Then John just now sees you.
i) Ławilt niisdit nagwadu. — And just now my father has seen him, her, it.
j) Ławilt lu'niidzimt noon. — And just now your mother has seen us.
k) Ławilt lu'niidzisimt Meli. — And just now Mary has seen you.

2. In some temporal designations, e.g., perfect, a different set of pronominals is used for the absolutive. This second set is said to be marked because an -'n- is placed between the verb and the pronominal. The -'n- thus "marks" the pronominal.

	singular	plural
first person	-'nu	-'nm
second person	-n	-'nsm
third person	-t	-t

Notice that for the third person and for the second person singular the marked and unmarked forms are the same.

a) Nah baa'nu. — I used to run.
b) Nah k̲'ol'nm. — We used to run.
c) Nah b̄aan, 'nii. — You used to run, didn't you?
d) Nah k̲'ol'nsm, 'nii. — You used to run, didn't you?
e) Nah b̄aat. — He, she, it used to run.
f) Nah k̲'olt. — They used to run.

g) Nat 'niidza'nu ol. — The bear saw me.
h) Nat 'niidzn ol. — The bear saw you.
i) Nat 'niisda ol. — The bear saw him, her, it.
j) Nat lu'niidza'nm ol. — The bear saw us.
k) Nat lu'niidza'nsm ol. — The bear saw you.
l) Nat luniisda ol. — The bear saw them.

The sentence patterns for marked absolutives with marked TEMP's are:

$$\text{TEMP}^{m}\ \text{VB}_{I}\text{+absPRO}^{m}$$

$$\text{TEMP}^{m}\text{+t}\ \text{VB}_{T}\text{+absPRO}^{m}\ \text{ERG}$$

If the ergative is a proper noun:

m) Nat 'niidza'nut Dzon. — John saw me.
n) Nat 'niidznt Dzon. — John saw you.

o) Nat niis nagwadu*.	My father saw him, her, it.
p) Nat lu'niidza'nmt noon.	Your mother saw us.
q) Nat lu'niidzasimt Meli*.	Mary saw you.
r) Nat lu'niisdit nagwadu.	My father saw them.

*These forms are irregular. In (o) niis is a contraction of niisdit. In (q) the pronominal is unmarked.

3. Which temporal designations take the marked absolutive pronominals is a matter of local and personal style. The various temporal designations can, however, be scaled in terms of which ones are most likely to take marked absolutive pronominals:

most likely to occur with marked absPRO^{m}	nah, nahɨa, nahɨa'al
	↑
	null TEMP
	|
	dm
	|
	ɨa'aldm
	|
	ɨa
	|
	ɨadm
	↓
least likely to occur with absPRO^{m}	wil, ɨawil, yagwa

The various sentence types in which absolutive pronominals occur can also be scaled in terms of which ones are most likely to take marked absolutive pronominals:

most likely to occur with absPRO^{m}	with a common noun ERG
	↑
	with a proper noun ERG
	↓
least likely to occur with absPRO^{m}	with a 3rd person pronominal ERG, intransitive sentences

4. The ordinary pronominals for ergatives are proclitics coming before the verb. They usually attach to the temporal designation. The unmarked ergative pronominals are:

	singular	plural
first person	-n-	-dip-
second person	-m-	-m-sm-
third person	-t-	-t-

The basic sentence pattern for unmarked ergative pronominals is:

TEMP+ergPRO VB_T+a ABS

Example sentences are:

a) ƚanwil niidza ol.	And just now I have seen a bear (ƚa- -wil TEMP; -n- ergPRO; niits VB_T; -a; ol ABS).
b) ƚadipwil lu'niidza ol awaan.	And just now we've seen those bears by you.
c) ƚamwil niidza ol, 'nii?	You've just seen a bear, haven't you.
d) ƚamsmwil niidza ol, 'nii?	You've just seen a bear, haven't you
e) ƚawilt niidza ol.	He, she, it, they have just seen a bear.

When the absolutive is a proper noun, the -as/-s enclitic is used.

f) ƚanwil niidzas Meli.	I've just now seen Mary.

5. Ergative pronominals may also be marked in certain temporal designations. An ergative pronominal is marked by using the same post-verbal elements as are used for the <u>unmarked</u> absolutives. The marked ergative pronominals are:

	singular	plural
first person	-u	-m
second person	-n	-sm
third person	-t	-t

The basic sentence pattern for marked ergative pronominals is:

$TEMP^m$ VB_T+$ergPRO^m$ ABS

Example sentences are:

a) Nah 'niidzu ol	I saw the bear
b) Nah 'niidzn ol, 'nii?	You saw the bear, didn't you?
c) Nah 'niisda* ol.	He, she, it saw the bear.

*This form is irregular in that the -a enclitic follows the marked ergative pronominal.

6. The temporal designations are scaled for marking ergatives in the same way as for marking absolutives (see #3 in this section). The sentence type scale for marking ergatives is:

most likely to occur with $ergPRO^m$	with a noun ABS
	↕
least likely to occur with $ergPRO^m$	with a pronoun ABS

In general ergatives are marked more readily than absolutives.

7. Occasionally a sentence may have an absolutive pronominal and a marked ergative pronominal. In such a sentence the absolutive pronominal precedes the ergative pronominal:

TEMP VB_T+absPRO+ergPRO^m

a) Nah dzakwdu (Nah TEMP: dzakw VB_T; -d- absPRO; -u ergPRO^m; *I killed it*).

8. Reflexive pronouns are expressed by the verbal proclitic la̲p- (the a̲ is pronounced as the a in "what").

a) La̲p'niidza'nu. — I see myself.
b) La̲p'niidza 'yuuta. — The man sees himself.

9. The indirect object pronominals are:

	singular	plural
first person	da k'oy	da k'wam
second person	da k'wan	da k'wasm
third person	dit 'niit	dit dip'niit,
	das 'niit	das dip'niit

a) K'yi'namt haasda k'oy. — He gave me a dog.

INDEPENDENT PRONOUNS

1. The independent pronouns have all the syntactic characteristics of proper nouns:

	singular	plural
first person	'nüüyu	'nüüm
second person	'nüün	'nüüsm
third person	'niit	dip'niit

THE ERGATIVE ENCLITIC WITH MARKED TEMPORAL DESIGNATIONS

1. In sentences with the more marked temporal designations as determined by the scale on page 64 the ergative enclitic -da may become -a, and the -t enclitic on the TEMP may be omitted.

a) Yagwat t'uusda 'yuuta hana'k̲.

The man is pushing the woman.

b) Nah t'uusa 'yuuta hana'k̲.

The man pushed the woman.

c) Yagwat luda̲mda 'yuuta hana'k̲.

The man is hugging the woman.

d) Nah luda̲m 'yuuta hana'k̲.

The man hugged the woman.

e) Nah luda̲mda 'yuuta hana'k̲.

The man hugged the woman.

When proper nouns occur in such sentences, they take the -s enclitic rather than the -t.

f) Yagwat t'uusdit Dzonit Meli.

John is pushing Mary.

g) Nah t'uusas Dzons Meli.

John pushed Mary.

In general in the more marked temporal designations the ergative takes on all the morpho-syntactic characteristics of the absolutive. This is true for both nouns and pronominals.

SUMMARY OF BASIC SENTENCE TYPES

1. Transitive sentences showing marking and pronominalization.

$TEMP^{m}$+t VB_{T}+$absPRO^{m}$(s) ERG

↑

$TEMP^{m}$ VB_{T}+$ergPRO^{m}$(s) ABS

↑

$TEMP^{m}$ VB_{T}+a(s) ERG+a(s) ABS

↑

TEMP+t VB_{T}+da(t) ERG+a(t) ABS

↓

TEMP+ergPRO VB_{T}+a(t) ABS

↓

TEMP+t VB_{T}+absPRO(s) ERG

↓

TEMP+ergPRO VB_{T}+absPRO

2. Intransitive sentences showing marking and pronominalization.

$TEMP^{m}$ VB_{I}+$absPRO^{m}$

↑

$TEMP^{m}$ VB_{I}+a(s) ABS

↑

TEMP VB_{I}+a(s) ABS

↓

TEMP VB_{I}+absPRO

TOPICALIZATION OF THE ERGATIVE

1. For special emphasis an ergative may be brought to the beginning of the sentence: this is called topicalization. Topicalized ergatives must be expressed by pronouns, never by nouns. Topical ergatives are either independent pronouns, demonstrative pronouns, interrogative pronouns, or relative pronouns. The basic sentence pattern for an independent pronoun topical ergative is:

$$\begin{array}{llll} & \text{TEMP+t} & \text{VB}_T\text{+dit ERG+a} & \text{ABS} \\ & \downarrow & & \\ \text{t+ergINDPRO} & \text{TEMP+t} & \text{in+VB}_T\text{+} \quad\quad \text{a} & \text{ABS} \end{array}$$

Some example sentences:

a) T'nüüyu dmt inbaa'n boot. — I am the one who will run the boat.

b) 'Nüüyu dmt inbaa'n boot. — I am the one who will run the boat.

c) 'Nüüyu dm inbaa'n boot. — I am the one who will run the boat.

Notice that (b) and (c) are progressive simplificiations of (a). The (a) variant of this sentence represents an older form of the language; it is also considered more formal and elegant. The simplifications are newer forms and are considered informal and casual.

2. The demonstrative pronoun is ni'ni. The basic sentence pattern for a topical ergative expressed as a demonstrative pronoun is:

$$\begin{array}{llll} & \text{TEMP+t} & \text{VB}_T\text{+dit ERG+a} & \text{ABS} \\ & \downarrow & & \\ \text{ni'ni} & \text{TEMP+t} & \text{in+VB}_T\text{+} \quad\quad \text{a} & \text{ABS} \end{array}$$

a) Ni'ni dmt inbaa'n boot. — This is the one that will run the boat.

3. The relative pronoun is naa.

$$\begin{array}{llll} & \text{TEMP+t} & \text{VB}_T\text{+dit ERG+a} & \text{ABS} \\ & \downarrow & & \\ \text{naa} & \text{TEMP+t} & \text{in+VB}_T\text{+} \quad\quad \text{a} & \text{ABS} \end{array}$$

a) Naa dmt inbaa'n boot. — He is the one who will run the boat.

4. The interrogative pronoun is naaɬ.

$$\begin{array}{llll} & \text{TEMP+t} & \text{VB}_T\text{+dit ERG+a} & \text{ABS} \\ & \downarrow & & \\ \text{naaɬ} & \text{TEMP+t} & \text{in+VB}_T\text{+} \quad\quad \text{a} & \text{ABS} \end{array}$$

a) Naaɬ dmt inbaa'n boot? — Who will run the boat?

5. sentences with topicalized ergatives may occur as dependent relative clauses in other sentences:

a) Ƚan 'niidza 'yuuta dmt inbaa'n boot.

I just saw the man who will run the boat.

also (less formal);

b) Ƚan niidza 'yuuta dm inbaa'n boot.

TOPICALIZATION OF THE ABSOLUTIVE

1. An absolutive may be topicalized as a noun or noun phrase:

TEMP+t VB_T+da ERG+a ABS
↓
ABS TEMP VB_T+a ERG

a) Waaba awaan nah dzabu. — That's the house I built.
b) Txa'ni manwineeya gwa'a naƚa meƚtu. — These are the main foods I have just talked about.

2. A topical absolutive may also be expressed with an independent pronoun:

TEMP+t VB_T+da ERG+a ABS
↓
absINDPRO TEMP VB_T+a ERG

a) 'niida nah 'niidza ol. — He's the one the bear saw.

3. A topical absolutive may also be expressed with the demonstrative pronoun ni'ni or 'nii:

TEMP+t VB_T+da ERG+a ABS
↓
(ni)'ni TEMP VB_T+a ERG

a) 'Nii silayawxgu ƚa twelve-o-clock. — That's the one I ate with at noon.
b) Ni'ni güüldm. — That's what we harvest.

4. The relative pronoun used to express a topical absolutive is gu or go with a -di enclitic on the demporal designation:

TEMP+t VB_T+da ERG+a ABS
↓
gu TEMP+di VB_T+a ERB

a) Gu nadi gyigyuunxga nag̲aniyaatgm. — That is what our grandfathers worshipped.

$$\text{TEMP} \quad \text{VB}_I\text{+a ABS}$$
$$\downarrow$$
$$\text{gu TEMP+di VB}_I\text{+a}$$

a) Gu nadi sunabaatga. That is what recently arrived.

Notice that whenever an absolutive is topicalized, the ergative is preceded by the -a enclitic, not its regular -da enclitic. Furthermore, if the ergative is a proper noun, it nevertheless does not take a proper noun enclitic. The enclitic -a attaches to the verb, even if it is intransitive and no noun phrase at all follows it.

5. Sentences with topical absolutives may occur as dependent relative clauses in other sentences. In such dependent clauses the relative pronoun is gu or go:

a) Nah gǜǜlda wineeya go dm gabat.

They used to harvest food they could eat.

INTERROGATIVES

1. One set of interrogative type sentences anticipates or expects a "yes" answer: these will be referred to as "positive interrogatives." A second set of interrogative type sentences anticipates or expects a "no" answer: the "negative interrogatives."

2. Intransitive positive interrogatives:

$$\text{TEMP V}_I\text{+a ABS}$$

becomes

$$\text{TEMP V}_I\text{+i ABS,}$$
$$\text{TEMP V}_I\text{+iɨ ABS.}$$

a) Yagwa baayɨ hana'a? Is the woman running?
b) Dm baayɨ hana'a? Will the woman run?
c) Nah baayɨ hana'k̲a Did the woman run?
d) Nah siipgi 'yuuta? Was the man in pain?

3. Intransitive positive interrogatives with pronominals.

$$\text{TEMP V}_I\text{+absPRO}$$
$$\downarrow$$
$$\text{TEMP V}_I\text{+absPRO+i}$$

a) Dm baayi? Will she run?
(Note: the third person pronoun is deleted)
b) Nah baayi? Will she run?
c) Nah siipgi? Did it hurt? Was he sick?

d) Dm siipgi?	Will it hurt?
e) Dm siipgn̲i̲?	Are you going to be sick?
f) Dm siipgā'nui?	Am I going to be sick?

4. Transitive positive interrogatives:

TEMP +t VB_T+da ERG+a ABS
↓
TEMP VB_T+dił ERG+i ABS

a) Nah dzakwdił oli haas?	Did the bear kill the dog?

5. Transitive positive interrogatives with ergative pronominals:

TEMP+erg PRO VB_T+a ABS	$TEMP^m$ VB_T+$ergPRO^m$ ABS
↓	↓
TEMP+ergPRO VB_T+ił ABS	$TEMP^m$ VB_T+$ergPRO^m$+ił ABS

a) Nah niidzanił wa̲n?	Did you see the deer?

6. Transitive positive interrogatives with absolutive pronominals:

TEMP+t VB_T+absPRO ERG
↓
TEMP+t VB_T+absPRO+ił ERG

a) Nat ts'alaaw̓kdił 'yuuta?	Did the man visit them?
b) Nat ts'alaaw̓dił 'yuuta?	Did the man visit them?

(Note: (a) is Kitkatla dialect, (b) is Hartley Bay dialect)

7. Transitive positive interrogatives with both pronominals:

TEMP+ergPRO VB_T+ absPRO
↓
TEMP+ergPRO+i VB_T+t+absPRO+i

a) Nahdi ts'alaaw̓kdi? (Kitkatla dialect)	Did he visit them?
b) Nahdi ts'alaaw̓di? (Hartley Bay dialect)	Did he visit them?

8. Intransitive negative interrogatives:

TEMP VB_I+a ABS
↓
ał TEMP VB_I+'di ABS

a) Ał baa'di haas?	Is the dog running?
b) Ał siipga'di 'yuuta?	Is the man sick?
c) Yagwał baa'di 'yuuta?	Is the man running?

9. Intransitive negative interrogative with pronominal:

TEMP VB_I+absPRO
↓
ał TEMP VB_I+absPRO+i

a) Ał dm sipsiipgami? Are we going to be sick?
b) Ał dm simaay'ni? Are you going berry-picking?
c) Ał dm simmaysmi? Are you going berry-picking?
d) Ał dm simaaymī? Are we going berry-picking?
e) Ał dm simaaydi? Is he going berry-picking?
f) Ał dm guu'oldi? Is she going bear-shooting?
g) Yagwał baa'di? Is she running now?
h) Ał baa'di? Is it running?
i) Ał siipgui? Am I sick?

10. Transitive negative interrogative:

TEMP+t VB_T+da ERG+a ABS
↓
ał TEMP VB_T+da ERG+i ABS,
ał TEMP VB_T+da ERG+ił ABS

a) Ał niisda łguwoomłgił haas? Does the child see the dog?
b) Ał gügüülda łguwoomłgi haas? Is the child looking for the dog?

11. Transitive negative interrogative with ergative pronominal:

TEMP+ergPRO VB_T+a ABS
↓
ał TEMP+ergPRO VB_T+dił ABS

a) Ał nam 'niisdił wan? Did you see the deer?

12. Transitive negative interrogative with absolutive pronominal:

TEMP+t VB_T+absPRO ERG
↓
ał TEMP+t VB_T+absPRO+ił ERG

13. Transitive negative interrogative with both pronominals:

TEMP+ergPRO VB_T+absPRO
↓
ał TEMP+ergPRO VB_T+absPRO+i

a) Ał nam niisdi? Did you see him?
b) Ał nam niisdui? Did you see me?
c) Ał müdm ts'alaaẅgami? Are you going to visit us?
d) Ał dmt ts'alaaẅgani? Are they going to visit you?
e) Ał dmt ts'alaaẅkdi? Is he going to visit her?

NEGATIVES

1. Negative sentences are related to affirmative declarative sentences according to the following models.

2. Transitive sentences:

TEMP+t VB_T+da ERG+a ABS
↓
ałga TEMP+dit VB_T+da ERG+ł ABS

a) Ałga nadit niisda łgu'yuutsł dziiẅ.
The child didn't see the dolphin.
b) Ałga dit niisda łgu'yuutał dziiẅ.
The child doesn't see the dolphin.
c) Ałganadit niisda 'yuutał ol.
The man saw no deer.

3. Transitive sentence with ergative pronominal:

TEMP+ergPRO VB_T+a ABS
↓
ałga TEMP+ergPRO+di VB_T+ł ABS

a) Ałga nandi düü'nł ol.
I killed no bears/ I didn't kill any bears.

4. Transitive sentence with absolutive pronominal:

TEMP+ t VB_T+absPRO ERG
↓
ałga TEMP+di+t VB_T+absPRO ERG

5. Transitive sentence with both pronominals:

TEMP+ergPRO VB_T+absPRO
↓
ałga TEMP+ergPRO+di VB_T+absPRO

a) Ałga nandi 'niidzn. I didn't see you.
b) Ałga nandi lu'niidzn. I wasn't staring at you.
c) Ałga ndmdi 'woon. I won't invite you.

6. Intransitive sentences:

TEMP VB_I+a ABS
↓
ałga TEMP+di VB_I+ł ABS

a) Ałga di baał wan gwasga. That deer isn't running.
b) Ałga di k̲'oł wan. The deer are not running.
c) Ałga nadī baałwan. The deer didn't run.
d) Ałga dmdi baałwan. The deer won't run.

7. Transitive sentence with pronominal:

TEMP VB_I+absPRO
↓
aɨga TEMP+di VB_I+absPRO

a) Aɨga dmdi baat. — It won't run.
b) Aɨga nadi baat. — He didnt run.
c) Aɨga di baan. — You're not running.

8. Negative sentences with aayn (<u>no</u>) may also be interrogative. Such sentences question the aayn <u>element</u> and anticipate a "yes" answer.

TEMP+t VB_T+da ERG+a ABS
↓
aayn+ɨ TEMP VB_T+diɨ ERG+i ABS

a) Aaynɨ nah dzagwdiɨ oli haas?
Didn't the bear kill the dog?

9. The relationships between affirmative and negative, declarative and interrogative sentences are summarized by the following models.

a) Transitive:

affirmative-declarative		TEMP+t	VB_T+da	ERG+a	ABS
		↓			
affirmative-interrogative		TEMP	VB_T+diɨ	ERG+i	ABS
		↓			
negative-interrogative	aɨ	TEMP	VB_T+da	ERG+i(ɨ)	ABS
		↓			
negative-declarative	aɨ+ga	TEMP+dit	VB_T+da	ERG+ɨ	ABS

b) Transitive with ergative pronominal:

affirmative-declarative		TEMP+ergPRO	VB_T+a	ABS
		↓		
affirmative-interrogative		TEMP+ergPRO	VB_T+diɨ	ABS
		↓		
negative-interrogative	aɨ	TEMP+ergPRO	VB_T+diɨ	ABS
		↓		
negative-declarative	aɨ+ga	TEMP+ergPRO+di	VB_T+ɨ	ABS

c) Transitive with absolutive pronominal:

affirmative-declarative		TEMP+t	VB_T+absPRO	ERG
		↓		
affirmative-interrogative		TEMP+t	VB_T+absPRO+iɨ	ERG
		↓		
negative-interrogative	aɨ	TEMP+t	VB_T+absPRO+iɨ	ERG
		↓		
negative-declarative	aɨ+ga	TEMP+dit	VB_T+absPRO	ERG

d) Transitive with both pronominals:

affirmative-declarative		TEMP+ergPRO	VB_T+ absPRO
		↓	
affirmative-interrogative		TEMP+ergPRO	VB_T+d+absPRO+i
		↓	
negative-interrogative	aɨ	TEMP+ergPRO	VB_T+d+absPRO+i
		↓	
negative-declarative	aɨ+ga	TEMP+ergPRO+di	VB_T+absPRO

e) Intransitive:

affirmative-declarative		TEMP	VB_I+a	ABS
		↓		
affirmative-interrogative		TEMP	VB_I+i(ɨ)	ABS
		↓		
negative-interrogative	aɨ	TEMP	VB_I+'di	ABS
		↓		
negative-declarative	aɨ+ga	TEMP+di	VB_I+ɨ	ABS

f) Intransitive with pronominal:

affirmative-declarative		TEMP	VB_I+absPRO
		↓	
affirmative-interrogative		TEMP	VB_I+absPRO+i
		↓	
negative-interrogative	aɨ	TEMP	VB_I+absPRO+i
		↓	
negative-declarative	aɨ+ga	TEMP+di	VB_I+absPRO

INTERROGATIVES WITH TOPICAL NOUN PHRASES

1. When a noun phrase is topicalized in an interrogative sentence, that topical element is what is being asked about and with emphasis. The proclitic modal element k'ap- (really) begins affirmative interrogative sentences with topicals.

a) K'ap hana'kaył siipgadi?	Is it really the woman who is sick?
b) K'ap 'yuutaył nah baadi?	Was it really the man who ran?
c) K'ap haasał niidzadi łguwoomłk?	Is it really the dog that the child sees?
d) K'ap olł nah guuyui?	Was it a bear that I shot?
e) K'ap haasał nah dzakwdidi ol?	Was it a dog that the bear killed?
f) K'ap olł nah indzagwadił haas?	Was it a bear that killed the dog?

2. Other interrogatives with topical noun phrases begin with aayn (no) followed by -ł. The indication is that the negation itself is being questioned, and therefore an affirmative response is anticipated.

a) Aaynł haasił na'ap dzakwdił ol?
Wasn't it a dog that the bear killed?

b) Aaynł olł nah'nt dzagwadił haas?
Wasn't it a bear that killed the dog?

TAG QUESTIONS

1. a) Nah siipk, 'nii?	He was sick, wasn't he?
b) Na'ap siipk, 'nii?	He was sick, wasn't he?
c) Ałga nahdi siipgat, 'nii?	He wasn't sick, was he?
d) Nah dzakwda ol haas, 'nii?	The bear killed the dog, didn't it?
e) Ałga di olł 'nt dzagwał hass, 'nii?	It wasn't a bear that killed the dog, was it?
f) Nah dzakwdidi wan, 'nii?	He killed a deer, didn't he?
g) Wan nah dzakwdit, 'nn?	He killed a deer, didn't he?
h) Ałgndit dzagwał wan, 'nii?	He didn't kill a deer, did he?

INTERROGATIVE PRONOUNS

1. Naa (who).

a) Na'nt dzagwadu ol?	Who killed the bear?
b) Nał'nt dzagwadu ol?	Who killed the bear?

(Note: (b) is considered older and more formal than (a))

c) Naayu nah baat?	Who was running?

d) Naayu siipgat?	Who is sick?
e) Dipnaayu sipsiipgat?	Who are sick?

2. Ksndaa (which).

a) Ksndadu sipsiipgat?	Which ones are sick?
b) Ksndayu sipsiipgat?	Which ones are sick?

3. Ndah . . . wil (where).

a) Ndaɫ habada?	Where did they go?
b) Ndeɫ nam wil niisdu ol?	Where did you see the bear?
c) Ndeɫ nam wil niisda?	Where did you see it?

4. Ndah . . . da (when).

a) Ndeɫ nam da niisda?	When did you see it?

5. Go (what).

a) Goɫ nah dzagwadu?	What was it they killed?
b) Godu di dzabn?	What are you making?
c) Godu gwa'a?	What's this?

IMPERATIVES

1. a) Baa!	Run! (singular)
b) Baan!	Run! (singular)
c) Baasm!	Run! (plural)
d) Giloodza baan!	Don't run! (singular)
e) Giloodza baasm!	Don't run! (plural)
f) Dzagwa ol awaan!	Kill that bear there by you! (singular)
g) Sm dzagwa ol awaan!	Kill that bear there by you! (plural)
h) Giloomdza dzagwa haas!	Don't kill the dog! (singular)
i) Giloomdza sm dzagwa haas!	Don't kill the dog! (plural)

VERB COMPLEMENTS

1. Verb complements come at the end of the sentence:

a) Aɫga dit da'axɫga wanɫ dm baat.
The deer can't run.

CONDITIONALS, MODALS, AND COMPLEX SENTENCES

1. Why, because.

a) Goyu na ganbaan?	Why were you running?
b) Nan ap sagabaxsga'nu.	Because I was frightened.
c) Gooɬ nam gandzagwadu haas?	Why did you kill the dog?
d) Na'ap siipk.	Because it was sick.
e) Dzakwdu haas nuwil k'ap siipgat.	I killed the dog because it was sick?
f) Nak'ap siipga haas, na gandzagwit.	Because the dog was sick, I killed it.

2. If, then.

a) Dzida sagagaxsgi, dm k'yeexga'nu.	If I am frightened, I will run away.
b) Dm k'yeexga'nu dzida sagabaxsgi.	I will run away if I am frightened.
c) Dzida siipgaɬ haas, dm dzakdu.	If a dog is sick, I will kill it.

3. When, then.

a) Ndawil sagabaxsgu, dm k'yeexga'nu.	When I am frightened, I will run away.
b) Ndawil siipga haas, dm dzakwdu.	Whenever a dog is sick, I will kill it.

4. In order that.

a) Nah dzakwdu dmt ɬa gyik 'wah ɬa'ka gyet.
   I killed it so it wouldn't bite anyone.
b) Nah dzakwdu opdzat ɬa'ka gyet.
   I killed it so it wouldn't bite anyone.

5. If not, then (unless).

Dzidam 'wah dü'ünɬ sipsiipgmhashaas, dm dagoy'tiksa hoshosk.
If you don't kill sick dogs, they cause trouble.

6. Subjunctive interrogatives.

a) K'ap sgüüɬ nandm dzagwadi?	Should I have killed it? (expects "yes" answer)
b) Aɬ sgüüɬ nandm dzagwadi?	Should I have killed it? (expects "no" answer)
c) Aɬgadi sgüüɬ nahdm dzagwat, 'niidi?	I shouldn't have killed it, should I?
d) Ndzit 'nüün nahdm dzakwdani?	If it had been you, would you have killed it?
e) Nahdm dzakwdni, ndzit 'nüün?	Would you have killed it had it been you?
f) Nahdm dzakwdni?	Would you have killed it?
g) Nahdm dzakwdn, 'nii?	You would have killed it, wouldn't you?

h) Aƚga namdm dzagwat, 'niidi?	You wouldn't have killed it, would you?

7. Tentative expressions.

a) Ndm al gyik niidzn, si'n.	I'll see you again, maybe.
b) Gidza ndm gyik niidzn.	I might see you again.
c) Aƚgandm al gyik niidzn, si'n.	I won't see you again, maybe.
d) Gidza aƚgandm al gyik niidzn.	I might not see you again.
e) Anoognƚ nm̱stuulni?	Would you like me to walk with you?

8. Time and place expressions.

a) Ƚa g̱anƚaaga wilt wasnda yeen g̱alts'ap.
   Just as it was morning, fog blanketed the village.

b) Lax likst'aa wilt wasnda yeen g̱alts'ap.
   It was on the island that fog blanketed the village.